William Annesley

Hagigah. A Translation Of The Treatise Chagigah From The Babylonian Talmud

William Annesley

Hagigah. A Translation Of The Treatise Chagigah From The Babylonian Talmud

ISBN/EAN: 9783744653473

Printed in Europe, USA, Canada, Australia, Japan

Cover: Foto ©ninafisch / pixelio.de

More available books at **www.hansebooks.com**

A TRANSLATION OF THE TREATISE

CHAGIGAH

FROM THE

BABYLONIAN TALMUD

WITH INTRODUCTION, NOTES, GLOSSARY, AND INDICES

BY

THE REV. A. W. STREANE, M.A.

FELLOW, AND DIVINITY AND HEBREW LECTURER, OF CORPUS CHRISTI COLLEGE, CAMBRIDGE, AND FORMERLY TYRWHITT'S HEBREW SCHOLAR.

CAMBRIDGE:
AT THE UNIVERSITY PRESS.
1891

[All Rights reserved.]

Cambridge:
PRINTED BY C. J. CLAY, M.A. AND SONS,
AT THE UNIVERSITY PRESS.

INTRODUCTION.

SINCE the publication of Deutsch's celebrated article[1], a large number of fragmentary portions of the Talmud have appeared in English. Such for example are to be found in Hershon's *Talmudic Miscellany*, 1880, his *Treasures of the Talmud*, 1882, and his *Genesis with a Talmudic Commentary*, 1883. A considerable portion of the Mishnah has also been translated, in particular, the treatise entitled *Pirḳe Aboth*, or *Sayings of the Jewish Fathers*. Numerous references to Dr C. Taylor's edition of that work with critical and illustrative notes[2] will be found in the following pages. Many other Mishnic treatises have also been more or less fully translated; e.g., by the Rev. D. A. de Sola and the Rev. M. J. Raphall[3], and, later, by the Rev. Joseph Barclay[4]. But no person, so far as I am aware, has hitherto undertaken to set any Talmudic treatise, with both Mishnah and Gemara, in its entirety before the English reader. I have accordingly ventured to think that such a work as this, corresponding to what has been already done by Drs E. M. Pinner, Chr. Ewald[5] and others[6] for German,

---

[1] 'The Talmud,' published in the *Quarterly Review*, Oct. 1867, and reprinted in his *Literary Remains*, London, 1874.

[2] Cambridge, 1877.   [3] London, 1843.

[4] London, 1878.

[5] Pinner's *B'rakhoth*, Berlin, 1842; Ewald's *Abodah Sarah*, 2nd ed., Nuremberg, 1868.

[6] See German translations of various treatises enumerated in Dr H. L. Strack's *Einleitung in den Thalmud*, p. 69.

and by L'Abbé L. Chiarini[1] and M. Moïse Schwab[2] for French readers, might not be without interest. This book then, unlike those to which I first referred, consists, not of quotations, however appropriately selected, but of a continuous whole.

Although perhaps no one who opens this volume is likely to "hold, with that erudite Capucin friar, Henricus Seynensis, that the Talmud is not a book but a man[3]," it may be well to sketch as briefly as possible the nature of that work, one of the treatises of which appears now for the first time in a non-Hebrew dress.

According to Jewish belief, in addition to the "Books of Moses," which formed the *written* Law (תּוֹרָה שֶׁבִּכְתָב), there was also delivered to the Israelitish leader an *oral* Law (תּוֹרָה שֶׁבְּעַל פֶּה)[4], which was held by the Jews in still higher veneration[5]. This oral Law, like the written, was held to have been faithfully transmitted through subsequent generations and all the vicissitudes of Jewish history, and the two together form the basis of all the discussion and exposition, of which the main substance of the Talmud consists. "Moses received the Torah from Sinai, and delivered it to Joshua, and Joshua to the elders, and the elders to the prophets, and the prophets to the men of the Great Synagogue[6]." "R. Simeon ben Laḳish said, What is that which is written, 'I will give thee tables of stone, and the law, and the commandment which I have written, to teach them' (Ex. xxiv. 12)? 'Tables,' these are the Ten Words; 'law,' this is the Scripture; 'and the commandment,' this is the Mishnah; 'which I have written,' these are Prophets

---

[1] *Le Talmud de Babylone, traduit en langue Française, et complété par celui de Jérusalem*, Vol. 1. Leipzic, 1831, contains *B'rakhoth*. No more appears to have been published.

[2] *B'rakhoth*, Paris, 1871. Other treatises have followed.

[3] Deutsch, *Lit. Rem.*, p. 3.

[4] "Not unlike the unwritten Greek 'Ῥῆτραι, the Roman 'Lex Non Scripta,' ...or our own Common Law," Deutsch, p. 18.

[5] See p. 47.

[6] *Sayings of the Jewish Fathers (Pirḳe Aboth)*, i. 1.

and K'thubhim; 'to teach them,' this is the Gemara; thus instructing us that all of these were given to Moses from Sinai[1]."

It is of course impossible to determine with any precision what substratum of truth may underlie this belief; in other words, to determine whether there may be preserved to us in the Talmud, as we now have it, any trace of precepts otherwise unknown but belonging to the age of Moses or to that of the Elders[2], or of the prophets who followed him. When we arrive however at the age indicated by the last words quoted above from the *Pirḳe Aboth*, the subject emerges into the light of history. From that time onwards we find that a certain class of men were charged from age to age with the custody of this Law, both while it was still in fact, as well as in name, oral, and subsequently, when it had been committed to writing. The title borne by these persons varied with the period, as did also the amount of deference paid to their successive expositions.

Ezra and 'the men of the Great Synagogue[3],' the last of whom, Simon the Just, died B.C. 300, handed on the tradition, to be cherished and amplified by the Sopherim (scribes), and these were succeeded in their guardianship by (*a*) the Tannāim[4] (A.D. 70—220), (*b*) the Amorāim[5] (from the death of Rabbi, A.D.

---

[1] *B'rakhoth*, 5 a, i. 13.

[2] Josh. xxiv. 3, Jud. ii. 7.

[3] Traditionally held to have been a college, consisting of 120 contemporary teachers. More probably the title was invented in a subsequent age to express collectively those learned in the Law, who belonged to the whole period comprised between the Return from the Captivity and B.C. 300. See Dr C. Taylor's *Sayings of the Jewish Fathers*, p. 124.

[4] *Repeaters, teachers* (תנא), also called Chakhamim, *wise men*, a title used to distinguish them from the Rabbanan, who (but see Glossary, RABBAN) were Gemaric teachers (Amoraim). Deutsch however (*Lit. Rem.* p. 21) adopts a classification which makes Banaim, (Master-) *builders* (בנאי), to be the name borne by the custodians of the oral Law from B.C. 220 to A.D. 220.

[5] *Speakers* (אמר). Hence they were men who *discussed* with authority, as opposed to their predecessors (Tannaim) who *taught* with authority. The Amoraim did not formulate new laws, unless they were compelled. Thus they

210 to R. Abina II., often called Rabena, head of the Academy at Sora in the latter part of the 5th century, the last who taught authoritatively on the basis of oral tradition), (c) the Sabborāim[1] (A.D. 500—689), and lastly, the Geonim[2] (A.D. 689—895).

During Old Testament times and till about B.C. 100 there appears to have existed nothing of the rivalry in the exposition of the Law which we find from that time onwards. Till the captivity all were either on the side of Israel's God or of idolatry, and after the Return several hundred years seem to have elapsed before any development of opposing schools took place. "The struggle for independence which was sustained, and brought to a successful issue, by the Maccabaeans with the help of the zealous adherents of the Law, tended to concentrate all political power in the hands of that party; whilst the Hellenist faction, who had brought the nation to the verge of ruin, must have lost all influence. But though subdued for a time, and in bad odour with the people, they succeeded in alienating John Hyrcanus and some of his successors from their opponents, who on their part sought to maintain themselves by the favour of the multitude. But since excessive zeal for the Law was the surest way of securing the attachment of the people, legal studies came to be regarded with deeper interest, and pursued with increasing energy, till with the multiplication of the disciples, divisions and endless disputes were developed[3]."

These differences of opinion as to the meaning of many of

---

stood in something of the same relation to the Tannaim as judges and counsel do to the legislature.

[1] *Reasoners* (סבר, to think, סָבְרָא, reason). They did not propound anything original, but reasoned upon the material left them by their predecessors, and so sought to obtain a clearer grasp of its meaning. Jose (who died A.D. 503) was the first of these, though he is sometimes reckoned as the last of the Amoräim. The last were 'Ina or Giza, and Simona. For a sketch of their times, see Etheridge, *Introd. to Heb. Lit.* p. 209 sqq.

[2] *Eminent* persons (גָאוֹן, excellent, noble). The word however also bears a narrower import as the title belonging to the heads of the Academy of Sora.

[3] Deutsch, p. 19.

the precepts in the written, and of the comments in the unwritten, Law had thus the natural effect of largely expanding the amount of matter to be transmitted. And again "the ever growing wants of the ever disturbed commonwealth necessitated new laws and regulations at every turn...Both for the promulgation of a new law and the abrogation of an old one a higher sanction was requisite than a mere majority of the legislative council. The new Act must be proved, directly or indirectly, from the 'Word of God'—proved to have been promulgated by the Supreme King—hidden and bound up as it were in its very letters from the beginning[1]."

Such was the state of things, when R. Jehudah the Holy[2], doubtless fearing that the Rabbinic schools might perish altogether in the hapless plight of the Jewish people, about A.D. 191 brought, or began to bring, into shape the Mishnah, i.e., the older of the two parts, of which the majority of the treatises forming the Talmud are each made up. The Mishnah is thus the (virtually common) basis of the two forms of the Talmud, known respectively as the Talmud of Jerusalem (more strictly, Tiberias) and of Babylon (Sora)[3].

Around this Mishnah, or commentary on the Biblical text, with its studied brevity suggestive of hastily taken lecture notes, there grew up a commentary or "critical expansion[4]," couched for the most part in language still more laconic and obscure, as well as still further removed in its form from Biblical Hebrew. This commentary on a commentary is called the Gemara[5], and forms the later, and by far the longer, of the two portions of an ordinary Talmudic treatise. The Gemara, unlike the two recensions of the Mishnah, differs considerably in the two forms of the Talmud.

The Talmud of Jerusalem is attributed to the editorship of

[1] Deutsch, p. 19.
[2] See p. 2, note 9.
[3] See further under MISHNAH in Glossary.
[4] Deutsch, p. 17.
[5] See Glossary.

R. Jochanan ben Eliezer (A.D. 184—279), but inasmuch as his death took place considerably more than a hundred years before the latest piece of Gemara contained in that Talmud, it is clear that he can only have given the impulse, which led to the putting together and completion of the whole. The same remark will apply to the tradition which ascribes the editing of the Talmud of Babylon to Ashi[1] (died A.D. 427), and Rabena[2], who were both much earlier than the last teachers therein named.

While both Talmuds, containing thus a commentary upon what is virtually the same body of Mishnic teaching, bear a strong similarity to one another, they have nevertheless conspicuous points of difference. The discussions in the Palestinian Talmud are briefer and more to the point. In it the learned give the opinions and decisions pronounced by their predecessors, but without the addition of the debates which led up to those decisions. It also contains more history and geography, as well as more of numismatology and archæology. We may add that in it Greek words needed, and accordingly received, no explanation.

The Talmud of Babylon on the other hand is three times the size of the other, bestows more care on legal and religious points, is the later, the more studied by the Jews themselves, and the more trustworthy. Lastly the Talmud of Babylon contains more Halachah, the Talmud of Jerusalem more Haggadah[3].

The following will probably strike the reader of any Talmudic treatise as its most prominent characteristics:

1st. Conciseness; frequently amounting to obscurity. This feature, noticeable in the Mishnah, is still more prominent in the Gemara. Both assume an intimate knowledge of the letter of the "Books of Moses," as well as a thorough familiarity with the details of ritual developed in the later days of the

---

[1] See p. 6, note 1.
[2] See p. viii.
[3] For these words, see Glossary.

Jewish state. This is largely accompanied by a brevity and baldness which utterly disregard all attempts at rhetorical effect or even attractiveness of style. If such a work is to be made at all intelligible in an English translation, it must be considerably amplified, as well by insertion in the course of the text, as by notes. Accordingly, while seeking to render the original as closely as the case permits, and while probably running the risk of reproducing but too faithfully in many cases its extreme baldness, I have felt it necessary to make the English text to be not only a literal translation, but to some extent a commentary, while reserving as much as possible for the notes everything of the nature of observations, strictly so called, on the text.

2nd. Disputation. Rabbis of opposing schools adduce their several opinions and support them both by older authority and by argument. It is hoped that the spaces (sub-paragraphs) which will be found throughout the text, may help to bring out this feature, and to render more apparent the thread of the discussion, which otherwise might occasionally be difficult to disentangle.

3rd. A desultory, disconnected style. Deutsch[1] speaks thus of the Talmudic student at the commencement of his investigation: "Schooled in the harmonizing, methodizing systems of the West—systems that condense and arrange and classify, and give everything its fitting place and its fitting position in that place—he feels almost stupefied here. The language, the style, the method, the very sequence of things (a sequence that often appears as logical as our dreams), the amazingly varied nature of these things—everything seems tangled, confused, chaotic." Often however the clue to the connexion between neighbouring paragraphs is to be found, not in any similarity in the subject-matter, but in the identity of the authority upon which they rest, or person quoted as having given utterance to them.

4th. Extraordinary methods of interpretation and subtle

[1] p. 16.

inferences from Biblical language. Examples will be found on pp. 5, 14, 16, etc.[1]

The Talmud however, apart from its literary features, and in spite of what we may consider as blemishes of substance or of style, can well claim a right to be regarded with profound interest, on account of the powerful influence which it has had upon the Jewish people, as exercising the strongest effect upon their imagination, as bound up for so many centuries with their history, and as inspiring them in many cases with an enthusiastic devotion to its contents. From the peculiar circumstances of their position, deprived of the natural outlets for the exercise of a nation's enthusiasm and interests, they devoted themselves for ages to this unique study, which accordingly throws a strong, if somewhat also of a fantastic, light upon their modes of thought and life for generations. More especially does the Book claim our attention, as containing the words of some, with whom we may feel morally certain that our Lord held converse, men with whose sayings He and those around Him were thoroughly familiar, men whose teaching, avowedly dependent as it was for its claims solely on the links connecting it with the *dicta* of their predecessors, was in such marked contrast with the words of Him who "taught them as one having authority, and not as their scribes[2]."

The Talmud of Babylon consists of sixty-three Tractates or Treatises, each of which bears the name of מַסֶּכְתָּא. These Treatises are arranged under six heads (סְדָרִים, orders). The second of these heads is called, The division of (or, concerning) festivals (סֵדֶר מוֹעֵד), and contains twelve treatises, of which CHAGIGAH (חֲגִיגָה) is the last[3]. We may summarise as follows

---

[1] "The mind of a Jew is never wholly intelligible to the mind of a Gentile." C. A. Vince, *Christian Conduct*, p. 108.
[2] Matt. vii. 29.
[3] This is according to the order of sequence laid down by Maimonides. For other arrangements, see Strack's *Einleitung in den Thalmud*, pp. 10—12.

the questions of which it treats; merely reminding the reader that the digressions from the main theme are numerous and lengthy:

Perek I. Who are bound to appear at Jerusalem at the three great annual Feasts? What is the amount which must be expended by them in offerings on the occasion? From what sources are these offerings to be drawn and of what are they to consist? Rules as to postponed offerings, and as to the dissolving of vows. Remarks on the rules concerning Sabbaths, Chagigah-offerings, and other matters.

Perek II, like the latter part of Perek I, treats of many matters which have little or no connexion with the main theme. On what things is instruction to be given? Into what things is investigation forbidden? Fragments of the story of Acher. The first dispute between Jewish Rabbis (Jose ben Joezer and Jose ben Jochanan). The names of the five *Pairs* (Presidents and Vice-Presidents of the Sanhedrin). Details connected with festival offerings. Rules relating to cleansing. Is a definite intention necessary, if cleansing is to be ceremonially valid? What are the degrees of purity?

Perek III. How far are hallowed things to be held as more honourable than heave-offering? And (in connexion with this enquiry, and returning thus to the main subject) how comes it that during the Feast the wine and bread of a strictly observant Jew are not defiled by the touch of a common person? How after the Feast are the vessels of the Sanctuary purified?

The text of the Talmud, besides presenting, in common with other ancient writings, unintentional variants (arising from errors of sight, of hearing, etc.), contains also a considerable number caused (*a*) by fear of the "Censor[1]" or representative of the secular power, or even by his actual direction, (*b*) by a desire to emphasize the differences between the Jewish and

---

[1] For interesting remarks upon the comparative influence of the "censure" upon the earliest printed editions of Talmudic treatises, according to the country of origin of the MSS. on which they were based, see Strack's *Einleitung, etc.* p. 53;

Christian religions. It is in the edition of Basel (A.D. 1578—1581) that the influence of the Censor comes into view. Owing to the wide-spread belief that the Talmud contained attacks upon Christianity, the word expressing a Christian Jew[1] was altered in many cases to that for Sadducee or for Epicurean[2], and the word for Gentile[3] to that for Cuthite (Samaritan).

The great majority however of the variants in this treatise are not of sufficient importance to merit attention. Consequently in the following pages it is only occasionally that any of them are dealt with in a note. Those who may desire to examine them further will find ample material to their hand in Rabbinovicz's *Variae Lectiones* noticed below.

Owing doubtless in part to the vicissitudes of Jewish history in mediaeval times, comparatively few MSS. including Gemara survive, although Mishnic treatises, especially that of the *Sayings of the Jewish Fathers* (Pirke Aboth), are fairly numerous[4]. The chief extant MSS. of the Talmud of Babylon are three:

1st. That of Munich[5]; the only MS. containing the whole of this Talmud. It was written A.D. 1369 at Paris by R. Solomon ben Simson,

2nd. The Roman[6], and

---

also for a list of passages in the Talmud, where the censure has obscured or obliterated references to our Lord, or to those immediately connected with Him, see Rabbinovicz's *Discourse* (מאמר) *on the printed editions of the Talmud*, appended to Part viii. of his *Var. Lect.*, pp. 24, 25, notes כה and בט.

[1] מִי׃. [2] See p. 22, note 3.

[3] גוֹי. See p. 134, note 1.

[4] We may here mention the unique Cambridge MS. of the Mishnah upon which the Talmud of Jerusalem rests, edited by the Rev. W. H. Lowe, M.A., Christ's College, Cambridge, 1883.

[5] Cod. Hebr. 95. See Steinschneider, *Die hebräischen Handschriften der K. Hof- und Staatsbibliothek in München*, München, 1875, p. 43. For further remarks and references in connexion with this MS. see Strack's *Einleitung, etc.*, p. 51, and Schwab's *B'rakhoth*, Introd., p. xlv. The latter places the MS. in the year 1342.

[6] See Assemani, *Biblioth. Apost. Vaticanae Codd. MSS. Catalogus*, Tom. i. clxxi. 34 (p. 139). Little seems known as to this MS., except that it belongs to

3rd. The Oxford[1] MS.

This last has many variations, for the most part minute, but in some cases interesting, and notably so in that part of this treatise which relates to Elisha ben Abuyah (Acher, see p. 83).

Twenty-three of the treatises forming the Talmud of Babylon were published at Soncino and Pesaro early in the 16th century (not later than 1519), but the first complete edition was that of Daniel Bomberg, Venice, 1520—31. Many of the errors of this edition were corrected in that of Justiniani, Venice, 1546—51. Several editions were produced during the period between the last-named and that of Basel, noticed above, and many followed the last-named. The variations of reading among the editions, at any rate as far as this treatise is concerned, are, generally speaking, insignificant.

The text followed here, except where an intimation to the contrary is given in the notes, is that of the edition published for the most part at Lemberg[2] in thirty-nine volumes. That which contains this treatise bears upon the title-page "Druck und Verlag des Salomon Sprecher, in Lemberg, 1867."

The references to the exact line in the original, which will be found at the top of the outer margin of each page in the translation as well as elsewhere in this work, will, it is hoped, be found useful. All Hebrew editions have been arranged to correspond with the pagination of the *editio princeps*, but in some, e.g., the Lemberg, two pages go to make one of the former. Accordingly in my notation the number in Arabic numerals, according as it is followed by a or b, denotes in the usual way the obverse or reverse of the page in the *editio*

---

that collection of Talmud-MSS., the greater part of which formerly belonged to the University of Heidelberg. See Strack, p. 50; Schwab, p. xlvii.

[1] "Mishnah and the Gemara of Babylon; Z'raim and Mo'ed...The Mishnah of the whole chapter precedes the G'mara.... Owner: Abraham ben Yizḥag hal-Levi אבקראט bought it at Cairo in the year 5317 = 1557.

"Neat squ. char.: 2 coll. large fol., vellum, ff. 184; last leaf injured. [Opp. Add. fol. 23.]" Neubauer's *Cat. of Heb. MSS. in the Bodl. Libr.*, Nr. 366. Oxford, 1886.

[2] But some volumes at Amsterdam.

princeps, while the further subdivision of each of these, e.g., in the Lemberg text, into two pages (right and left hand) is denoted by i and ii, and the individual line in i or ii by the number in Arabic numerals which follows.

It remains for me to express my obligations to those who in various ways have aided in the execution of my task.

This little book forms one more illustration of the frequency with which Prof. Cowell by his kindly advice and interest has stimulated others to literary effort. I had originally hoped that his name would have preceded mine upon the title-page, and, though the pressure of his other work has rendered this impossible, I cannot thank him too warmly for the first suggestion, as well as for the ready help and counsel which he has from time to time bestowed.

The book may be considered as the outcome of the lectures of the late Dr S. M. Schiller-Szinessy, the learned University Reader in Talmudic, of whose unwearied readiness, both in lecture and privately, to expound the difficulties of his subject I cherish a most grateful recollection.

To the Rev. R. Sinker, D.D., Librarian of Trinity College, I also tender my warmest thanks for his kindness in finding time to read the proofs of the work, and for many valuable hints on points of detail.

Lastly, my sincere acknowledgments are due to the Syndics of the University Press for undertaking the publication of the book, and for several suggestions respecting its form.

ERRATA.

Page 25, line 29. *For* Tanaim *read* Tannaim.
,, 39. At top of margin supply 8 b, i. 23.
,, 63, margin. *For* Deut. xxiii. 8 *read* Deut. xxxii. 8.

חגיגה
פרק א

MISHNAH.

I. (1) ALL are bound in the case of a holocaust[1] except a deaf man, a fool, and a child, and one of doubtful sex, and one of double sex, and women, and slaves who are not manumitted, the lame man, and the blind man, and the sick man, and the old man, and him who is not able to go up on his feet. What is the definition of a child?[2] Every one who is not able to ride upon his father's shoulders, and to go up from Jerusalem to the mountain of the House. These are the words of the house of Shammai. But the house of Hillel[3] say, Every one who is not able to take hold of his father's hand, and to go up from Jerusalem to the mountain of the House, as it is said, Ex. xxiii. 14. "three footgoing times[4]."

---

[1] ראייה (ראה, to see; in Niph'al, to appear) is an abbreviated expression for עוֹלַת רְאִיָּה, burnt-offering (holocaust) of the appearing (i.e., before God at one of the three great Feasts, Passover, Weeks, Tabernacles). See further in Glossary at the end of this volume.

[2] איזהו קטן, lit., Who is this child?

[3] Hillel succeeded Shema'iah as President (נָשִׂיא) of the Sanhedrin, probably about 32 B.C., and held office till his death, about A.D. 8. Shammai was successor to Hillel's colleague Menachem, and was accordingly somewhat junior to his rival. For these two see Dr C. Taylor's *Sayings of the Jewish Fathers*, notes on pp. 34, 35, 37, 107, and Wolf's *Biblioth. Heb.* ii. 824, 859; iv. 380.

[4] From the use of the word רְגָלִים, here denoting "times," but having the primary sense of *feet*, the house of Hillel inferred that no child, too young to walk, could keep the command.

CHAGIGAH.

2a, ii. 1. (2) The house of Shammai say, The holocaust involves two pieces of silver and the chagigah a meah[1] of silver, but the house of Hillel say, The holocaust involves a meah of silver and the chagigah two pieces of silver.

GEMARA.

What is the expression *all* to include[2]? It is to include him who is half a slave and half free. But according to Rabena[3], who says, He who is half a slave and half free is exempt from the holocaust, what is the expression *all* to include?

It is to include him who is lame on the first day and well[4] on the second day. This agrees with him who says, All of them[5] are transferable from one day to another; but according to him who says, All of them are transferable as from the first day only[6], what is the expression *all* to include? It is to include the blind in one eye. But this is not in accordance with the following Baraitha[7]. For Jochanan ben Dahăbai[8], saying it in the name of Rabbi[9] Jehudah, taught, He who is blind in one eye is

---

[1] The sixth part of the דִּינָר (denarius), and equivalent to the Biblical גֵּרָה (*gerah*, e.g., Exod. xxx. 13, = $\frac{1}{20}$ of a shekel), which weighed sixteen grains of barley.

[2] לְאֲתוֹיֵי (infin. Aph‘el of אתא with prefix לְ) for לְאַיְתוֹיֵי, the י (a frequent substitute in late Hebrew for א as first root letter) being irregularly omitted.

[3] There were two of this name. The elder was a pupil of R. Joseph, for whom see p. 17, note 5. The younger was the last of the Gemaric teachers (Amoraim), and died A.D. 474. See Wolf's *Biblioth. Heb.* ii. 880.

[4] נִתְפַּשֵּׁט, lit., stretched out (in limb).

[5] The sacrifices.

[6] And therefore are not to be offered, if on that first day the person was legally (e.g., by lameness) incapable of offering, however soon afterwards he may have become capable.

[7] ודלא כי האי תנא דתניא, lit., But no; for thus it is taught, for there is a Baraitha. For this word see Glossary.

[8] A second-century teacher.

[9] "The title of RABBI κατ' ἐξοχήν was given to Jehudah ben Simon III., who was also called Jehudah *ha-Nasi* (the prophet) and Rabbenu *ha-Ḳadosh* (the Holy). To him is attributed the compilation of the MISHNAH, but the MISHNAH as we have it is a later recension, as may be inferred from the way in which 'Rabbi' himself is introduced." Dr C. Taylor's *Sayings etc.* p. 41, note 1; see also Wolf, ii. 839; Smith and Wace, *Dict. Chr. Biog.* iii. 342; and Etheridge *Introd. to Heb. Lit.* p. 86. Rabbi died, aged 60, circ. A.D. 210.

exempt from the holocaust, as it is said, "He shall be seen," or "He shall see¹." As he went to see, so he went to be seen; as to see with both his eyes, so to be seen with both His² eyes. 2 a, ii. 15.
Ex. xxiii.
17, Deut.
xvi. 16.

And, if you like, I will fully grant you what they have said from the beginning³. But you will say, Rabena's saying⁴ constitutes a difficulty. There is no difficulty. One opinion is according to the older Mishnah, the other⁵ according to the later Mishnah.

For there is a canonical Mishnah⁶, He who is half a slave and half free serves his master one day and himself the other day. These are the words of the house of Hillel. The house of Shammai said to them, You have settled it well for his master⁷, but you have not settled it well for himself. Does he wish to marry a slave woman? he is not able; a free woman? he is not able; to abstain from marriage? but was not the world created only that men might be fruitful and multiply? as it is said, "he created it not in vain; he formed it to be inhabited." But⁸ for the sake of the maintenance of the world⁹ they force his master and make him a free man¹⁰, and he writes for him a bill on half his property, and the house of Hillel comes round to teach according to the words of the house of Shammai. Baba
Bathra,
13 a, i. 11.

2 b

Is. xlv. 18.

*Except a deaf man, a fool, and a child etc.*¹¹ There is a Baraitha, A deaf man is like a fool and a child. As a fool and a child are not responsible for their actions, so a deaf man is not responsible for his actions. And we learn, as we are taught by a canonical Mishnah, A deaf man, as wise men have everywhere said, is one who does not¹² hear and does not speak. Lo, you will Niddah,
13 b, ii. 17.

---

¹ For the sense see p. 32, note 5.   ² God's.
³ Viz., that the word *all* is to include him who is half a slave and half free.
⁴ See p. 2.
⁵ That of Rabena.
⁶ See Glossary, under MISHNAH. The Mishnah quoted has no direct connexion with the question of exemption from the holocaust, but only relates to the general position of one who is half a slave and half free, suggested by such a person's having just been under discussion.
⁷ By thus securing to him the services of his slave for at least half his time.
⁸ Owing to the force of these considerations urged by the house of Shammai.
⁹ Through the institution of marriage.
¹⁰ That he may be able to marry, while yet his master has the benefit of his labour.
¹¹ See p. 1.
¹² i.e., *cannot*, and so in all subsequent cases.

2 b, ll. 2. say then, He who speaks and does not hear, or he who hears and does not speak, is bound. Yes, for there is a Baraitha for this. For our Rabbis have taught, He who speaks and does not hear is deaf, he who hears and does not speak is dumb. Both one and the other are to be treated as capable persons in all that relates to them. And whence do you infer that he who speaks and does not hear is deaf, and that he who hears and does not speak
Ps.xxxviii. is dumb? Since it is written, "But I as a deaf man hear not;
14. and I am as a dumb man, who openeth not his mouth." And, if you like, I will say, according to the proverbial saying, A man stumbling in his words[1]. He who speaks and does not hear, or he who hears and does not speak, is bound. But, lo, there is a Baraitha, viz., He who speaks and does not hear, or he who hears and does not speak, is exempt. Rabena, or it may have been[2] Rabba[3], said, There is a hiatus[4] here. And there is a Baraitha[5] to this effect, All are bound as regards the holocaust, and as regards the rejoicing[6], except a deaf man. He who speaks and does not hear, or he who hears and does not speak, is exempt from the holocaust. But although he is exempt from the holocaust, he is bound as regards the rejoicing; but as for him who does not hear and does not speak, and as for a fool and a child, he is exempt also from the rejoicing, inasmuch as these are exempt from all the commandments which are contained in the Law.

There is also a Baraitha to this effect, All are bound as regards the holocaust and the rejoicing except a deaf man. He who speaks and does not hear, and he who hears and does not speak, are exempt from the holocaust. But although he is exempt from the
3 a holocaust, he is bound as regards the rejoicing; but as for him who does not hear and does not speak and as for a fool and a child,

---

[1] As a mnemonic מילוליה תקיל איש.

[2] ואיתימא, lit., Or, if thou sayest (thou mayest be right).

[3] A friend of Abai. He is said to have died on the day that Ashi was born, A.D. 353. He was a pupil of his father-in-law Chasda. See Wolf, ii. 880.

[4] חַסּוֹרֵי is the infin. Pa'el, and מִיחַסְּרָא the participle Ithpa'al, the infin. exercising the intensifying force common also in earlier Hebrew. To decide that there must be a hiatus or lacuna in the teaching received was the last resort of the Rabbis, when confronted, as here, with two conflicting streams of tradition.

[5] Which suggests another way of reconciling the apparently conflicting statements.

[6] Reckoned as an integral part of the Feast.

they are exempt also from the rejoicing, inasmuch as these are 3 a, i. 3. exempt from all the commandments which are contained in the Law.   What is the difference in the nature of holocaust, that they are exempt, and in the nature of rejoicing, that they are bound?   As regards the nature of holocaust we are taught by the recurrence of the word[1] from the passage intitled "Assemble," as it is written, "Assemble the people, the men and the women Deut. and the little ones," and it is written, "when all Israel is come to xxxi. 12. appear."   And that point, whence do we get it[2]?   Because Deut. xxxi. 11. it is written, "that they may hear and that they may learn." And Deut. there is a Baraitha as follows, "That they may hear," this ex- xxxi. 12. pression excludes him who speaks and does not hear; "and that they may learn," this expression excludes him who hears and does not speak.   Is this to say, that he who cannot talk cannot learn? No; for this suggests[3] the case of the two dumb men who were in the neighbourhood of Rabbi[4], viz., the sons of R. Jochanan ben Gudgodah's[5] daughter; and the sons of R. Jochanan's sister say concerning it, that every time that Rabbi went up to the College, they went up and sat before him[6], and shook their heads, and moved their lips, and Rabbi asked for mercy for them, and they were examined[7], and it was ascertained that they were perfect in knowledge of Halachah[8] and Siphra and Siphre[9] and all the Talmud[10].   Mar Zot'ra[11] said, The reading there is, "in order

[1] Deut. xvi. 16 יִרְאֶה and xxxi. 11 לִרְאוֹת, each involving the verbal root from which ראייה comes.

[2] והתם מנלן, lit., And there, whence (does it appear) to us? viz., that the above-mentioned classes of persons are exempt from holocaust.

[3] Lit., is.

[4] For Rabbi see p. 2, note 9.

[5] He flourished before the destruction of the second Temple, and was an arithmetician and an astronomer. See Wolf, ii. 844.

[6] For קמיהו the reading of the printed texts (the Munich MS. omits the clause), קמיה (=קָמֵיהּ) is given in the margin of the Lemberg edition as conjectural emendation. קם is shortened by syncope from קדם.

[7] Ethpa'el (=Hithpa'el הִתְנַסּוּ) of נסה.

[8] See Glossary.

[9] Siphra and Siphre are Midrashim (Commentaries), the former on Leviticus, the latter on Numbers and Deuteronomy. Siphra is by some ascribed to Akiba. See Etheridge, p. 67.

[10] Lit., the six orders (divisions of the Talmud).

[11] Head of the Academy at Pumbeditha (for which place see p. 69, note 5), A.D. 402–410.

that they may teach." R. Ashi[1] said, Assuredly it is, "in order that they may teach"; for, if you imagine that it is, "in order that they may learn," then, since he who does not talk does not learn[2], and since he who does not hear does not learn, this sense of *learn* comes out of the words, "in order that they may hear[3]," but assuredly it is here, "in order that they may teach."

R. Tanchum[4] said, He that is deaf in one ear is exempt from the holocaust, as it is said, "in their ears." And this expression "in their ears" must mean, in the ears of all Israel, for this comes out of the words "before all Israel." How "before all Israel"? I should say, that, although they could not all hear, the Merciful One wrote it in their ears, and the fact that they heard comes out of the expression "in order that they may hear."

R. Tanchum said, He that is lame in one foot is exempt from the holocaust, as it is said, "footgoing times[5]." And this expression, "footgoing times," must mean to exempt men with wooden legs. This comes out of the expression "steps," for there is a Baraitha, viz., Steps are not steps but feet[6], and so He[7] says, "The foot shall tread it down, the feet of the poor, the steps of the needy," and He says, "How beautiful are thy steps in shoes[8], O prince's daughter!" Rabba expounds thus, What is the meaning of that which is written, "How beautiful are thy steps in shoes, O prince's daughter"? It means, How comely are the feet of Israel at the

Margin references: 3 a, l. 24. Deut. xxxi. 11. Is. xxvi. 6. Cant. vii. 1.

---

[1] He was born on the day of Rabba's death, A.D. 353 (see p. 4, note 3), and became at the age of 14 head of the Academy at Sora, which post he held for 60 years. Sora at the modern *Mosaib* on the Euphrates is the ancient Sepharvaim (Σίππαρα) through the intermediate forms Sifra and Sivra. See Rawlinson in the *Athenæum*, July 21, 1855 (p. 846). Five years after Ashi's succession to the headship, R. Papa, head of the neighbouring Academy of Neresh (see p. 12, note 3), died. Ashi is called an editor of the Babylonian Talmud. See R. Abram Zacuti's *Liber Juchassin* (Lexicon Biogr. et Hist.), p. 112 *b*. London and Edinb. 1857.

[2] The word thus rendered in this and the next clause is that from which Gemara (see Glossary) is derived.

[3] And therefore cannot occur again, for this would be tautology, which is impossible in Holy Writ.

[4] A second century teacher.

[5] See p. 1, note 4.

[6] i.e., behind the word for steps (פעמים) there lies the notion of feet (רגלים).

[7] God, i.e., Holy Writ.

[8] i.e., behind the word for shoes (נעלים) there lies the notion of feet (רגלים).

time when they go up to the feast¹! "Prince's daughter" means 3 a, ii. 16. daughter of Abraham our father, who is called prince, as it is said, "The princes of the peoples are gathered together to be the people Ps. xlvii. 9. of the God of Abraham:" "God of Abraham," and not God of Isaac and Jacob, but "God of Abraham"; for he was the first of the proselytes².

R. Kohăna³ said, R. Nathan bar Minyumi⁴ expounded in the name of R. Tanchum thus, What is the meaning of that which is written? "And the pit was empty, there was no water in it." Gen. From the literal sense, as it is said, "And the pit was empty," do I xxxvii. 24. not know that there was no water in it? Nay, but it means that though there was no water in it, there were serpents and scorpions in it.

Our Rabbis have taught, There is a matter with regard to R. Jochanan ben Beruka⁵ and R. El‘azar ben Chisma⁶, viz., that they went to visit⁷ R. Joshua⁸ in Pekiin⁹. He said to them, What

---

¹ רֶגֶל, properly, a foot, may denote in Talmudic Hebrew one of the three great Feasts, to which Israel went up on foot.

² Isaac and Jacob on the other hand had been taught by their fathers.

³ There were two of this name. The elder was disciple and colleague of Rab. The younger, who is here meant, was a contemporary of Ashi, and was also a priest, as was probably the elder. See Wolf, ii. 877.

⁴ A disciple of Rab and of Tanchum.

⁵ Father of Ishmael and a contemporary of El‘azar ben Azariah in Jabneh (Jamnia), A.D. 80. See Wolf, ii. 844. Jabneh (2 Chr. xxvi. 6, called Jabneel in Josh. xv. 11, the Jamnia of Greek writers) is placed by Josephus (*Bell. Jud.* iv. xi. 5) between Ashkelon and Joppa. It was probably a conspicuous seat of Jewish learning before the destruction of the second Temple. It was long the meeting-place of the Sanhedrin, which however in the time of Bar Kokh'ba and once again subsequently was removed to Osha (אוּשָׁא) in Galilee. See further in Neubauer, *Géog. du Talmud*, pp. 73 sqq.

⁶ A disciple of Akiba, thus flourishing at the beginning of the second century. The latter part of his name denotes *the muzzled one*. He was unacceptable to the congregation, because he had not sufficient memory to enable him to pronounce the marriage benediction.

⁷ Lit., to place themselves over against the face of.

⁸ His full name was R. Joshua ben Chănania, a disciple of Jochanan ben Zakkai, and vice-president (אַב בֵּית דִּין) in the presidency of Gamaliel (A.D. 80—115). A story is told of him somewhat later (p. 22) in connexion with the emperor's court. See Wolf, iv. 407; Dr C. Taylor, p. 39, note 39; Etheridge, pp. 63 sqq.

⁹ Otherwise called Bekiin. It lay between Jabneh (see note 5) and Lod (Lydda, Diospolis, see p. 9, note 11).

news was there in the College to-day? They said to him, We are thy disciples, and of thy waters we drink. He said to them, Although it be so, it is impossible for the College to be without something new. Whose Sabbath was it? It was the sabbath of R. El'azar ben Azariah[1]. And on what was the discourse to-day? They said to him, On the section, "Assemble." And how did he explain it[2]? "Assemble the people, the men and the women and the little ones"; if men, they come to learn; if women, they come to hear; but little ones, wherefore do they come? in order to get a reward for those that bring them. He said to them, There was a fair jewel in your hand, and ye sought to deprive me of it.

And again, he expounded the passage, "Thou hast avouched the LORD this day," "and the LORD hath avouched thee this day." The Holy One, blessed be He, said to Israel, Ye have made me a glory in the world, and I will make you a glory in the world. Ye have made me a glory in the world, for it is written, "Hear, O Israel: the LORD our God is one Lord," and I will make you a glory in the world, for it is said, "Who is like thy people Israel, a nation that is alone in the earth?"

And he also opened his mouth and expounded the passage, "The words of the wise are as goads, and as nails planted are the words of the masters of assemblies, which are given from one shepherd." Wherefore are the words of the Law likened to goads? It is to tell thee, that as a goad is what keeps the heifer in her furrows, so as to produce sustenance for the world, so the words of the Law keep the learners of them from the ways of death for the ways of life. If you say, that as a goad is what moves, so the words of the Law will move; no, for the teaching says "nails." If you say, that as a nail is a thing which diminishes and does not add[3], so the words of the Law diminish and do not add; no, for the teaching says "planted." As planting is a thing

---

[1] A disciple of Jochanan ben Zakkai, a priest and rich. Three years before his death, which occurred A.D. 82, he was appointed to succeed Rabban Gamaliel II., who was deposed from the presidency of the Academy at Jabneh. After Gamaliel had been re-admitted and allowed to address the congregation three Sabbaths in the month, El'azar as vice-president was still given the last Sabbath. See Wolf, ii. 812; Taylor, pp. 39, 74, 75, notes.

[2] Lit., What did he expound in it?

[3] e.g., a nail driven into a wall diminishes rather than adds to its substance. So the Law is by its very nature restrictive.

which is fruitful and multiplies, so too the words of the Law are 3 b, 1. 14. fruitful and multiply. "Masters of assemblies." These are the disciples of wise men, who sit by companies and study in the Law, some declaring unclean and others declaring clean, some binding and others loosing[1], some disqualifying and others pronouncing ceremonially pure. Perhaps a man may say, How under those circumstances[2] am I to learn the Law? The teaching says, All of them "are given from one shepherd." One God gave them, one pastor[3] uttered them from the mouth of the Lord of all that is made[4], blessed be He, for it is written, "and Ex. xx. 1. God spake all these words." Also do thou make thine ear as the upper millstone[5], and procure for thyself an understanding heart to hear the words of those who declare unclean and the words of those who declare clean, the words of those who bind and the words of those who loose, the words of those who disqualify and the words of those who pronounce ceremonially pure. On the same occasion[6] he said to them, It is not an orphan generation in the midst of which El'azar ben Azariah lives. And why did they[7] not tell[8] him without hesitation? It was on account of the matter that occurred. For there is a Baraitha, A matter occurred with regard to R. Jose, son of a Damascene woman[9], viz., that he went to visit[10] R. El'azar in Lod[11].

[1] Cf. Mt. xviii. 18.
[2] היאך מעתה, lit., How from (things as they are) now?—i.e., seeing that experts thus differ.
[3] Moses.   [4] Lit., the works.
[5] So as to receive and prepare for profitable use the good food of the Law. The word rendered millstone is perhaps the Greek ἐπίχυσις (wine-pitcher, Menander, Φιλαδ. i.) and may denote the funnel, through which corn descended into the mill. So Rashi, who lived at Lunel in Provence (see Eth. p. 282), explains by טירמוי״א=Provençal tremueia. See Diez, Etymol. Wörterb. etc. Pt. i. p. 419. Bonn, 1861.
[6] Lit., In the same utterance.   [7] The two disciples.
[8] Lit., And would that they had told! ל gives the optative force to the future (3rd plural of אמר).
[9] He was a disciple of Eliezer ben Hyrkanus. See p. 45, note 3.
[10] See p. 7, note 7.
[11] The Old Testament form (e.g., 1 Chron. viii. 12) of the name; afterwards (e.g., Acts ix. 32) Lydda, and later, Diospolis, a town near Joppa, and within a day's journey of Jerusalem. It was an important centre of Jewish learning, apparently as early as the period while the second Temple was yet standing. According to Talm. Bab. Sabbath, 104 b, Talm. Jer. Sanhedrin, vii. 16, Lod was the seat of a tribunal which had the power of pronouncing capital sentences,

3 b, l. 30.   He[1] said to him, What was there new in the College to day? He said to him, They voted[2] and decided, Ammon and Moab[3] are to pay the tithe for the poor in the seventh year.   He said to him, Jose, stretch out thine hands, and lose[4] thy sight.   He stretched out his hands and lost his sight.   R. El'azar wept
Ps. xxv. 14. and said, "The secret of the LORD is with them that fear him, and his covenant to make them know it." He said to him, Go, say to them, Ye need not have hasted to vote. For thus I have received by tradition from Rabban[5] Jochanan ben Zakkai[6], who heard from his teacher, and his teacher from his teacher, that it is a teaching of Moses from Sinai, Ammon and Moab are to pay the tithe for the poor in the seventh year. What is the reason? Those who came up from Egypt subjugated many fortified cities, while those who came up from Babylon did not subjugate many, because the first consecration was a consecration for but a short time, and not a consecration for the future permanently[7]; and so they[8] left it an open question, that the poor of the people might be sustained upon them

inasmuch as the impostor Ben Stada (for whom see Josephus, *Bell. Jud.* II. xiii. 5, and cf. Acts xxi. 38) was there condemned to death. Lod was in a fertile region and the centre for a considerable amount of commerce. Its Rabbinic school included Eliezer ben Hyrḳanus (see p. 45, note 3), and Tarphon (see p. 48, note 3). Aḳiba (see p. 15, note 8) also sometimes stayed there. It suffered severely from persecution, probably in Hadrian's time. In the 3rd century, and after the Sanhedrin had been removed to Galilee, the fixing of the intercalary month still took place at Lod. Its importance, however, in connexion with Judaism declined with the growth of Christianity. See further in Neubauer's interesting notice, *Géog. du Talmud*, pp. 76 sqq.

[1] El'azar.
[2] Niph'al of מנה.
[3] i.e., the Jews living in those parts.
[4] Lit., *receive*, a euphemism, to avoid an ill omen.
[5] Rabban was a title reserved for the seven immediate descendants of Hillel, who were presidents (נְשִׂיאִים) of Rabbinic schools.

[6] A contemporary of Simeon, son of Hillel. The latter had eighty disciples, of various degrees of merit. Of these however Jochanan ben Zakkai was considered the least. The exact dates of his birth and death are unknown. Towards the end of his life (which is said to have lasted 120 years), he became president of the Academy of Jabneh (see p. 7, note 5) and is considered its founder. "He was distinguished as a scrupulous adherent of the old paths rather than a theoretical reformer." Taylor, p. 46. See also Wolf, iv. 391—6, and Etheridge, pp. 48—50.

[7] Hence those returning from Babylon were not bound to imitate it.
[8] The Rabbis.

in the seventh year[1]. There is a Baraitha, that after that his mind had been appeased, he said, Let there be mercy, that the eyes of Jose may return to their place; and they returned.   3 b, ll. 12.

Our Rabbis have taught[2], Who is it who is a fool[3]? He who goes out alone at night[4], and he who passes the night in a cemetery, and he who tears his clothes. It has been reported that R. Hunna[5] said, So long as they all take place at one time[6]. R. Jochanan[7] said, Even in the case of one of them taking place. Explain this[8]. If he have done them in the way of folly, even though he confined himself to one, yet he is guilty; but if he have not done them in the way of folly, even though he have done them all, yet he is not guilty. Granting fully that he has done them in the way of folly, then as for him who passes the night in a cemetery, it may be said[9], He does it that there may rest upon him a spirit of uncleanness[10]; and as for him who goes out alone

---

[1] Which they could not be, if the land, as subject to the Jewish Law, had no cultivation, and therefore no produce, and therefore no tithing, in the seventh year. Therefore Moses must have contemplated the suspension of the Law of the sabbatical year in Ammon and Moab, as not to be permanently conquered and possessed by the people after either the Egyptian or Babylonian deliverance. Further it is implied that this suspension cannot be carried out, when the Jews are restored, and have full dominion over a land, including Ammon and Moab, consecrated thenceforth for ever.

[2] This phrase (תְּנוּ רַבָּנָן), mentioning no name, always introduces something pre-Christian. See the same expression on pp. 4, 7, etc.

[3] i.e., in the eye of the law.

[4] Thus incurring danger from Lilith, an evil spirit, sometimes taking the form of a bird. See Buxtorf's *Lex. Chald. etc.* p. 1140.

[5] Predecessor of Chasda as head of the Academy of Sora (he had previously been head of that of Nehardea; see p. 20, note 3) from about A.D. 290 till his death ten years later. See Wolf, ii. 870.

[6] Lit., one blow.

[7] Jochanan ben Eliezer, called also "son of a blacksmith" (בֶּן נַפְחָא), lived A.D. 184—279. He was a pupil of Rabbi, Jannai, Oshaia and others, and is said to have been head of the Academy at Tiberias for 80 years. He gave the chief impulse to the formation of the Jerusalem Talmud, but was not, as some have thought, its author. For further notices of him see *Juchassin*, p. 150 b; Wolf, ii. 874; Etheridge, p. 144.

[8] הכי דמי, lit., How is this to be compared? i.e., Illustrate this. It is a phrase which always expresses a request for more information.

[9] Lit., it is being said.

[10] And therefore he acts not as a fool, but with deliberation. It was supposed that by such means special communications from the devil were obtained. Cf. LXX. in Is. lxv. 4, Ἐν τοῖς μνήμασι...κοιμῶνται διὰ ἐνύπνια.

3 b, ll. 26.   at night it may be said that the Gandrippus[1] has seized him; and as for him who tears his clothes it may be said that he is lost in
4 a   thought[2]. But in case men have done them all, they are like the ox that has gored an ox, an ass, and a camel, and has been made a precedent of warning for all men.   R. Papa[3] said, If R. Hunna had heard that this is the Baraitha, viz., Who is a fool? it is he who destroys all that is given to him, he would have recalled his words.   It is a question[4] as regards his recalling of his words, whether he would have recalled his words only in the case of the man who tears his clothes, in consideration of the Baraitha which is like it[5], or whether he would have recalled them in the case of all three.   The matter was left undecided[6].

And one of doubtful sex and one of double sex etc.[7] Our Rabbis have taught[8], The use of the word, "male[9]," is to exclude the women; "thy males" to exclude the one of doubtful and the one of double sex; "all thy males" to include the children.   The Mishnah teacher[10] said, Male is to exclude the women. But why do I need a verse as above, to teach me this?   Inasmuch as[11] it is a case of a positive precept in which the time determines. And from all positive precepts in which the time determines, women are

Ex. xxiii. 17, Deut. xvi. 16.

---

[1] = κυνάνθρωπος, melancholy madness, Germ. *Wolfsmuth*.

[2] Lit., he is possessed of thoughts.

[3] Head of the Academy of Neresh (perhaps = Nahras, W. of Tigris. See Neubauer, *Géog. du Talmud*, p. 365) circ. A.D. 353.

[4] איבעי is Ithpe'el. The phrase in the text always means that some of the Academy asked others of that body.

[5] viz., who destroys all that is given him.

[6] תיקו, an expression of obscure derivation, either (i) Quaestio haec manet in *theca* sua, i.e., dubia, or (ii) an abbreviation for תשבי יתרץ קושיות ובעיות, (Elijah) the Tishbite will explain difficulties and problems, or (iii) (reversing the order of the letters) ואתה קדוש יושב תהלות (Ps. xxii. 4), "But thou art holy inhabiting praises." See Buxtorf, p. 2588, who prefers (i). Levy (*Neuheb. u. Chald. Wört.* s.v.) however considers it as shortened from תְּקוּם or תִּיקוֹם (root קוּם), thus meaning, (The question) remains (unanswered).

[7] See p. 1.

[8] See p. 11, note 2.

[9] As involved in the expression "thy males," which is but one word in the Heb.

[10] מר, a lord, i.e., an unnamed Rabbi.

[11] מִבְּדִי contracted from מָן־כְּד־הִי *from* (the fact) *that it* (is so), to be distinguished (see Levy, s.v.) from מִכְּדִי a particle of comparison "than," a contraction of מָן־כְּד־דִי.

exempt. Nay, but it is needed. You might have thought[1], 4a, l. 16. We learn of a twofold appearing before the Lord from the section, "Assemble." As in the one case women are bound, so in the other case women are bound[2]. We learn it[3] from this.

The Mishnah teacher said, The expression "thy males" is to exclude the one of doubtful and the one of double sex. It is all right[4] as regards the latter. This was necessary. You might have imagined that, since he has a shred of virility, he is bound[5]. We learn from this that his case is one *sui generis*. But as for the former, this was a dubious case. How was a verse necessary to remove the doubt[6]? Abai[7] said, Si eius ovaria externa sunt[8].

The Mishnah teacher said, The expression "all thy males" is to include the children. But there is a canonical Mishnah, Chag. 2a, Except a deaf man, a fool and a child. Abai said, There is no i. 1. difficulty. The one case has to do with a child who has reached the age for initiation in the law, the other with a child who has not reached the age for initiation. A child who has reached the

---

[1] סלקא דעתך אמינא, lit., Your thought perhaps arises in this form, viz., "I might say."

[2] The two passages referred to are Deut. xvi. 16 (יֵרָאֶה), xxxi. 11 (לִרְאוֹת). The former has to do with the three great annual feasts, the latter refers to the assembling once in seven years, and is in immediate connexion with the section "Assemble" which begins at verse 12. The argument is: It might have been inferred from the word *appearing* (ראייה), which occurs (see above) by implication in both passages, that women, inasmuch as they are expressly (v. 12) bidden to come in the latter case, are bound to come in the former also. Against such an inference the word "males" (זָכוּר) protects us. That word is therefore not superfluous, but necessary.

[3] viz., the true state of the case.

[4] בשלמא and הניח are synonymous, but the former is used in reference to a superior sort of authority (e.g., of Scripture) as compared with that indicated by the use of the latter.

[5] Therefore a verse was necessary to exclude him.

[6] Because we should have thought, that, *quâ* dubious case, he was not bound.

[7] His mother having died in giving him birth, his father's brother, Rabba bar Nachmani, the "rooter up of mountains," brought him up, and called him Abai from the first letters of the original of Hos. xiv. 4 (E. V. 3), "For in thee the fatherless findeth mercy." He was head of the Academy at Pumbeditha before Rabba (for whom see p. 4, note 3). They were both pupils of Joseph bar Chia (for whom see p. 17, note 5). See also Wolf, ii. 867.

[8] Then it is a doubtful case, whether he is bound to go up, and so a verse was necessary.

4 a, ll. 6. age for initiation—this is Rabbinical only¹. Even so, and the expression² is a mere supporting peg³. But why does the expression come? To correspond with what the others⁴ said. For we have a Baraitha⁵, Others say, the cordwainer and the smelter in bronze and the tanner⁶ are exempt from the holocaust, because it is said "all thy males," i. e., he who is able to go up with all thy males. They are exempt, who are not fit to go up with all thy males.

Ex. xxiii. 17, Deut. xvi. 16.

*Women and slaves who are not manumitted etc.*⁷ This is all right as regards women, as we have said, but slaves—how do we get them here⁸? R. Hunna says, The scripture says "before the LORD God." This expression can only apply to him who has but one Lord. He is excluded who has another lord. But why do I need a verse for it? Surely by every precept by which a woman is bound a slave is bound, and by every precept by which a woman is not bound a slave is not bound. The teacher learns it from the case of a woman through the double occurrence of the words "unto her⁹." Rabena said, It¹⁰ is only needed for one who is

Ex. xxiii. 17, Deut. xvi. 16.

---

¹ As opposed to Mosaic.   ² "All thy males."

³ The object of the verse (for, being a part of Holy Writ, it of necessity had some object) must have been to exclude cordwainers, etc. It was not for the purpose of including children, for this law about children was Rabbinic, and therefore not such as would be found laid down either explicitly or by implication in the Law. The verse therefore is only "a supporting peg." This kind of citation, as characteristically Jewish, cannot be wholly left out of account (although it would be easy to assign too much weight to it), in considering the character of some N.T. quotations, e.g. (Mt. ii. 15), "Out of Egypt did I call my son."

⁴ viz., R. Nathan. He had laid an ineffectual trap for a teacher, in consequence of which the decree went forth that his name should not be mentioned. So, e.g., p. 34, note 4.

⁵ This is the rendering of the conjectural emendation in the margin of the Lemberg edition. The text has the word which introduces a *canonical* Mishnah.

⁶ βυρσεύς.   ⁷ See p. 1.

⁸ Lit., slaves, whence (are they) to us?

⁹ The two passages are (Lev. xix. 20) "nor freedom given *unto her*" (לָהּ), viz., a bondmaid, and (Deut. xxiv. 3) "shall write *unto her* (לָהּ) a bill of divorcement." The argument is that the occurrence of לָהּ in both passages is a hint that they are connected, and, the connexion once granted, it further shews that the divorce (Deut.) is equivalent to "freedom" (Lev.). Therefore if the woman be not divorced (Deut.), she is a slave (Lev.), and so has a slave's status and disabilities.

¹⁰ The expression, "before the Lord God,"

half a slave and half free. This is precisely too what the teaching of the Mishnah is, *women and slaves who are not manumitted.* What is the meaning of the addition, *who are not manumitted?* If I should say that it means, who are not manumitted at all, then the words ought to be simply, slaves, but do you not think that it means, those who are not completely manumitted? and who are such? He who is half a slave and half free. Learn from this the meaning. 4a, ii. 23.

And[1] the lame man and the blind man and the sick man and the old man. Our Rabbis have taught[2], The expression "steps[3]" excludes people with wooden legs. Another explanation is, The expression "steps" excludes the lame man, and the sick man, and the blind man, and the old man, and the one who is not able to go up on his feet. *And the one who is not able to go up on his feet,* what is this expression to include? Rabba said, It is to include the delicately nurtured, as it is written, "When ye come to appear before me, who hath required this at your hand, to trample[4] my courts?" 4 b Is. i. 12.

There is a Baraitha, The uncircumcised person[5] and the unclean person are exempt from appearing. This is all right as regards an unclean person, for it is written, "And thither thou shalt come: and thither ye shall bring." Every one who belongs to the category of coming belongs to the category of bringing, and every one who does not belong to the category of coming does not belong to the category of bringing[6]. But "the uncircumcised person," whence do we get it[7]? Behold, this comes not from a text but from R. Akiba[8], Deut. xii. 5, 6.

[1] The *and* is an insertion. See p. 1. Similar minute differences, not affecting the sense, may be seen in subsequent quotations of the Mishnah.

[2] See p. 11, note 2.

[3] Lit., "footgoing times" (Exod. xxiii. 14). See p. 1.

[4] רמס an expression of contempt, and taken here by the Rabbis to apply to those who, as having been delicately nurtured, refused to uncover their feet (Exod. iii. 5) even on holy ground.

[5] Such a case for instance as that of a third child left without the rite, because the wound had proved fatal to two older ones.

[6] And bringing implies ceremonial cleanness.

[7] viz., that he is included.

[8] "One of the greatest lights of Judaism both before and after the death of Gamaliel II." (A.D. 115), Dr C. Taylor, *Sayings etc.*, p. 67. See his whole note, and Etheridge, pp. 66, 67, 76. Ben Joseph Akiba was a pupil of Eliezer ben Hyrkanus (see p. 45, note 3), and of Nachum of Gimzo (see p. 62, note 1). Succeeding Gamaliel, he became head of the Academy at B'ne Berak (Ibn

16   CHAGIGAH.

4 b, l. 9. who includes an uncircumcised person as unclean. For there is a
Lev. xxii. Baraitha, viz., R. Aḳiba says, The expression "each man¹" is to
4. include the uncircumcised person.   Our Rabbis have taught,
The unclean person is exempt from appearing, for it is written,
Deut. xii. "And thither thou shalt come : and thither ye shall bring." Every
5, 6. one who belongs to the category of coming belongs to the category
of bringing, and every one who does not belong to the category of
coming does not belong to the category of bringing.

    R. Jochanan ben Dahăbai says in the name of R. Jehudah, A
man blind in one eye is exempt from appearing, for it is said, "he
shall be seen," "he shall see²." As he comes to see, so he comes
to be seen. As he comes to see with both his eyes, so he comes
to be seen with both His eyes³.

    R. Hunna, when he came upon this passage "he shall be seen,"
"he shall see," wept. He said, Should a servant whose master is
looking out to see him, absent himself from him? as it is written,
Is. i. 12. "When ye come to appear⁴ before me, who hath required this at
your hand, to trample my courts?"

Deut.   R. Hunna, when he came upon this passage, wept, "And thou
xxvii. 7. shalt sacrifice peace-offerings and shalt eat there." Should a servant,
whose master is looking out for him to eat at his table, absent him-
Is. i. 11. self from him? For it is written "To what purpose is the multitude of your sacrifices unto me? saith the Lord."

Gen.xlv.3.   R. El'azar⁵, when he came upon this passage, wept, "And his

---

Ibrak), near Joppa (T. B. *Sanhedrin*, 92 b). He is said to have been descended from Sisera on the father's side, and to have spent the first forty years of his life as a shepherd, and wholly devoid of interest in Jewish learning. Then, fired by the determination to prove himself worthy of the marriage which he had secretly contracted with the daughter of a rich Jew (disinherited by her father on his account), he studied and became a Rabbi. He was put to death on the suppression of Bar Kokh'ba's rebellion. See also *Dict. Chr. Biog.* i. 67; Wolf, ii. 858; iv. 410—16. For him as one of the הֲרוּגֵי מַלְכוּת (slain on account of the kingdom, i.e., martyred to the cause of the Jewish Church at the bidding of Roman emperors), see Wolf, ii. 832, and compare p. 22, note 1, and p. 27, note 1 in this vol.

    ¹ אִישׁ אִישׁ E.V. "what man soever."

    ² The consonants may be pointed either as Niph'al or as Ḳal (יִרְאֶה, יְרָאֶה).

    ³ i.e. God's eyes; which parity of action necessarily falls to the ground in the case in question. Cp. *Israel=videns Deum* in St Aug., e.g., *De C. D.* xvi. 39.

    ⁴ Lit., to be seen.

    ⁵ El'azar ben Shammua' is the El'azar κατ' ἐξοχήν of the Talmud. He was teacher of Rabbi (see p. 2, note 9).

brethren could not answer him; for they were troubled at his 4 b, ii. 8. presence." And is then the rebuke of flesh and blood such? how much more the rebuke of the Lord!

R. El'azar, when he came upon this passage, wept, "And 1 Sam. Samuel said to Saul, Wherefore hast thou disquieted me, to bring xxviii. 15. me up?" And was then Samuel the righteous dismayed at the Judgment[1]? How much more should we be! As for Samuel, what is that which is written? "And the woman said unto Saul, 1 Sam. I saw gods coming up." The expression "coming up[2]" shews that xxviii. 13. there were two persons. Samuel was one, and there was another, for Samuel went and brought Moses with him. He said to him, Peradventure, though God forbid, we are wanted for the Judgment; rise with me, for there is nothing that thou hast written in the Law, which I have not kept.

R. Ami[3], when he came upon this passage, wept, "Let him put Lam. iii. his mouth in the dust: perhaps there may be hope." He said, All 29. this to be done, and the result a mere "perhaps."

R. Ami, when he came upon this passage, wept, "Seek right- Zeph. ii. 3. eousness, seek meekness; perhaps ye shall be hid in the day of the LORD's anger." He said, All this and—"perhaps."

R. Asi[4], when he came upon this passage, wept, "Hate the evil Am. v. 15. and love the good, and establish judgment in the gate: perhaps the LORD, the God of hosts, will be gracious." All this, and—"perhaps."

R. Joseph[5], when he came upon this passage, wept, "But there Prov. xiii. is that is destroyed without judgment." He said, Who is that who 23. is taken before his time? It is possible that this may have to do with R. Baybi bar Abai[6]. He used to visit the Angel of

---

[1] Supposing that the Last Day was come.

[2] Being plural in the Hebrew.

[3] A priest, pupil (as were Asi and Dimi) of Jochanan (for him see p. 11, note 7), whom he succeeded (A.D. 279) as head of the Academy of Tiberias. He died A.D. 300. See Wolf, ii. 869.

[4] A priest, colleague of Ami (see previous note) and joined with him in the presidency of the Academy at Tiberias. See also Wolf, ii. 869.

[5] Born at Shili in Babylonia, A.D. 259. His full name was Joseph bar Chia. One of his teachers was Nachman bar Jacob, who was himself a pupil of Samuel the colleague of Rab. See p. 20, note 3 and p. 45, note 5. He was head of the Academy at Pumbeditha. In his latter days, in spite of blindness, he composed a Targum on the Hagiographa. For references to him see Wolf, ii. 876; Etheridge, pp. 165, 166.

[6] Baybi's date may be approximately gathered from that of his father Abai, for whom see p. 13, note 7.

4 b, ll. 27. death. He¹ said to his attendant, Go, bring me Mary of Magdala², the women's hairdresser. He went and brought him Mary of Magdala, who taught children. He said to him, I bid thee bring Mary of Magdala, the women's hairdresser. He said to him, If so, I will bring her back. He said to him, Since thou hast brought her, let her be included. But how didst thou get hold of her?

5 a He answered, She was holding the poker in her hand, and was stooping down and clearing out the stove. She took it and put it upon her foot and was burned, and her evil star was in the ascendant³, and I have brought her. R. Baybi bar Abai said to him, Have ye⁴ permission to do thus? He said to him, And

Prov. xiii. 23. is it not written, "There is that is destroyed without judgment"? R. Baybi said to him, There is also the passage, "One

Eccles. i. 4. generation goeth, and another generation cometh." The Angel said, I shepherd⁵ them, till they have fulfilled the generation, and again I hand them over⁶ to Dumah⁷. He said to him, But in the final result what hast thou done with the years⁸? He said, If there is a mighty Rabbi, who does not fulfil his threats⁹, I add them to him, and so there is compensation.

Job ii. 3. R. Jochanan, when he came upon this passage, wept, "And thou incitest me against him, to destroy him without a cause." A slave, against whom men incite his master, and he allows it¹⁰, is there any help¹¹ for him?

Job xv. 15. R. Jochanan, when he came upon this passage, wept, "Behold, he putteth no trust in his holy ones." If He putteth not trust in His holy ones, in whom will He put trust? One day he was walking in the way. He saw a certain man, who was gathering figs. He was leaving what were ripe, and gathering what were not

---

¹ The Angel.

² This story is thought by some to involve a confused reference to the mother of our Lord.

³ Lit., her star (fate) was for evil.

⁴ You and your ministers.

⁵ i.e., correct their mistakes.

⁶ להן conjectural emendation for MS. reading לו'.

⁷ The god of Silence.

⁸ Which are as it were in hand, taken from those cut off before their time.

⁹ Lit., who passes by his words, i.e., one who, although hasty of temper, so far checks himself, as not to translate his harsh language towards his pupils into action.

¹⁰ Lit., is incited.   ¹¹ Lit., restoration.

ripe. He said to him, Dost thou not think that those are much 5 a, 1. 20.
better? He said to him, As regards their use, they are for a
journey. The one will keep and the other will not keep. He
said, This is what is written, "Behold, he putteth no trust in his
holy ones[1]." Is it so? and yet there is the case of that disciple, who was in the neighbourhood of R. Alexandri[2], and died
while yet young[3], and he said, If this one of our Rabbis had
wished[4], he would have been alive now; or perhaps he was one of
those who are referred to in the passage "he putteth no trust in
his holy ones"; but no, for he was one who kicked against his
teachers[5].

R. Jochanan, when he came upon this passage, wept, "And I Mal. iii. 5.
will come near to you to judgment; and I will be a swift witness
against the sorcerers, and against the adulterers, and against false
swearers; and against those that oppress the hireling in his wages."
A slave whose master drags him to his judgment-seat and hastens
to witness against him, is there any help for him? R. Jochanan ben Zakkai said, Alas for us, for Scripture weighs out for us
both light and heavy.

Resh Lakish[6] said, Every one who turneth aside the judgment
of the stranger is as though he turned aside the judgment of God;
for it is written "ומטי the stranger," and the word is מטי[7]. ibid.

R. Chanina bar Papa[8] said, "Every one who doeth a thing and
repenteth of it is forgiven at once, for it is said, "and they fear ibid.
not me." Lo, if they do "fear me," it follows that they are forgiven at once.

R. Jochanan, when he came upon this passage, wept, "For Eccles.
xii. 14.

[1] He gathers them unripe, lest they should fall away from their excellence. "The grey-hair'd saint may fail at last," etc. Keble, 8th S. a. Trin.

[2] Flourished in the time of R. Chanina bar Papa and of R. Abai. See
Juchassin, p. 112 b.

[3] אל־ד־זוטר.

[4] i.e., had repented.

[5] A rebellious pupil.

[6] ריש לקיש (chief of robbers), so called, because at one time he took the
leadership of a band of outlaws, but was brought back to honourable ways by
his wife's brother, R. Jochanan. They were Palestinian teachers, and often
discussed points together. See Wolf, ii. 881.

[7] These letters may be vocalised either as מַטֵּי (so Massoretes), "that
turn aside," or as מַטֵּי, "that turneth Me aside."

[8] We can only infer his date from that of his father. See p. 12, note 3.

5 a, ll. 2. God shall bring every work into judgment concerning every hidden thing." A slave, whose master punishes[1] sins of error as though they were sins of presumption—is there any help for him? What is the meaning of "concerning every hidden thing"? Rab[2] said, This means the man who kills a louse in the presence of his neighbour, so that he is disgusted at it. But Samuel[3] said, This means the man who spits in the presence of his neighbour, so that he is disgusted. What is the meaning of "whether it be good or whether it be evil"? The men of the house of R. Jannai[4] say, This is he that gives a coin[5] to a poor man publicly[6]. For this story is told of R. Jannai himself. He saw a man[7] who gave a coin to a poor man publicly[6]. He said to him, It had been better that thou hadst not given it to him now, for thou hast given it to him and hast put him to shame. The men of the house of R. Shila[8] say, This is he that gives alms to a woman secretly, because he brings her into suspicion. Rabba said, This is he that sends home to his wife meat that is not bled[9] on the eve of the sabbath[10]. But lo, on the other hand, Rabba himself sent such home. Ah,

---

[1] Lit., weighs out to him.

[2] Called the greatest of all the Gemaric teachers, and hence named Rab *par excellence* (also called Abba. See p. 39, note 5). He was a Babylonian, nephew to R. Chia, and disciple of R. Jehudah. He founded the Academy of Sora (see p. 6, note 1), of which he was president for twenty-four years, dying in A.D. 243. See Wolf, ii. 879, and (for his works) Etheridge, p. 157.

[3] Often mentioned, as here, along with his contemporary Rab. Samuel excelled in the civil, and Rab in the other parts of the Jewish Law. The former was also an astronomer. He was born at Nehardea, the most ancient Jewish community in Babylonia (Neubauer, *Géog. du T.* p. 350), succeeded Shila in the headship of that Academy, and died A.D. 250. See Wolf, ii. 881, for his various titles. He was court physician and teacher to Sapor I., king of Persia, who died circ. A.D. 273 (to be distinguished from Sapor, son of Hormouz : see next p.). See Gibbon, ch. xi. Samuel is often called in the Talmud Sapor, also Aryoch (lion, king, teacher).

[4] Jannai was a contemporary of Chia. See *Juch.* p. 155.

[5] The original word (זוּזָא, zouza) denotes a small silver coin, the value of which was a quarter of a (biblical) shekel. See Levy, s.vv. זוּזָא, קֶלַע.

[6] The Greek παρρησία in a Heb. dress.

[7] Lit., *the* man.

[8] Flourished at the beginning of the 4th century.

[9] Lit., cut.

[10] On the Friday afternoon there is a bustle in preparing for the Sabbath, and the wife may perhaps assume that her husband has already made sure of the animal's being killed in a manner which accorded with Jewish requirements.

but it was a different matter as regards the daughter of R. Chasda[1], for he was certain about her, as being a woman of experience. 5 a, ll. 19.

R. Jochanan, when he came upon this passage, wept, "And it shall come to pass, when many evils and troubles are come upon them." A slave, whose master brings upon him evils and troubles —is there any help for him? What is the meaning of "evils and troubles"? Rab said, Evils which become troubles counterbalancing one another, as in the case of the wasp and the scorpion[2]. But Samuel said, This refers to him who bestows money upon the poor man in the hour of his extreme distress[3]. Rabba said, This agrees with the proverb, Money[4] for corn standing in the field is not found, for corn hanging up it is found[5]. Deut. xxxi. 21.

"Then my anger shall be kindled against them in that day, and I will forsake them, and I will hide my face from them." R. Bardala bar Tabyumi[6] said that Rab said, Every one who is not included in the "hiding of the face" is not of them; every one who is not included in the words "and they shall be devoured" is not of them. Our Rabbis said to Rabba, Master, thou art not included in the "hiding of the face," and thou art not included in the "devouring." He said to them, How know ye how much I send out secretly to king Shabor[7]? And still our Rabbis fixed their eyes upon him. While this was going on, there came a message[8] from the house[9] of king Shabor, and they spoiled him. He said, Deut. xxxi. 17. Deut. xxxi. 17. 5 b

---

[1] Succeeded Hunna as head of the Academy of Sora, a post which he held A.D. 290—300. Sora, like Nehardea and Pumbeditha, gave its name to one of the districts of Babylon.

[2] Hot and cold water cure respectively the pain of the scorpion's bite and of the wasp's sting. But if a man is both bitten and stung on the same spot, it is a case of "troubles counterbalancing one another."

[3] As opposed to an earlier stage, when help might have been of permanent use.

[4] Lit., A zouza.

[5] For hanging up, i.e., in store, lest the rats should get it, even though no money was forthcoming to obviate risks accruing at an earlier stage.

[6] Beyond what is implied by the fact of his being a pupil of Rab his date is uncertain.

[7] See Gibbon, cc. xviii., xxiv., xxv., for Sapor (Shabor), the king of Persia whose accession preceded his birth. He was son of Hormouz, and reigned A.D. 310—380. He warred against Rome, which to the Jews represented Edom, their traditional foe.

[8] שְׁדרוּ for שָׁדרוּ. See Goldammer's Luzzatto, *Grammar etc.*, p. 64 (New York, 1876), and Wright's *Comp. Gr. of Sem. Langs.*, p. 169 (Cambridge, 1890).

[9] Equivalent to the Greek οἱ περί κ.τ.λ.

5 b, l. 7. This agrees with the Baraitha, viz., Rabban Simeon ben Gamaliel[1] said, Every place on which wise men have fixed their eyes[2] is the scene of a death or calamity.

Deut. xxxi. 18. "And I will surely hide my face in that day." Rabba said, The Holy One said, Even if I hide mine eyes from them, I will speak to him by a dream.   R. Joseph said, His hand is stretched out
Is. li. 16. over us, as it is said, "and I have covered thee in the shadow of my hand."

R. Joshua ben Chănania was in the house of Caesar. That infidel[3] shewed him a people whose Lord had turned[4] His face from them. He[5] shewed him in return His hand stretched out over us. Caesar said to Rabbi Joshua, What did he shew thee? He replied, A people, whose Lord has turned away His face from them, and I shewed him His hand stretched out over us. They said to that heretic[6], What didst thou shew him? He replied, I shewed him a people, whose Lord had turned away His face from them. They said to him, And what did he shew thee? He said, I know not. They said to him, A man, who does not know what he is shewn by a sign, shall he interpret[7] before a king? They cast him out and slew him.

When the soul of R. Joshua ben Chănania was departing, they

---

[1] He succeeded his father Gamaliel as head of the Sanhedrin at Jerusalem, A.D. 58, and was one of the הרוּגי מַלְכוּת (see p. 15, note 8). For further particulars cf. Wolf, iv. 899.

[2] To fix the eyes denotes to invoke evil or punishment.

[3] Lit., Epicurus, a frequent word in the Talmud for an unnamed unbeliever, whether of Jewish or Gentile blood. For the mention of both these classes, as well as for a play upon the word, as though derived from פקר, to act without restraint, to be restless, see *Sanhedrin*, 38 b, ii. 2. The word is often applied to Christians, who are also called מִינִין (see note 6 below) and צְדּוּקִין (Sadducees).

[4] אַחְדְרִינְהוּ. The pronom. suffix is attached to the past Aphel of הדר, which, however, as though it were a participle, has the plural masc. suffix, as attracted to the grammatical number of אַפֵּיה. For this last the more regular form would be אַפּוֹהִי.

[5] Joshua.

[6] מִינָא, the most frequent name for Christians in the Talmud. It comes from an Arabic root, meaning to speak falsely (so Levy, s.v.), but according to Jewish etymologists it is an abbreviation of מַאֲמִין a believer (so called in irony), or, less likely still, formed from the initial letters of the three words מַאֲמִין יֵשׁוּעַ נוֹצְרִי, a believer in Jesus of Nazareth.

[7] Lit., shew.

said to him, O our Rabbi, what will become of us at the hands of the Epicureans?" He said to them, "Is counsel perished from the sons¹, is their wisdom vanished?" When counsel has perished from the sons, the wisdom of the peoples of the earth has vanished. Or, if you like, draw comfort from this passage, "And he said, Let us take our journey and let us go, and I will go before thee²." 5 b, l. 18. Jer. xlix. 7. Gen. xxxiii. 12.

R. Ela³ was mounting a ladder in the house of Rabbah bar Shela⁴; he heard a child who was reading, "For, lo, he that formeth the mountains and createth the wind, and declareth unto man what is his thought." Ela said, A slave, whose master declareth to him what is his thought, is there any help for him? What is the meaning of the expression, What is his thought? Rab said, Even the superfluous talk between a husband and his wife is told a man⁵ in the day of his death. Is it so? and yet Rab Kohăna hid himself under the nuptial couch of Rab and heard him talk and laugh and do as he had a mind. He said, The mouth of Rab is like that of one who has not tasted broth⁶. He⁷ said to him, Kohăna, get out, these are not good manners⁸. There is no difficulty. In the one case it was needful to procure her favour, in the other it was not needful to procure her favour. Amos iv. 13.

"But if ye will not hear it, my soul shall weep in secret places for your pride." R. Samuel bar Inia⁹ in the name of Rab said, The Holy One, blessed be He, has a place, and its name is "secret places." What is the meaning of "for your pride"? R. Samuel bar Isaac¹⁰ said, For the glory of Israel, because it was taken away from them and given to the peoples of the world. R. Samuel bar Nachmani¹¹ said, On account of the glory of the kingdom of heaven. And how is there¹² weeping in the presence of¹³ the Jer. xiii. 17.

---

¹ The Hebrew words for "sons" and for "prudent" (E.V.) are identical in form.

² Thus indicating that Jacob, even though the weaker, will always take the lead of Esau (=Edom=Rome).

³ He lived in Jabneh. See Wolf, iii. 809.

⁴ A contemporary of Hunna and Chasda, i.e., in the latter part of the 3rd cent. See Wolf, ii. 880, *Juchassin*, p. 183 b.

⁵ i.e., the angels tell him.

⁶ An expression denoting a newly-married man.

⁷ Rab.   ⁸ Lit., the way of the world.

⁹ His exact date is unknown.

¹⁰ A contemporary of Zerah (for whom see p. 26, note 2).

¹¹ Date uncertain.   ¹² i.e., can there be?

¹³ A euphemism for *on the part of*.

<small>5 b, l. 32.</small> Holy One, blessed be He, seeing that R. Papa said, There is no tribulation in the presence of the Holy One, blessed be He. For <small>Ps. xcvi. 6.</small> it is said "Honour and majesty are before him, strength and beauty are in his sanctuary." There is no difficulty. The one has to do with the inner, the other with the outer side of the Divine Being. Is there then no weeping on the outer side? And yet <small>Is. xxii. 12.</small> it is written, "And in that day did the Lord, the LORD of hosts, call to¹ weeping and to mourning and to baldness and to girding with sackcloth." That is a different matter, viz., the destruction of the Temple², for for this even the angels of peace wept, as it is <small>Is. xxxiii. 7.</small> said, "Behold, their valiant ones cry without: the angels of peace weep bitterly."

<small>Jer. xiii. 17.</small> "And mine eye shall weep sore, and run down with tears, because the Lord's flock is taken captive." R. El'azar said, Wherefore these three tears³? One for the first Temple, and one for the second Temple, and one for Israel, because they are gone into captivity from their place. And there are some who say, One for the neglect of the Law. This is all right according to those who explain, For Israel, because they are gone into captivity. This is that which is written, "because the Lord's flock is taken captive." But according to those who explain, For the neglect of the Law, <small>Jer. xiii. 17.</small> what is the connexion of this with "because the LORD's flock is taken captive"? Since Israel are gone into captivity from their place, thou canst have no neglect of the Law greater than this.

Our Rabbis have taught⁴, There are three persons, over whom the Holy One, blessed be He, weepeth every day, viz., over him who can study in the Law and does not study it, and over him who cannot properly study the Law, and yet does study it⁵, and over a president⁶ who deals arrogantly with the congregation.

Rabbi took up the Book of Lamentations and read in it. When <small>Lam. ii. 1.</small> he came upon this verse "He hath cast down from heaven unto the earth," the Book fell from his hands. He said, From the high roof to the deep pit!

---

¹ i.e., proclaim.   ² A matter *sui generis.*

³ דִּמְעָה, תִּרְמַע, דָּמַע.

⁴ See p. 11, note 2.

⁵ i.e., who has not, properly speaking, the ability or opportunity, yet makes an effort in that direction.

⁶ Of a Rabbinic school.

Rabbi and R. Chia[1] were discussing and walking along a road. **5 b, ii. 15.**
When they came to a certain place, they said, If there is a powerful
Rabbi here, let us go and visit him. They said, Is there a powerful
Rabbi here? And the reply was, Yes, but he is blind. R. Chia
said to Rabbi, Stay here; thou shalt not make little of thy princely
dignity; I will go and visit him. But he[2] laid hold of him and
went with him. When they were coming away from him, he said
to them, Ye have visited a face, which is seen but sees not; may
ye be held worthy to visit the Face which sees and is not seen. He[2]
said to him[3], Now see[4], thou wouldst have deprived me of this
blessing.   They said to him, Whence hast thou heard it?   From
the sayings of R. Jacob[5] have I heard it. For R. Jacob, a man
of K'phar Chatyah[6], used to visit his teacher every day. When
he was old, the teacher said to him, My lord need not do this, for
my lord is not able. R. Jacob said, Is this a small thing that is
written with respect to our Rabbis? "And he shall live on for ever, **Ps. xlix.**
he shall not see destruction, when he seeth that wise men die." **10, 11;**
But what[7]? He who seeth wise men in their death shall live; **E.V. 9, 10.**
how much more he who sees them in their life!

R. Idi[8], father of R. Jacob bar Idi, was accustomed to spend
three months on his journey and one day in the house of Rab,
and our Rabbis used to call him Rab's schoolboy of a day. He
became broken-hearted[9]. He read to himself the passage, "I am as **Job xii. 4.**
one that is a laughing-stock to his neighbour, etc." R. Jochanan
said to him, In the prayer that comes from thee do not injure our
Rabbis.

[1] More fully Chia Rabbah, son of Abba Sela, whence he is sometimes called
Chia bar Abba. He was a pupil of Rabbi, and his date about A.D. 218. He is
by some reckoned among the Mishnic (Tanaim), by others among the Gemaric
teachers (Amoraim).   See Wolf, ii. 872.

[2] Rabbi.   [3] Chia.

[4] Lit., Behold now. For examples of the use of אִיבָּא see a good note in
Goldammer's Luzzatto, *Grammar etc.* p. 111.

[5] His date is not accurately known.

[6] Perhaps to be identified with *Hattin* (Robinson, *Bibl. Researches*, iii. 34),
N.W. of Tiberias. See Neubauer, *Géog. du T.* p. 207.

[7] וּמַה always introduces something of an argument.

[8] For the story here told of him see *Juch.* p. 110 b. For the sake of one
day's instruction from Rab he spent six months in the double journey, i.e., all
the time between Passover and Tabernacles, on both which occasions a married
Jew is obliged to be with his wife.

[9] More lit., faint (with vexation).   Cf. use of ἀθυμεῖν, Col. iii. 21.

<small>5 b, ii. 28.</small>
<small>Is. lviii. 2.</small>

R. Jochanan went into the College and expounded thus, "Yet they seek me daily, and delight to know my ways." And while they seek Him by day, do they not seek Him by night also? Yes, but it is to inform thee that every one who studieth in the Law even one day in the year, the Scripture reckoneth it to him, as if he studied all the year; and so in the case of punishments, as it is written, "After the number of the days that ye spied out the land." And was it that they sinned forty *years*? Was it not forty *days* that they sinned? but it was to inform thee, that every one who committeth a transgression even one day in the year, the Scripture reckoneth it to him, as if he had transgressed all the year.

<small>Numb. xiv. 34.</small>

What is the definition of a child? Every one who is not able to ride upon his father's shoulders[1]. Rabbi[2] Zera objects to this, and enquires, Who brought him hither[3]? Abai said to him, As his mother was bound by the law of rejoicing, his mother brought him hither. Henceforward[4], if he can go up, holding by the hand of his father, from Jerusalem to the mountain of the House, he is bound; but if not, he is free. R. [Zera[5]] replied, I take the side of the house of Hillel against the words of the house of Shammai. For we read, "But Hannah went not up; for she said to her husband, Not until the child be weaned, then I will bring him." But Samuel was able to ride upon his father's shoulders. Abai[6] said to him, Even according to thine own argument there is a difficulty for thee. How was not Hannah in her own person bound

<small>6 a</small>

<small>1 Sam. i. 22.</small>

---

[1] The view of the house of Shammai. See p. 1.

[2] Rabbi was the Palestinian, Rab the Babylonian title. Zera, though properly holding the latter, as being a pupil of R. Hunna at Sora, yet after Hunna's death (A.D. 300) returned to Palestine and died at Tiberias. There he is said to have been called קְטִינָא as a synonym for זְעֵירָא, *small*. See Wolf, ii. 871. See also a long note on him in *Juch.* p. 132 b, where the story is told that being desirous of ascertaining by anticipation whether the fires of Gehenna would have power to hurt him, he caused himself to be put into an oven, whereupon the Rabbis who looked upon him saw that his feet were singed.

[3] i.e., from his home to the city of Jerusalem. The question now is whether he is to go up from the city to the Holy House. But, says Zera in effect, if the house of Shammai's definition be the right one, the child could not have been brought by his father to Jerusalem at all, and thus the question could not arise. Therefore, he argues, we take the definition of the house of Hillel.

[4] The remainder of the way.

[5] The proper name seems to have dropped out of the Talmud text.

[6] אבו is an obvious error.

by the law of rejoicing? But the real explanation is that 6 a, i. 12. Hannah saw great delicacy in Samuel, and was uneasy about Samuel in respect to the fatigue of the journey.

R. Simeon[1] asked[2], What of a child that is lame, according to the words of the house of Shammai, or one that is blind, according to the words of both of them? Explain this[3]. If we are to speak of the case of a lame person, who cannot stretch out his limb, or a blind person, who cannot open his eye, see now, an adult is free, why should we ask about a child? It is not necessary to discuss such a case. But in the case of a lame person, who can stretch out his limb, or a blind person who can open his eye, what of this case? Abai said, Wherever the adult is bound according to the Law, we educate the child in it also according to our Rabbis, and wherever the adult is free according to the Law, the child also is free according to the Rabbis.

The house of Shammai say, The holocaust involves two pieces of silver etc.[4] Our Rabbis have taught thus, The house of Shammai say, The holocaust involves two pieces of silver, and the Chagigah a meah of silver; for the holocaust is all a burnt-offering to the Most High, which is not the case with the Chagigah; and besides we find that at the Feast of Weeks[5] the Scripture enjoins more burnt-offerings than peace-offerings. But the house of Hillel say, The holocaust involves a meah of silver and the Chagigah two pieces of silver, for the Chagigah is older than the Decalogue, which is not the case with the holocaust; and besides we find in the case of "the princes" that the Scripture enjoins more peace- Numb. vii. offerings than burnt-offerings. What then is the reason that the 15, 17, etc. house of Hillel do not agree with the house of Shammai? Inas-

[1] One of the הַרוּגֵי מַלְכוּת. See p. 15, note 8; also Wolf, ii. 861.
[2] A question of learned ignorance.
[3] "Explain this" (lit., How is this to be compared, or pictured? See p. 11, note 8) forms the Talmud teacher's reply to Simeon. For (it says) if these defects be incurable, there is no need of entering on the question. Because it would be of no use to bring him up when a child, seeing that, *quâ* lame or blind, he would not, even though adult, be allowed to enter, but would be פָּטוּר.
[4] See p. 2.
[5] A post-biblical meaning of the word in the original (עֲצֶרֶת). In the Bible it either has the general sense of *assembly* (e.g., Jer. ix. 1), or refers to the last day of Passover (Deut. xvi. 8) or of Tabernacles (Lev. xxiii. 36, Numb. xxix. 35).

6 a, ll. 5. much as thou sayest that a holocaust is better, for it is all a burnt-offering to the Most High, on the contrary[1] a Chagigah is better, for there are in it two feastings[2]; and in that thou sayest, Let us learn from the Feast of Weeks, I reply that we are to judge an individual gift[3] by comparison with an individual gift[4], and we are not to judge an individual gift by comparison with the gift of a congregation[5]. What then is the reason that the house of Shammai do not agree with the house of Hillel? In that thou sayest that a Chagigah is superior, because it is older than the Decalogue, a holocaust also is older than the Decalogue; and in that thou sayest, Let us learn from "the princes," we are to judge a thing that lasts for ever[6] by comparison with a thing that lasts for ever, and we are not to judge a thing which lasts for ever by comparison with a thing which does not last for ever[7]. And how does the house of Hillel come to teach that the Chagigah is older than the Decalogue, but the holocaust not? Because[8] it is written, "and they sacrificed sacrifices of peace-offerings[9]." There must have been a holocaust also. Lo, it is written, "and they offered burnt-offerings." The house of Hillel consider that the burnt-offering which Israel offered in the wilderness was the "continual burnt-offering[10]," but the house of Shammai consider that the burnt-offering which Israel offered in the wilderness was a holocaust. Abai said, The house of Shammai and R. El'azar and R. Ishmael[11] all consider that the burnt-offering which Israel offered in the wilderness was a holocaust. And the house of Hillel and

Exod. xxiv. 5.

Exod. xxix. 42.

---

[1] Lit., (I rest my argument) upon what is superior (על ד רבה).
[2] One for God and one for the offerer and his friends.
[3] Such as the holocaust.
[4] Such as that of the princes.
[5] Such as that of Weeks.
[6] Such as the Chagigah.
[7] Such as the offering of the princes.
[8] Against that view of the house of Hillel.
[9] Here therefore we have peace-offerings and (see next sentence) holocausts apparently instituted together at a time subsequent to the giving of the Decalogue (Exod. xx.).
[10] This "continual burnt-offering," the house of Hillel would say, is the burnt-offering referred to in the passage, which the Talmud has just adduced against them. That passage therefore, they would argue, does not affect their position.
[11] An associate of Akiba. For further particulars about Ishmael and his school see Wolf, ii. 849, 877.

R. Aḳiba and R. Jose the Galilaean[1] all consider that the offering which Israel offered in the wilderness was the "continual burnt-offering." The house of Shammai hold this view according to what we have said. R. Ishmael agrees, for there is a Baraitha, viz., R. Ishmael says, The general directions only were given to Moses on Sinai, and the details afterwards in the Tabernacle of the Congregation[2]. But R. Aḳiba said, General directions and details were alike given him on Sinai, and they were repeated in the Tabernacle of the Congregation, and given for the third time in the plains of Moab[3]. And if thou dost imagine that the burnt-offering which Israel offered in the wilderness was the "continual burnt-offering," how should there be anything, which at the first did not need to be flayed and divided[4], but at the end did need to be flayed and divided[5]? R. El'azar agrees, for there is a Baraitha, viz., In commenting on the passage, "continual burnt-offering, which was ordained in Mount Sinai," R. El'azar says, Its ordinances were told in Mount Sinai, but it was not itself offered. R. Aḳiba says, It was offered and never ceased again. But how then am I to explain[6] the passage, "Did ye bring unto me sacrifices and offerings in the wilderness forty years, O house of Israel?" The explanation is that the tribe of Levi, which had not served idols, they offered them.

The house of Hillel hold the view which we have mentioned. R. Aḳiba also holds the view which we have mentioned. R. Jose the Galilaean agrees with them, for there is a Baraitha, viz., R. Jose the Galilaean says, Three commands have been put upon Israel when they go up to a feast, viz., the holocaust, and the Chagigah, and the rejoicing. There is in the holocaust what there is not in the other two, and there is in the Chagigah what there is not in the other two, and there is in the rejoicing what there is not in the other two. There is in the

_____

[1] He flourished about the time of Aḳiba's death.
[2] i.e., Leviticus.
[3] i.e., Deuteronomy.
[4] See Exod. xxix. 38—40.
[5] As did the perpetual burnt-offering (Lev. i. 6). The argument is, That which was to be offered twice a day would have all its details explained as early as possible. This whole Baraitha however, though adduced in support of the opinion ascribed to Ishmael, is far from proving the point, a fact which is admitted a few sentences later in the Talmud itself. See p. 30, note 3.
[6] Lit., to establish.

holocaust what there is not in the other two, for the holocaust is a whole burnt-offering to the Most High, which is not the case in the other two. There is in the Chagigah what there is not in the other two, for the Chagigah is older than the Decalogue, which is not the case in the other two[1]. There is in the rejoicing what there is not in the other two, for the rejoicing has to do with women as well as men, which is not the case in the other two.

And what is the reason that R. Ishmael is represented as expressing an opinion agreeing with the house of Shammai? viz., "If thou dost imagine that the burnt-offering which Israel offered in the wilderness was the continual burnt-offering, how should there be anything which at the first did not need to be flayed and divided, but in the end did need to be flayed and divided[2]?" But then R. Jose the Galilaean said, The burnt-offering which Israel offered in the wilderness was the "continual burnt-offering." At the first it did not need to be flayed and divided, but in the end it did need to be flayed and divided. For there is a Baraitha, viz., R. Jose the Galilaean says, The burnt-offering which Israel offered in the wilderness was not subject to flaying or dividing. inasmuch as the regulations for flaying and dividing were only from the time of the Tabernacle of the Congregation and henceforward. Strike out R. Ishmael[3].

R. Chasda enquired, What is the meaning of this verse? "And he sent young men of the children of Israel, which offered burnt-offerings," lambs, "and sacrificed peace-offerings of oxen unto the Lord." Or perhaps both these and those were oxen. What comes out of it all then[4]? Mar Zot'ra says, It depends upon the division[5] of the verse by the accents[6]. R. Acha, the son of Rabba[7], said, It is important for a man who says, Behold, I vow

---

[1] This is the one clause in R. Jose's speech, which bears upon the point at issue.

[2] A repetition of a portion of the Baraitha adduced just before, but unsuccessfully, as a proof of Ishmael's view.

[3] i.e., the tradition, as regards him, is a false one.

[4] i.e., Is there any use in the whole discussion? And the answer is, Yes, for Mar Zot'ra etc.

[5] Lit., the breaking.

[6] For other early notices of accentuation see Wickes, *Heb. Prose Accents*, p. 1, note 2 (Oxford, 1887).

[7] He appears to have been the associate of Ashi and to have been head of the Academy at Sora A.D. 410. The date of his death is probably A.D. 413. See Wolf, ii. 868.

a burnt-offering like the burnt-offering which Israel offered in the wilderness. What was it? Were they oxen or lambs? The matter was left undecided[1].

There is a Baraitha here, These are the things that have no prescribed limit, the corner of a field[2], and the first-fruits[3] and the appearing before the Lord[4], and the conferring of kindnesses[5] and the teaching contained in the Law.   R. Jochanan said, We were of opinion that the appearing before the Lord had no superior limit but had an inferior limit, until R. Oshaia[6], in the name of a great teacher[7], came and taught that appearing before the Lord has no limit either superior or inferior.   But wise men say, that the holocaust involves a meah of silver, but the Chagigah two pieces of silver.   What does the appearing mean? R. Jochanan said, The presenting of oneself in the Court, but Resh Lakish said, The presenting of oneself with an offering.   All the world is agreed that on the first day it means, the presenting of oneself with an offering, but men differ as regards the remainder of the days of the Feast. Every time that a man comes and brings an offering, all the world agrees that we are to receive it from him, but men differ in the case of one who comes and does not bring; for R. Jochanan considers that the presenting of oneself in the Court is sufficient, because it is not necessary, every time that he comes, to bring an offering; but Resh Lakish says, The presenting oneself with an offering is the meaning, for it is necessary, every time that he comes, to bring an offering.   Resh Lakish put this difficulty to R. Jochanan, "None shall appear before me empty." He said to him, Yes, but only on the first day of the Feast. He[8] put this further difficulty to him.   The passage "None shall appear before me empty" refers to coming with sacrifices.   If thou sayest,

6 b, ii. 17.

7 a

Exod. xxiii. 15.

---

[1] See p. 12, note 6.
[2] Lev. xix. 9, xxiii. 22.
[3] Exod. xxiii. 19.
[4] i.e., the offering in connexion with that appearing. The word in the original occurs only in this passage of the treatise, but is cognate with ראייה (R'iyyah), for which see p. 1, note 1 and Glossary.
[5] גְּמִילוּת חֲסָדִים is the general expression, of which kindness to the poor (צְדָקָה) is a species.
[6] A disciple of Rabbi. See Wolf, ii. 871.
[7] רַבִּי. The expression, though in itself indefinite, yet in each case seems to have had reference to some definite person well known at the time.
[8] Resh Lakish.

7 a, ll. 9. With sacrifices? perhaps not, but with birds and meal-offerings; then here is an argument against thee. The Chagigah is assigned to a private person, but the appearing is assigned to the Most High. As the Chagigah, which is assigned to a private person, involves sacrifices, so must the appearing, which is assigned to the Most High, involve sacrifices[1]. And what are these sacrifices? They are burnt-offerings. If thou sayest, Burnt-offerings? perhaps not, but peace-offerings; then here is an argument against thee. The Chagigah is assigned to a private person, and the appearing is assigned to the Most High. As the Chagigah, which is assigned to a private person, is suited to him, so must the appearing, which is assigned to the Most High, be suited to Him[2]. And so it is fitting[3] that thy table should not be full and the table of thy Master empty. He[4] said to him, Yes, but only on the first day of the Feast. R. Jose[5], in the name of R. Jehudah, put this difficulty to him, saying, Three times in the year Israel was commanded to go up to a Feast, viz., at the Feast of the Passover, and at the Feast of Weeks, and at the Feast of Tabernacles, and they must not appear by halves, inasmuch as it is said, "all thy males," and they must not appear empty, inasmuch as it is said, "none shall appear before me empty." He said to him, Yes, but only on the first day of the Feast.

Exod. xxiii. 17; Deut. xvi. 16.
Exod. xxiii. 15.
Exod. xxiii. 17; Deut. xvi. 16.

R. Jochanan put this difficulty to Resh Lakish; "he shall be seen," "He shall see[6]." As I[7] am seen freely, so shall ye see me freely. But every one who comes and does not bring an offering, all the world agrees that he goes up and allows himself to be seen and goes away. But they differ in the case of one who comes and brings an offering. R. Jochanan says, The simple

---

[1] And not merely, as in the case of birds, the wringing of the neck.

[2] And therefore it must involve offerings which shall be wholly devoted by fire to God, and not shared in, as peace-offerings etc., by the worshipper or others.

[3] Lit., with justice.

[4] Jochanan.

[5] This name, when it stands as here, without addition, always denotes Jose ben Chelpetha or Chalaphta, associated with Simeon, Jehudah (Rabbi), Meir, and El'azar ben Shammua' at the Academy of Tiberias. He is believed to have written the book סֵדֶר עוֹלָם. See Wolf, ii. 846.

[6] See p. 3. The Heb. consonants in each passage may be vocalised, so as to have either sense.

[7] God.

presenting of oneself in the Court is the real presenting of oneself, and so has no limit of times prescribed, while on the contrary the presenting of oneself for an offering has a limit of times prescribed. But Resh Laḳish said, The presenting of oneself with an offering is alone the real presenting of oneself, for if it be the case of an offering also, there is no limit[1]. He[2] put this difficulty to him[3], "Let thy foot be seldom in thy neighbour's[4] house." But here it has to do with sin-offerings and trespass-offerings. So is the opinion of R. Levi[5]. For R. Levi adduces[6] the passage, "Let thy foot be seldom in thy neighbour's house," and[7] the passage, "I will come into thy house with burnt-offerings." There is no difficulty. In the one case it has to do with sin-offerings and trespass-offerings, in the other with burnt-offerings and peace-offerings. There is a Baraitha also to this effect, viz., "Let thy foot be seldom in thy neighbour's house:" the passage speaks of sin-offerings and trespass-offerings; if thou sayest, Of sin-offerings and trespass-offerings? perhaps not, but of burnt-offerings and peace-offerings, as he says, "I will come into thy house with burnt-offerings, I will pay thee my vows," for see, they actually speak[8] there of burnt-offerings and peace-offerings; Nay, but look thou how I explain, "Let thy foot be seldom in thy neighbour's house," viz., that the passage is speaking of sin-offerings and trespass-offerings.

And they must not appear by halves etc.[9] R. Joseph thought to explain thus, If a man has ten sons, they are not to go up five at this time and five to-morrow[10]. Abai said to him, Of course[11]. For

7 a, ll. 22.

Prov. xxv. 17.

Ps. lxvi. 12.

Ps. lxvi. 12.

7 b

---

[1] Therefore he must present one every time that he appears during the Feast.
[2] Jochanan. [3] Resh Laḳish. [4] i.e., God.
[5] Levi placed absolutely denotes Levi bar Sisi, a disciple of Rabbi, for whom see p. 2, note 9. For Levi see Wolf, ii. 877.
[6] Lit., throws out for consideration.
[7] As contrasted with it.
[8] אָמוּר for אָמְרוּ. See p. 21, note 8.
[9] This however is not really a section of the Mishnah upon which the Gemara is commenting, but is part of Jose's teaching. See p. 32.
[10] Fear of the evil eye might have prevented them from allowing themselves to be all seen together. Comp. "unbeschrieen!" (i.e., Wir wollen es unbeschrieen lassen! We would leave it unbewitched!), an exclamation still uttered by Ashkenazi parents when their children are admired.
[11] פשיטה, lit., This is a simple thing.

otherwise the question would arise, Which of them wilt thou cause[1] to be sinners, and which of them wilt thou cause to be obedient[2]? But wherefore then does the passage come[3]? It is to correspond to the saying of others[4]. For there is a Baraitha, viz., Others say, The cordwainer, and the smelter in bronze and the tanner[5], are exempt from the holocaust, for it is said, "all thy males[6]," i.e., he who can go up with all thy males. These are excluded, for they cannot go up with all thy males.

Exod. xxiii. 17, Deut. xvi. 16.

Mishnah.

I. (3) Burnt-offerings on a middle holiday[7] come from things not previously consecrated, but the peace-offerings from the tithe. On a high holiday, which is the first day of the Passover, the house of Shammai say that they come from things not previously consecrated, but the house of Hillel say that they come from the tithe.

(4) Israelites generally fulfil their duty with vows[8] and freewill-offerings[9] and with tithe of cattle, and the priests by the eating of sin-offerings, and of trespass-offerings, and by the firstborn, and by the wave breast and heave shoulder, but not by the eating of birds[10] or of meal-offerings.

---

[1] Hiph. participle of שׁוה with pron. suffix.

[2] Lit., prompt, alert.

[3] i.e., What is its use? And the answer is, that it is to fall in with the injunction that all must go, except the class is specially exempted.

[4] See p. 14, note 4.   [5] See p. 14.

[6] זְכוּרְךָ lit., thy malehood.

[7] The מוֹעֵד is contrasted with a Great Festival (מִקְרָא הַקֹּדֶשׁ "a holy convocation"). For example, the first and seventh days of Passover are holy convocations, but the intermediate ones are "middle holidays" (מוֹעֲדִים). But מוֹעֵד is also used in the Bible (e.g., Lev. xxiii. 4) as a generic term to include great and intermediate holidays alike.

[8] נֶדֶר was a vow consisting of a certain number of animals not individually selected beforehand. For this and the following word see Lev. xxii. 23.

[9] נְדָבָה was a vow consisting of animals from the first individually selected.

[10] The priest who wrung the neck of a bird offered by another in sacrifice, might eat it along with the blood, but this, the Talmud says above, does not count to him as an offering on his part.

Gemara.

But according to this it is burnt-offerings on a middle holiday that come from things not previously consecrated. Well, then, it follows that on a high holiday they come from the tithe. But why? For surely it is obligatory, and everything which is obligatory comes only from that which is not previously consecrated. And if thou sayest, Then this teaches us that burnt-offerings are offered on a middle holiday, and are not offered on a high holiday[1], with whom will this view correspond? With the house of Shammai. For there is a canonical Mishnah, viz., The house of Shammai say, Men bring peace-offerings and do not lay their hands on them, but not burnt-offerings; but the house of Hillel say, Men bring both peace-offerings and burnt-offerings and lay their hands on them[2]. There is a hiatus here[3], and this is the real teaching. It means that burnt-offerings, vows and freewill-offerings are brought on a middle holiday; on a high holiday they are not brought, but the burnt-offering of a holocaust is brought even on a high holiday. And when it[4] is brought, it is only brought from things not previously consecrated, but peace-offerings of joy are brought even from the tithe. And the Chagigah of a high holiday, which is the first day of the Passover, the house of Shammai say, is from things not previously consecrated, but the house of Hillel say, From the tithe. There is also a Baraitha to this effect, Burnt-offerings, vows and freewill-offerings are brought on a middle holiday; on a high holiday they are not brought, but the burnt-offering of a holocaust is brought even on a high holiday. And when it is brought, it is only brought from things not previously consecrated, but peace-offerings of joy are brought even from the tithe. And the Chagigah[5]

Marginalia: 7 b, l. 13. Beytsah, 19 a, ii. 2, and elsewhere.

---

[1] If thou sayest, This is only another way of telling us that it is not allowed to offer burnt-offerings on a high holiday (a Sabbath in the wider sense of that term), but only on a middle holiday.

[2] To lay the hands on the head of an animal was a breach of the Sabbath, because it so far prevented the animal from having rest (Exod. xxiii. 12). The requirement of the house of Shammai, that the hand be laid on the head of the animal, when offered as a burnt-offering, involved, as far as their followers were concerned, the restriction of such offerings to middle holidays, as opposed to high holidays (i.e., to Sabbaths in the wider sense).

[3] i.e., the Mishnah is defective. See p. 4, note 4.

[4] The burnt offering of a holocaust.

[5] This Chagigah was a sacrifice supplementary to the Passover lamb, though not itself necessarily a lamb, for, while a lamb (Exod. xii. 3) was necessary for

7 b, ll. 17. of a high holiday which is the first day of the Passover, the house of Shammai say, is from things not previously consecrated, but the house of Hillel say, From the tithe. How is the Chagigah of a high holiday which is the first day of the Passover, different from that of any other high holiday? R. Ashi said, See, we learn from this that the Chagigah of the fifteenth day[1] is taken from
8 a things not previously consecrated, but the Chagigah of the fourteenth not[2]; consequently he[3] must from the beginning have had the opinion that the Chagigah of the fourteenth day is not an enactment of the Law. The Mishnah teacher said, *The house of Hillel say, From the tithe*[4]. But why? For surely it is obligatory, and everything which is obligatory comes only from that which is not previously consecrated. Ola[5] said, This is so in[6] the case of one making a supplementary offering. Hezekiah[7] said, Men may supplement beast with beast, but they may not supplement money with money. But R. Jochanan said, Men may supplement money with money, but they may not supplement beast with beast. A Baraitha supports R. Hezekiah, and a Baraitha supports R. Jochanan. A Baraitha supports R.
Deut. xvi. 10. Jochanan[8], viz., The word "tribute" teaches that a man is to

the *Passover* of the fourteenth, the passage, Deut. xiv. 26, was held to show that sheep or oxen were permissible for the *Chagigah* of that day. Finally, the Passover lamb itself came to be merely supplementary, and was served out in very small portions after each person had made his actual meal on the Chagigah. Compare the Lord's Supper following on the ἀγαπαί in the first age of the Church. See further in Glossary, CHAGIGAH.

[1] The fifteenth day of Nisan (which consisted of the fourteenth night and fifteenth day according to our reckoning) was the first day of the Passover.

[2] On the fourteenth day, just before the sunset (Exod. xii. 6) which introduced the fifteenth, at the end of the meal, the Passover lamb was distributed, about the size of an olive being given to each person. The full meal which preceded this distribution was "the Chagigah of the fourteenth." *This* Chagigah, not being the ceremony of the day, might be taken from tithe. The Chagigah of the next morning ("of the fifteenth day"), also making a full meal, must be from things not previously consecrated, inasmuch as *it* was the ceremony of the day.

[3] viz., the person who puts the question.   [4] See p. 34.

[5] Ola Rabba (his full name) was a friend of Rabbi, and had the same teacher, viz., El'azar. See p. 16, note 5; *Juch.* 178 *b*; Wolf, ii. 878.

[6] i.e., The statement of the house of Hillel refers to.

[7] Son of Chia bar Abba. For approximate date see p. 25, note 1.

[8] The order of Hezekiah's and Jochanan's views is here reversed in accordance with the Rabbinic maxim, End with that with which you begin.

bring his duty offering from things not previously consecrated; 8a, 1. 12.
and whence have we got it that if he wishes to mix things, he
may mix¹? The teaching says, "According as the Lord thy Deut. xvi. 10.
God shall bless thee." A Baraitha supports R. Hezekiah, viz.,
The word "tribute" teaches that a man is to bring his duty offering
from things not previously consecrated. The house of Shammai
say, The first day from things not previously consecrated, thenceforward from the tithe, but the house of Hillel say, Only the first
meal from things not previously consecrated, thenceforward from the
tithe. And all the rest of the days of the Passover a man is to fulfil
his duty with the tithe of a beast². On a high holiday what is
the reason that he should not do the same? R. Ashi said,
Lest perhaps, if this were allowed, he might go to tithe upon a high
holiday, for it is impossible to tithe upon a high holiday on account
of the red chalk³. What passage is there to shew that
"tribute" is a word that denotes things not previously consecrated? The passage, "And king Ahasuerus laid tribute⁴ Esth. x. 1.
upon the land."

*Israelites generally fulfil their duty with vows and freewill-
offerings*⁵. Our Rabbis have taught⁶ thus, "And thou shalt rejoice Deut. xvi. 14.
in thy feast." This means to include in the word joy all kinds
of joy. Hence wise men have said, Israelites generally fulfil
their duty with vows and freewill-offerings and with tithe of
cattle, and the priests by the eating of sin-offerings and trespass-offerings, and by the firstborn, and by the wave breast and
heave shoulder. I should have thought that they might have
done it also with birds and meal-offerings. The teaching says,
And thou shalt rejoice in thy *Feast*, meaning things only from which 8 b

---

¹ The use of the word "mix," as excluding beasts and including money (since money may be mixed without our knowing it, but beasts cannot), is the one point for which the Talmud adduces this Baraitha, as thus shewn to support Jochanan's contention.

² The use of the word "beast," and the mention, just above, of a meal, since *money* cannot be eaten, are the two points for which the Talmud adduces this Baraitha, as thus shewn to support Hezekiah's contention.

³ Chalk was used to distinguish the animals selected for tithe, and to mark them with it was to work, and so was prohibited on the Sabbath.

⁴ Inasmuch as, from the nature of the case, this was an addition to all claims in connexion with ritual.

⁵ See p. 34.

⁶ See p. 11, note 2.

8 b, l. 1. the Chagigah may come. These¹ are excluded, for the Chagigah does not come from them. R. Ashi said, This comes out of the expression "and thou shalt rejoice." These are excluded, for there is no joy in them. And R. Ashi said, Pray, for what purpose does the expression "in thy feast" occur? It is to serve the same purpose as it served with R. Daniel bar Kattinah². For R. Daniel bar Kattinah said that Rab said, How is it that men do not take them wives on a middle holiday? Because it is said, "and thou shalt rejoice in thy feast," and not in thy wife.

MISHNAH.

I. (5) He who has many to eat with him and few possessions, brings many peace-offerings and few burnt-offerings. He who has many possessions and few to eat with him, brings many burnt-offerings, and few peace-offerings. If a man have little of both, to his case applies the saying about the meah of silver and the two pieces of silver³. If he have much of both, to his case apply the words, "every man shall give as he is able⁴, according to the blessing of the LORD thy God, which he hath given thee."

Deut. xvi. 17.

GEMARA.

Many peace-offerings—whence does he bring them? For behold, he has them not. R. Chasda said, He supplements⁵, and brings a large bullock. R. Shesheth⁶ said to him, Behold, they say, Men supplement beast with beast. What did he mean? If you

---

¹ Birds and meal-offerings.
² Towards the end of the 2nd century.
³ As a minimum. See p. 2.
⁴ Lit., "according to the gift of his hand."
⁵ i.e., He sells the small bullock, and *adding some money* to the price, purchases a larger animal.
⁶ A pupil of Hunna. He flourished at the end of the 3rd and beginning of the 4th centuries. He was blind, and, as it was essential that those who taught from the Law should *read* its words, he (like other blind Rabbis) learned the Targum by heart, that he might base his expositions on it, as representing the sense and being the nearest approximation to the words of the Law. See *Juch.*, p. 196 a; Wolf, ii. 882.

say, He meant this, viz., Behold, they say, Men supplement beast with beast, but not money with money, then he ought to have said to him, Men do not supplement money with money. But this is what he meant, viz., Behold, they say, Men *also* supplement beast with beast¹. To whose teaching is this to be attached? For it does not accord with Hezekiah, and it does not accord with R. Jochanan². And if you say, It is Gemaric teachers who are at variance, but the Mishnic teachers are not at variance, I reply that there is a teaching³ which says, The first meal shall come from things not previously consecrated. In what sense is the expression "the first meal" used here? It means, The money equivalent of the first meal shall come from things not previously consecrated.

Ola said that Resh Lakish said, If a man set apart ten beasts for his Chagigah, he may bring five on the first high holiday, and may again bring five on the second high holiday⁴. R. Jochanan said, When he has finished, he cannot bring again. R. Abba⁵ said, But they⁶ do not really differ. The one is the case where he

¹ i.e., He could sell the small bullock, and, adding its price to other money, buy a larger one, or, he could buy another small one and offer the two.

² See p. 36.

³ See p. 37, where the house of Hillel say it. The argument is, It does not seem merely a matter of dispute between Gemaric teachers. In Mishnic times also there appears to have been a difference of opinion on the point. For on the one hand Jochanan, a Mishnic teacher (see for his date p. 11, note 7), says that "men supplement money with money, but they may not supplement beast with beast" (p. 36), while on the other hand the house of Hillel speak of a *meal*, and does not this word (see p. 37, note 2) exclude the idea of money? The reply, reconciling the two teachings, is that the word *meal* may be taken to include its money equivalent.

⁴ It may here be noted that it became the practice among the Jews in Babylon and throughout the world generally, first in the case of the New Year festival, and then in that of all the great Feasts (not Fasts), to keep two consecutive days, in order that they might insure the inclusion of the right time, which those in Palestine ascertained by actual observation of the new moon. See Edersheim, *The Temple, its Ministry*, etc., pp. 170—172. A reason which is assigned for the continuance of this custom in times when astronomical error on the subject was no longer possible, is to enable Jews, even though living on opposite sides of the globe, and therefore subject to a difference of as much as twelve hours in local time, thus to keep at least one day in common.

⁵ When this name is used thus absolutely it is equivalent to Rab, for whom see p. 20, note 2.

⁶ Ola and Jochanan.

8 b, ii. 6. keeps silence, the other where he declares his intention. This expression, When he keeps silence—explain it¹. Perhaps there was not time in the day to bring them. In that case they are not brought, because there was not time in the day. But² perhaps he has none to eat with him³. In that case they are not brought, because he has none to eat with him. No; this is not such a case; and so far as this goes, it is necessary that he should bring them. For there is time in the day, and he has people to eat with him. Inasmuch as he did not bring them at the earlier time⁴, learn from this that he left them behind intentionally; and this also is the purport of the story, how when Rabbin⁵ came, R. Jochanan said, If a man set apart ten beasts for his Chagigah, he may bring five on the first high holiday, and may again bring five on the second high holiday. They⁶ are in appearance difficult to reconcile⁷, but in reality not. For learn from this that the one is the case when he keeps silence, the other when he declares his intention⁸. Learn from this that the point has been also distinctly

9 a settled. R. Shemen⁹ bar Abba said that R. Jochanan said, They have only taught this¹⁰, when it is not ended¹¹, but if it is ended, he may bring again. What is ended? If you say, It means that he has ended *his offerings*, how can he bring any more? But the teaching means, When *the day* is not ended, but if the day is ended, he may bring again.

¹ See p. 27, with note 3.

² וְ+אֶלָּא.

³ And the meat would not all keep until the next day.

⁴ Read מדבקמא (= קמא+ד+ב+מן).

⁵ For notices of him, connecting him also with Abai, Ami, Asi, and Jeremiah, see *Juch.*, p. 187 *a*.

⁶ The two statements of Jochanan.

⁷ אַהֲדָדֵי, invicem.

⁸ Of bringing them on different days.

⁹ Spelt שימן when it occurs again in this treatise. For reference see Index. He was a disciple of Jochanan, for whom see p. 11, note 7.

¹⁰ viz., that the man may not postpone any part of his offerings.

¹¹ viz., (as it is subsequently explained in the text) when the approach of sunset has not yet necessarily brought offerings to an end for that day.

MISHNAH.

I. (6) He who has not observed the Feast on the first high holiday of the Feast, may keep the Feast during any part of its extent, even including the last high holiday of the Feast; but if the whole period be passed, and he have not observed the Feast, he is not bound afterwards. It is with reference to such a person that the words are used, "That which is crooked cannot be made straight: and that which is wanting cannot be counted."

9 a, 1. 5.

Eccles. i. 15.

(7) R. Simeon bar Manassea[1] says, Who is this that is crooked, that cannot be made straight? This is he who forms an incestuous connexion and begets therefrom a bastard child. If you should say, Nay, it has to do with theft and plunder; but no, for he could make restitution of it, and be made straight. R. Simeon ben Jochai[2] says, Nothing is called crooked but that which was straight at the beginning and has become crooked, and what is this? This is a learned pupil, who severs himself from the Law.

GEMARA.

Whence do you gather this[3]? R. Jochanan said in the name of R. Ishmael, The same word, Restraint[4], is used of the seventh day of Passover[5], and of the eighth day of the Feast of Tabernacles[6]. What is true of the former as regards postponement[7] of payments,

---

[1] Flourished in the time of Rabbi. See p. 2, note 9, and *Juch.*, p. 79 *a*.

[2] A pupil of Akiba (for notice of whom see p. 15, note 8). S. ben Jochai's "whole life was absorbed in the study of Kabala, in which science he has ever been regarded as one of the most eminent masters." Etheridge, whose account of him see (pp. 80—83).

[3] מנהני מילי, lit., Whence these words? viz., the first part of the Mishnah, down to the words, "the last high holiday of the Feast."

[4] עֲצֶרֶת.

[5] Deut. xvi. 8. A.V. and R.V. "a solemn assembly," A.V. marg. "restraint," R.V. marg. "closing festival."

[6] Lev. xxiii. 36, Numb. xxix. 35, A.V. and R.V., as in Deut.; A.V. marg. in Lev. "day of restraint."

[7] Lit., things transferable, substitutions; in other words, things that are valid, though offered on days subsequent to the first day. See p. 2, note 5.

9 a, i. 22.	the same is true of the latter. The word is used in an unrestricted way[1]. For if it were not used in an unrestricted way, the force of the argument drawn from it might have been broken by saying, Whereas the seventh day of Passover is not separated from those that precede it, you may say that the eighth day of the Feast of Tabernacles is separated from those that precede it[2]. Assuredly, it is used in a wholly unrestricted sense. What does restraint really mean? That one is restrained from acts of work. But we
Deut. xvi. 8.	have the passage, "Thou shalt do no work[3]." Why then has the Merciful One written me Restraint? But learn from it that it was to give the unrestricted sense of the word[4]. And a Baraitha brings out the same thing thus. For there is a Baraitha,
Lev. xxiii. 41.	"And ye shall keep it a feast unto the Lord seven days." One might have thought from this passage that one was to go on sacrificing all seven days. No, for the teaching says "it." Thou art to sacrifice "it," and thou art not to sacrifice all seven days. If so, why have we seven stated as the number of the days of the Feast? For postponements of payments; and whence do you gather that if a man has not observed the Feast on the first high holiday of the Feast, he is to go and sacrifice during any part of its extent, even
Lev. xxiii. 41.	including the last high holiday? Because the teaching says, "Ye shall keep it in the seventh month." If it had merely said, In the seventh month, one might have thought that one was to go and sacrifice the whole month. No; for the teaching says "it." Thou art to sacrifice "it" and thou art not to sacrifice further.

And what about postponed offerings? R. Jochanan says, Postponed offerings are from[5] the first day; but R. Oshaia says,

---

[1] The word עֲצֶרֶת being applied to the closing day of both, and not in any limited or special sense in either passage, it follows that, in the absence of any such limitation, all things that are true of the one are true of the other, save those six things, which are particularly mentioned elsewhere as distinguishing them. Otherwise עֲצֶרֶת, thus applied to both, would be unfitly used, a thing impossible in Holy Writ.

[2] On the 8th day of Tabernacles, the Jews do not sit in the tabernacle, in which they take their meals during the earlier days.

[3] If therefore עֲצֶרֶת were used in that sense here, it would be superfluous, which is impossible. This then cannot be its meaning.

[4] That so you might be able to argue from the 7th day of Passover to the 8th day of Tabernacles.

[5] Lit., for, i.e., with reference to that day only.

Postponed offerings are on any one day for another[1]. What practical difference is there between them? R. Zera said, If a man is lame on the first day and cured on the second day, here is a difference between them. R. Jochanan said, Postponed offerings are from the first day. Inasmuch as he was not fit on the first day, he is not fit on the second day; but R. Oshaia said, Postponed offerings are one day for another; although he was not fit on the first day, he was fit on the second.

But how could R. Jochanan have said this? For surely Hezekiah said, A Nazirite, if again polluted on the eighth day, must bring an additional offering[2], but if in the previous night, he need not bring it[3]; but R. Jochanan said, Nay, in the latter case[4] also he must bring it. R. Jeremiah said, A case of defilement is a different matter[5], for payments postponed from it are made at a second Passover[6]. R. Papa objects to[7] this and says, It will be all right according to him who says, The second Passover admits of offerings postponed from the first; but according to him who says, The second is an independent Festival, where is your argument[8]? But R. Papa said, that R. Jochanan considered that the

---

[1] i.e., for *any* preceding day, not only 2nd for 1st, but also 3rd for 2nd, etc.

[2] Because he has come out of his former uncleanness, and incurred a fresh uncleanness.

[3] Because he has not come out of his former uncleanness, and therefore that which he has now contracted may be dealt with as a continuation of the former.

[4] Lit., in the night. Jochanan's reason was, that in the previous night the man was to all intents and purposes clean, though, to offer the sacrifice of purification, sunrise must be awaited. He will therefore now be obliged to make his offering not only for the former, but also for the newly incurred uncleanness. The bearing of this upon the case which is in course of discussion in the text consists merely in the fact that Jochanan was thought thus virtually to have admitted the principle that payments are "one day for another," and not "for the first day only."

[5] i.e., different from the kind of postponed offering hitherto treated of.

[6] This later passover (פֶּסַח קָטֹן), based on Numb. ix. 10 sqq., differed from the earlier in the following points: 1°. It lasted but one day. 2°. It was not required that the Hallel should be sung before the meal, but only when the lamb was slain. 3°. It was not necessary that leaven should be removed from the houses. See *Dict. of Bible*, s. v. "Passover," where *Pesachim* ix. 3 is quoted.

[7] Lit., lays hold of.

[8] Lit., What is there to say?

9 b, 1. 4.   night is not to be included in the seven days of cleansing¹. But how could R. Jochanan have said this? For lo, R. Jochanan said elsewhere, If a man has had one emission in the night and two in the day, he must bring an additional offering²; if two in the night and one in the day, he need not bring it³; and if thou dost imagine that R. Jochanan considered that the night is not to be included⁴, then, if there were two in the night and one in the day, he must bring. But, it is answered, R. Jochanan was adopting the words of the other speaker, viz., that the night is to be included. "Adopting the words of the other speaker," say you? Of course there would then be nothing further to argue about. No; two in the day and one in the night were necessary for him⁵. I might otherwise have taught that it would be according to the view⁶ of R. Shisha son of R. Idai; but we learn from this that it is according to R. Joseph⁷.

Eccles. i. 15.   If the Feast has passed and he has not offered, he is not bound to make another offering, and with regard to this it is said, "That which is crooked cannot be made straight: and that which is wanting cannot be counted." Bar He He⁸ said to Hillel, This expression to "be counted⁹" must mean to "be filled¹⁰." Nay, but this is the sense. His fellows counted upon him to fulfil a positive command and he was not counted among them.

There is a Baraitha, Thus also is explained, "That which is

---

¹ Lit., is not lacking the time, i.e., the time requisite to qualify for the complete fulfilment of a duty. In this case then it means that Jochanan considered that the man was already clean, although, the morning not having come, his sacrifice had not yet been offered. To take a different kind of case, a lame man is lacking time, because the time which must pass before he is qualified to offer (which time in his particular case lasts as long as he is lame) has not elapsed, and consequently he has no duty to fulfil.

² Because to all intents and purposes he has been cleansed already.

³ Because that appears to be a prolonged uncleanness.

⁴ Lit., is not lacking the time, i.e., that as soon as the sun has set, the man is clean.

⁵ Jochanan.

⁶ Lit., grip or grasp.

⁷ Their views are given in בְּרִיחֹת 8 a.

⁸ Also on the principle of Gematria, or substitution of letters (see Wolf, ii. 820), called Ben Bag Bag (He = ה = 5 = 2 + 3 = ב + ג), a contemporary of Hillel and Shammai. See Dr Taylor, p. 111, note 50, for further notices of him.

⁹ להימנות.

¹⁰ להמלאות.

crooked cannot be made straight." This means the man who has 9 b, l. 17. failed in reading the Sh'ma' of the morning, or in reading the Sh'ma' of the evening, or who has failed in the morning prayer or in the evening prayer. "And that which is wanting cannot be counted." This means the man whose fellows counted upon him to fulfil a positive command, and he was not counted among them.

Bar He He said to Hillel, What is that which is written, "Then shall ye return and discern between the righteous and the Mal. iii. 18. wicked, between him that serveth God and him that serveth Him not"? The righteous and he that serveth God are identical terms, the wicked and he that serveth Him not are identical terms. He said to him, He that serveth Him and he that serveth Him not are both absolutely righteous, but he that repeateth his portion a hundred times is not like him that repeateth his portion a hundred and one times. He said to him, Then by reason of one time is he called "him that serveth Him not"? He said to him, Yes, go and learn from the mule-drivers' market how they say, Ten parasangs for a zouza[1], but eleven parasangs for two zouzas.

Elijah[2] said to Bar He He, but some say, to R. Eliezer[3], What is the meaning of the passage, "Behold, I have refined thee, but not Is. xlviii. 10. as silver; I have tried thee in the furnace of affliction"? It means that the Holy One, blessed be He, searched out[4] all good qualities to give to Israel, and found only poverty. Samuel, or, if you like, R. Joseph[5], said, This accords with the proverbial saying, Poverty befits a Jew, as a red leather trapping a white horse.

R. Simeon ben Manassea says, What sort of person is this, that is crooked and that cannot be made straight? This is he who forms an incestuous connexion and begets therefrom a bastard child,

---

[1] For zouza see p. 20, note 5.

[2] The prophet was believed to appear suddenly from time to time on earth and address himself to some Rabbi. Cf. p. 12, note 6.

[3] The name, thus used absolutely, stands for Eliezer ben Hyrkanus, the famous pupil of Jochanan ben Zakkai (p. 10, note 6), and teacher of Akiba (p. 15, note 8). He founded a school at Lod (see p. 9) in rivalry to that of Jabneh, and in course of time suffered excommunication. For further particulars of him and specimens of his sayings see Dr Taylor (who styles him "the typical traditionalist"), pp. 47—50 with notes; Wolf, iv. 403—5; Etheridge, pp. 61, 62.

[4] Lit., went round for.

[5] Samuel's pupil's pupil. See p. 20, note 3.

9 b, ii. 24. etc.[1] If he beget, yes[2]; if he do not beget, no.   And lo, there is a Baraitha[3]. R. Simeon ben Manassea says, In case of a thief it is possible that he may restore that which he has stolen, and so it may be made good; in case of a robber, it is possible that he may restore his plunder, and so it may be made good; but he that approaches a man's wife, and so makes her unfit for her husband, is cut off from the world, and goes to his own place[4].

R. Simeon ben Jochai says, One does not say, Investigate a camel, investigate a pig[5], but investigate a lamb. And what kind of person is this? This is the pupil of a wise man, who has separated himself from the Law.   R. Jehudah ben Lakish[6] said, Every pupil of a wise man, who has separated himself from the Law, to him does the passage refer, which says, "As a bird that wandereth from her nest, so is a man that wandereth from his place," and that which says, "What unrighteousness have your fathers found in me, that they are gone far from me?"   There is no difficulty[7]. The one case has to do with his unmarried sister, the other with another man's wife[8]. And, if you like, I will say that both of them have to do with another man's wife, and yet there is no difficulty. The one is the case of a man who has to use violence,

10 a the other of one whose approaches are admitted. And, if you like, I will say that both are cases of one who has to use violence, and yet there is no difficulty. The one is the case of the wife of a priest, the other that of the wife of an ordinary Israelite.

Zech. viii. 10. "Neither is there any peace to him that goeth out or to him that cometh in." Rab says, It means when a man leaves off[9] from

Prov. xxvii. 8.
Jer. ii. 5.

---

[1] See p. 41. The quotation is not made with strict verbal accuracy.

[2] Because in that case he cannot get rid of the results of the sin.

[3] In which, unlike the passage immediately preceding, Simeon condemns the act as sinful in itself without any reference to its results. This constitutes an apparent difficulty which is presently cleared up.

[4] Lit., goes (to the place meet) for him.

[5] For these are, and always were, obviously unclean, while the case which the passage under discussion refers to is that of one who has *become* crooked.

[6] A contemporary of Rabbi (end of 2nd and beginning of 3rd century). See p. 2, note 9, and Wolf, ii. 874.

[7] In reconciling the apparently conflicting traditions as to Simeon ben Manassea's view.

[8] If it be a married woman whom he approaches, the man goes *ad diabolum*, whether a child (מָמְזֵר) be born or not; if it be his unmarried sister, then, only if a child is born, and so for the two cases which immediately follow.

[9] Lit., goes out.

speaking Halachah[1] to speak Bible only, he has no more peace; but 10 a, 1. 5. Samuel said, This is he who deserts the Talmud[2] for Mishnah. But R. Jochanan said, Even if he go from one Talmud to the other[3].

Mishnah.

I. (8) The rules concerning the dissolving of vows fly about in the air, and there is nothing upon which they can rest. The Halachoth concerning Sabbath, Chagigoth, and trespasses[4], behold, they are as mountains suspended by a hair, for lo! the Bible teaching is little and the Halachoth manifold. The legal decisions[5] and the Temple services, the things clean and unclean, and cases of unlawful unions, have something on which they may rest, and these are the principal things of the Law.

Gemara.

There is a Baraitha. R. Eliezer says, They[6] have something upon which they may rest, for it is said, "when he shall separate," Lev. xxvii. 2, Numb. vi. 2. "when he shall separate," twice[7]. One separation has to do with binding and one separation with dissolving. R. Joshua says, They have something upon which they may rest, for it is said, "Wherefore I sware in my wrath." In my wrath I sware, and I relented[8]. Ps. xcv. 11. R. Isaac[9] says, They have something upon which they may rest, for

---

[1] See Glossary.   [2] i.e., Gemara.
[3] From the Jerusalem to the Babylonian Talmud, or *vice versâ*. For passages further illustrating the Rabbinic view as to the respective merits of Scripture and tradition see Hershon, *Talmudic Miscellany*, chap. xi. no. 33, with note and references; also Longfellow's *Golden Legend*,
    "The Kabala and Talmud hoar
    Than all the prophets prize I more,
    For water is all Bible lore,
    But Mishna is strong wine."
[4] The appropriation of holy things to secular uses.
[5] On the part of the courts, as dealing with ordinary offences.
[6] viz., the dissolving of vows.
[7] Used on each occasion in reference to vows.
[8] Lit., I turned round in myself. Upon this verse accordingly may be founded teaching as to the dissolving of vows.
[9] He was a contemporary of Jochanan ben Eliezer (=ben Naphcha; see p. 11, note 7), of Ami (see p. 17, note 3), and of Nachman ben Jacob, an associate of Hunna (see p. 11, note 5).

10a, 1. 17. it is said, "Whosoever is of a willing heart." Chănaniah[1], nephew
Exod. xxxv. 5. of R. Joshua, says, They have something on which they may rest,
Ps. cxix. 106. for it is said, "I have sworn and have fulfilled it, that I will
observe thy righteous judgments."   R. Jehudah said that R.
Samuel said, If I had been there, I would have said to them, Mine
Numb. xxx. 3, E.V. 2. is much better than yours, for it is said, "He shall not break his
word." He is not to break it, but afterwards it may be broken[2]
for him.   Rabba said, There is an objection to all of them
except Samuel's, for there is no objection to his. For if we take
that of R. Eliezer, perhaps the truth rests with R. Jehudah, who
said it in the name of R. Tarphon[3], for there is a Baraitha, R. Jehudah says in the name of R. Tarphon, I grant fully that neither
of them is a Nazirite, for the state of a Nazirite is not given except
on condition of separation[4]. If we take the words of R. Joshua,
perhaps the meaning is this, I sware in my wrath, and I will not
relent. If we take the words of R. Isaac, perhaps it is to exclude
the explanation of Samuel, for Samuel said, If a man has determined in his heart, it is further needful that he should utter it
with his lips. Lo, we learn from this[5], that even though he has
not uttered it with his lips[6], he is bound. If we take the words
of Chănaniah, nephew of R. Joshua, perhaps it is as R. Gidel[7]
reported that Rab said; for R. Gidel said that Rab said, Whence

---

[1] In the first half of the 2nd century.

[2] i.e., dissolved.

[3] Head of the Academy of Lod (see p. 9, note 11), a contemporary of Aḳiba. He was a priest, and wealthy. There are no grounds for identifying him with the Tryphon with whom Justin Martyr held a disputation. One of his sayings (see *Pirḳe Aboth* ii. 19) may be considered sufficiently noteworthy to quote here. "The day is short, and the task is great, and the workmen are sluggish, and the reward is much, and the master of the house is urgent. He said, It is not for thee to finish the work, nor art thou free to desist therefrom." He was present at the death of Jochanan ben Zakkai. See p. 10, note 6, and for further particulars Wolf, ii. 836, 409.

[4] It is only the last clause of Tarphon's statement which is germane to the matter in hand. The point is that one of the two occurrences of separation (see above) is accounted for, inasmuch as this expression is thus applied to the Nazirite. As there is but one other occurrence of it in the Bible, and as that one must be applied to the binding of vows, it follows that there is none left to apply to the dissolution of vows. In Numb. A.V. renders יָפֵר as above, not so in Lev.; and R.V. differs in both.

[5] From Isaac's words.

[6] But only willed it in his heart.

[7] About A.D. 250. See Wolf, ii. 870.

do we find that an oath is meritorious[1]? Because it is said, "I have sworn and have fulfilled it that I will observe thy righteous judgments." But the words of Samuel are open to no objection. Rabba said, or, if you like, R. Nachman bar Isaac[2] said, This accords with the proverbial saying, Better is one grain of pepper than a basket full of dates.

Halachoth concerning Sabbath. But there is much in Holy Writ concerning it[3]. Nay, but it was necessary[4], so as to agree with the words of R. Abba, for R. Abba said, He who digs a hole on the Sabbath, when it is only needed for the sake of the earth from it[5], is permitted to do so. According to whom is this teaching? According to R. Simeon, who said, A work which is not necessary for its own sake[6] is permitted. If thou sayest, According to R. Jehudah, his teaching is that there are two cases to be distinguished, and that in the one the man does something which effects good, in the other harm. What is the meaning of the expression, *as mountains suspended by a hair?* It refers to the fact that the traditional Law forbids work requiring thought[7], whereas Holy Writ makes no mention of work requiring thought.

Chagigoth. But there is much in Holy Writ concerning them.

Nay, but it was necessary, so as to agree with what R. Papa said to Abai, viz., Whence is it that the passage, "and ye shall keep it a feast to the Lord" involves sacrifice? Perhaps the Merciful One meant merely, Celebrate a Feast without sacrifice. But that sacrifices are meant we learn from this passage, "That they may hold a feast unto me in the wilderness." But, it may be replied, here also it only means, Hold a Feast. But if thou sayest, Here also it only means, Hold a Feast, yet there is the

_____

[1] Lit., is fulfilling the commandment. This then, according to Rab, is the point of the expression "and have fulfilled it," and it is not, as Chănaniah thought, to suggest the possibility of non-fulfilment of the vow, in other words, of its dissolution.

[2] A contemporary of Ami and Asi. See p. 17, note 3 and 4; also *Juch.* p. 70; Wolf, ii. 878.

[3] How then can the above Mishnah speak of it as scantily dealt with therein?

[4] For the Mishnah to put it in that way.

[5] And not for the sake of the hole itself.

[6] And accordingly on this principle it is permitted to dig a hole, unless it is to be made direct use of, as e.g., for the foundations of a house or for burial.

[7] e.g., the various kinds of work which were included in the making of the Tabernacle, and which on the above-mentioned principle were prohibited.

10 b, 1. 9. Exod. x. 25.	passage, "And Moses said, Thou must also give into our hands sacrifices and burnt-offerings." But the objector may say, Perhaps here the Merciful One meant merely, Eat and drink and keep the Feast before Me. Thou art not to think so, for it
Exod. xxiii. 18.	is written, "neither shall the fat of my feast remain all night until the morning." And if thou dost imagine that this is a mere Feast, Does fat belong to a mere Feast? But perhaps you will object, the Merciful One meant only this, viz., that the fat which comes at the time of a Feast shall not remain. But that such is not the meaning we learn from this consideration, viz., The fat which comes at the time of a Feast shall not remain. Shall then
Lev. vi. 2, E. V. 9.	all that which comes all the rest of the year remain? "All night unto the morning" is what is written. Perhaps, if the argument were drawn from that passage only, I might have said, The
Lev. vi. 2. Exod. xxiii. 18.	Merciful One wrote the one as an affirmative, and the other as a negative commandment[1]. But, it is replied, the Scripture has
Deut. xvi. 4.	other negative commandments[2] to the same effect, e.g., "Neither shall any of the flesh, which thou sacrificest the first day at even, remain all night until the morning." But perhaps it was to impose upon him two negative commandments[3] and one positive. But[4] there comes in two passages the word "wilder-
Exod. v. 1.	ness," "wilderness." It is written in the one, "That they may hold a feast unto me in the wilderness," and it is written in the
Amos v. 25.	other, "Did ye bring unto me sacrifices and offerings in the wilderness?" As in the latter there are sacrifices mentioned, so in the

---

[1] So as the better to secure that the command should be carried out. For the breach of a negative commandment is punished with stripes, of an affirmative only with rebuke. For the person may conceivably be still *about* to perform the latter, while he cannot plead a similar defence when found doing something which he has been told not to do.

[2] Therefore this cannot have been its object here.

[3] Two; for one of the negative commandments (viz., Exod. xxiii. 18), as standing in the immediate neighbourhood of a positive one (ver. 17), could not be punished with stripes; therefore the Lord may have thought it necessary to introduce another which should not be weakened by such contiguity.

[4] The argument is, All this is not needed. The point is settled by the occurrence of the word "wilderness" (מִדְבָּר) in two passages, evidently relating to the same subject. For the first clearly has to do with the Feast, the nature of which is under discussion, while the second passage expressly mentions the offering of *sacrifices*. Therefore, linked as they are by the occurrence of the above-mentioned word in both, the first of them must involve the duty of sacrificial offering.

former there are sacrifices meant. And what is the meaning of the expression, *as mountains suspended by a hair?* Nay, but we do not learn the words of the Law from the words of tradition[1].

Trespasses. But there is much in Holy Writ concerning them.

Rami bar Chama[2] said, It was only necessary in order to agree with the following Mishnah, If the messenger has done his commission[3], it is the master of the house who has trespassed; if the messenger has not done his commission, the messenger has trespassed. But if he has done his commission, how has the master trespassed? And is it possible that the one should be guilty and the other liable to the punishment? This is as mountains suspended by a hair. Rabba said, But what is the difficulty? Perhaps a trespass is different[4]. But one learns the law on this subject from the analogy of the two words, viz., "sin" in the present case, and "sin" used of the heave offering. As in the one case[5], the man's messenger represents him[6], so in the other[7] the man's messenger represents him. But Rabba said, It was only necessary in order to agree with the Baraitha, The master of the house remembered and the messenger did not remember[8]. The messenger has trespassed. What then has the

10 b, l. 27.

Kiddushin, 42 b, ii. 12, N'darim, 54 a, ii. 7, M'ila, 20 a, ii. 13, K'thuboth, 28 b, ii. 16.

---

[1] The point of this rejoinder is, that as one of these passages containing the word מָרְבָּר is only in a prophet, and not in the Books of Moses, it is worthless for the argument. For other cases in which passages of Scripture outside the Torah are spoken of as tradition see Dr C. Taylor's *Sayings etc.* Exc. I.

[2] Father-in-law of Ashi (p. 6, note 1), and son-in-law of Chasda (p. 21, note 1).

[3] e.g., by expending on common things money, the whole or a part of which should have been devoted to sacred uses, his master having forgotten this circumstance when he despatched him on the errand.

[4] From other offences in this respect.

[5] Viz., the heave-offering.

[6] The argument is this. In Numb. xviii. 28, 29, where the subject is the heave-offering (תְּרוּמָה), we have the verb in the plural (תָּרִימוּ) "ye shall offer," while the end of verse 32 (תְּמֻתוּ, "ye shall die") implies that a sin in connexion with the offering will be punished with death. The plural shews that in the case of the sin offering a man's servants represent him, and *all* are punished. But the word "sin" (חֵטְא) is used both in this context (vv. 22, 32) of heave-offering, and elsewhere (seeing that the substantive is implied in the verb חטא, Lev. v. 15) of trespass (מַעַל=מְעִילָה). Therefore what is true of the one is true of the other.

[7] viz., the trespass.

[8] viz., that the money given to him to apply to the master's occasions was money already dedicated to sacred uses.

4—2

<small>10 b, ii. 15.</small> poor messenger done? This is as mountains suspended by a hair.

Rab Ashi said, What is the difficulty? Perhaps it is more difficult than in the case of one who takes sacred money for ordinary uses. But Rab Ashi said, It was only necessary in order to agree with the canonical Mishnah, If a man have taken a stone or a <small>M'ilah,9 b,</small> beam of the sanctuary[1], behold, he has not trespassed. If he have <small>ii. 16, Baba Kamma,</small> given it to his neighbour, he has trespassed, but his neighbour has <small>20 b, ii. 24,</small> not trespassed. But most assuredly he has appropriated it[2]. <small>Baba M'tsia', 99 b, ii. 3.</small> What is it to me whether it be the man himself or his neighbour? This is as mountains suspended by a hair. And what is the difficulty? Perhaps it is in accordance with the words of Samuel. <small>11 a</small> For Samuel said, It is thus in the case of a treasurer. We give in charge to him the stones of a building, so that all which is thus placed, is placed at his disposition. But at the end he has built some of it into his house. Behold, he has not trespassed, until he has dwelt under it to the worth of a farthing. But most assuredly he has altered the stone[2]. What is it to me whether he has dwelt in it or not? This is as mountains suspended by a hair.

And what is the difficulty? Perhaps it is in accordance with the words of Rab; for Rab said, For example, if a man have placed it upon the opening of a roof-window, then, if he have dwelt in it, yes; if he have not dwelt in it, no. But granting fully that it is as Rabba said, yet thou findest more difficulty here than in the case of him who drew sacred money for common uses; in that case he knows well that they are coins belonging to the sanctuary. It was a matter for him to watch what he was doing. But in this case how should he know[3]? This is as mountains suspended by a hair.

The Bible teaching is little, but Halachoth are manifold. There is a Baraitha, viz., Concerning stripes and uncleanness connected

---

[1] And applied it to his own purposes. For it can be recovered from *him*, and so the case is not parallel to that in which he has lost control over it by giving it to his neighbour. In the latter case it is a trespass, and a trespass, unlike *a sin*, which can be atoned for by simple restitution, will require in addition the payment of the fifth part of the value and a guilt-offering besides.

[2] By building it into his house. Therefore (it is implied) he should be severely dealt with. Compare the case of the stolen ox, ass, or sheep (Exod. xxii. 1, 4). If the animal was found alive, the stealer was less severely punished than if he had killed it.

[3] For he may be very inexperienced.

with tents[1] the Bible teaching is little, but Halachoth are manifold. 11a, 1. 17.

Concerning stripes is the Bible teaching little? Concerning stripes there is manifold Bible teaching. R. Papa said, This is the right reading[2], Concerning stripes the Bible teaching is manifold, but Halachoth are few. Concerning tents Bible teaching is little, but Halachoth are manifold. But what comes out of this[3]? If thou art in doubt on the subject of stripes, look in the Bible; if thou art in doubt on the subject of tents, look in the Mishnic teaching.

Legal decisions. But there is much in Holy Writ concerning them. It was only necessary in order to agree with the words of Rabbi. For there is a Baraitha, viz., Rabbi says, "Life for life" Exod. xxi. 23. means money. Thou sayest, money, but it may not be so, but life in the literal sense. Nay; but the word *giving* is used in connexion with life in a succeeding and in a preceding passage. rv. 30, 22. As there it means money, so here it means money.

Temple Services. But there is much in Holy Writ concerning them. It was only necessary with a view to the bringing of the blood. For there is a Baraitha, "and they shall present[4]." Lev. i. 5. This is the receiving of the blood. And the Merciful One expressed it[5] by a word which denotes "bringing[6]," as it is written, "And Lev. i. 13. the priest shall present the whole and shall burn it upon the altar." But the Mishnah teacher said, This refers to the bringing of limbs[7] to the steps[8], and the object of the passage is to shew that the bringing did not take it out of the *genus* receiving.

Things clean. But there is much in Holy Writ concerning them. It was only necessary in order to calculate a religious bath, the size of which is not determined in Holy Writ. For there is a Baraitha, "and he shall wash his flesh in water"[9], i.e., in Lev. xv. 5, 6 sqq.

---

[1] e.g., the question whether tents, as being in a sense houses, are rendered unclean by the presence of a dead body.

[2] Lit., This is what it says.

[3] ומאי נפקא מינה. i.e., Is it not an unimportant remark for the Mishnah to make? The answer is, Not so, for it is equivalent to the following precept.

[4] The offering of the blood was a priestly function.

[5] The receiving.

[6] For bringing implies receiving.

[7] Not blood.

[8] Of the altar.

[9] The words in the text however (ורחץ את בשרו במים) are not a perfectly accurate quotation of any of these passages.

11 a, ii. 6. the waters of a religious bath all his flesh, water into which his whole body shall enter. And what amount must they reach? Cubit upon cubit to the height of three cubits, and wise men have calculated the waters of a religious bath to be forty seahs.

Things unclean. But there is much in Holy Writ concerning them. It was only necessary in order to determine that a creeping thing should be the size of a lentil¹; for this is not determined in Holy Writ. For there is a Baraitha, "In them²." One might have thought it meant among them all, but that the teaching says, "of them." One might have thought it meant from a portion of them, but that the teaching says, "among them." But how is this? It is to include the case of a man's touching the extremity of it³, for this is equivalent to the whole of it. Wise men calculated that a lentil should be the minimum for comparison. For a snail at first is about the size of a lentil.   R. Jose in the name of R. Jehudah says, As the tail of a lizard.

Lev. xi. 26, 43.

Lev. xi. 32, 33.

Unlawful unions. But there is much in Holy Writ concerning them.   Nay, it was necessary to meet the case of the daughter of a woman, whom a man had forced⁴, for this is not determined in Holy Writ.   Rabba said, R. Isaac bar Abdimi⁵ said to me, There comes in each passage the word "they," "they," and there comes the word "crime," "crime⁶."

11 b

---

¹ In order to make unclean.

² The preposition in the original may bear the sense of *in, with, among*. In the earlier of the two passages ("every one that toucheth, etc."), our idiom does not admit of the introduction of any preposition between the verb '*touch*' and its object. In the later, the rendering of the A. V. and R. V. is "neither shall ye make yourselves unclean with them." The original preposition however, the Talmud says, might, but for the correction "*of* them," used twice elsewhere in the passage, be taken as implying that uncleanness is not communicated, unless the whole of the unclean thing is touched. On the other hand the converse conclusion might be erroneously drawn, if we had only the expression "of them." Hence the need of both expressions.

³ The unclean thing.

⁴ The question would arise, Was he forbidden to marry *her*, as he would be to marry the daughter of his *wife*?

⁵ For his approximate date, as fixed by that of Rabba, see p. 4, note 3.

⁶ The argument, stated briefly, is this. When we compare three passages, viz., Lev. xviii. 10, 17, xx. 14, we find that the first and second have הֵנָּה, "they," the second and third זִמָּה, "crime." This, says the Talmud, shews that the case just mentioned is included under the Biblical prohibition.

These are the principal things of the Law. Are *these* principal 11 b, 1. 4. things, and not *those*[1]? But I may say, These and those are the principal things of the Law.

May our return be to thee "All are bound etc[2]."

פרק ב

MISHNAH.

II. (1) Men are not to expound unlawful[3] unions with a company of three, nor the work of Creation with two, nor the Chariot[4] with one; but if a man do so, he must be a wise man, and one who has much knowledge of his own[5]. Everyone who meddles with these four things that follow, it were better for him that he had not come into the world, viz., what is above and what is beneath, what is before and what is after[6]. And every one who does not revere the glory of his Maker, it were better for him that he had not come into the world.

[1] i.e., Can we admit such a distinction as primary and secondary among the precepts of the Law? Surely not.

[2] הַדְרָן וגו׳ (*au revoir*), Inf. Pi'el of הדר with pron. suf. of 1st pers. pl.; a formula which concludes each section (פֶּרֶק), and indicates the wish both for the sake of piety and of a good omen, that this may not be the last time of its perusal. Others explain, Make these matters return to thee, i.e., Repeat them over again to thyself. In that case read הַדְרֵן, imperative Pi'el of the same verb with pron. suf. of 3rd pers. pl.

[3] i.e., incestuous.

[4] The opening vision of Ezekiel (see p. 81, note 1). This, as taken to contain the mysteries belonging to the *government* of the world, and the beginning of Genesis, as setting forth the story of its *creation*, were favourite subjects for Ḳabbalistic investigation, but were not to be discussed before men in general. Accordingly there was no Commentary on Genesis corresponding to those on the Books that follow (מְחִלְתָּא on Exodus, סִפְרָא on Leviticus, סִפְרֵי on Numbers and Deuteronomy). Abarbanel in the Preface to his Commentary on Ezekiel, has given the chief explanations of "the Chariot," which have commended themselves to Jewish teachers. There is also a summary of them in J. H. Hottinger, *De Incestu*, etc. pp. 41—48.

[5] One who will not ask for many explanations, for this would involve discussion.

[6] "Above," i.e., God; "beneath," i.e., Gehenna; "before" the Creation; "after" the end of the world.

Gemara.

11 b, l. 15. Thou saidst at first, *Nor the Chariot with one*, and again thou saidst, *But if a man do so, he must be a wise man, and one who has much knowledge of his own.* This is its meaning. Men are not to expound unlawful unions to three others, nor the work of Creation to two others, nor the Chariot to one other, but if they do, he must be a wise man, and one who has much knowledge of his own. Men are not to expound unlawful unions with three. What is the reason? Shall we say, It is on account of the passage, "each man to any that is near of kin"? "Each man[1]" is equivalent to two, "that is near of kin" is equivalent to one; and the Merciful One said, "Ye shall not approach etc."[2] But regard it thus; as it is written, "each man that curseth his God," "each man that giveth of his seed unto Molech," so it is with this passage also; but as these last must mean[3] to include the strangers, who are cautioned for cursing the Lord, and for idolatry, like Israel, so that first quoted also must mean to include the strangers who are cautioned for unlawful unions, like Israel. But do we get it from the passage, "therefore shall ye keep my charge?" "Therefore shall ye keep" implies two, "my charge" one; for the Merciful One in this passage was forbidding the practice of "abominable customs." But as it is written, Ye therefore shall keep the Sabbath, "and ye shall keep the Unleavened Bread," "and ye shall keep the charge of the sanctuary," so it is with this passage also[4]. But R. Ashi said, How are we to explain, *Men are not to expound unlawful unions with three?* It means that they are not to expound the details of the subject with[5] three others. What is

Lev. xviii. 6.
Lev. xxiv. 15.
Lev. xx. 2.
Lev. xviii. 30.
ibid.
Exod. xxxi. 14.
Exod. xii. 17.
Numb. xviii. 5.

---

[1] אִישׁ אִישׁ = *two* men, as a *minimum*.

[2] i.e., ye shall not explain this.

[3] In using אִישׁ אִישׁ, an expression which after all includes *any* number of men taken severally. The argument is that from the reference to strangers which the words אִישׁ אִישׁ must bear in these two passages we may gather that they have the same reference in the passage concerning unlawful unions.

[4] i.e., the expression "ye shall keep" is in such general use, where no question of a minimum number is concerned, that it cannot be supposed in the particular case now being dealt with (Lev. xviii. 30) to have any special significance in that direction.

[5] Read however, with the margin of the Lemberg text, לשלשה, *to* three others.

the reason? The probability is that when two sit before their Rabbi one is wholly occupied[1] with his Rabbi, and the other inclines his ear to instruction, but if there are three, one is wholly occupied with his Rabbi, but the other two are wholly occupied with each other, and know not what their Rabbi is saying, and they go forth from his lecture to allow[2] things that are prohibited in the matter of unlawful unions. But if this be so, the whole Law should also by parity of reason come under this rule. No, for unlawful unions are different from other subjects. For the Mishnah teacher said, As for robbery and unlawful unions, a man's soul coveteth and lusteth for them. But if it be so, robbery also should come under the rule. No, for in the case of unlawful unions, whether the temptation is visible or not visible, the man's propensity is strong, but in the case of robbery, when the temptation is visible, his propensity is strong; when it is not visible, the propensity is not strong.

Nor on the work of Creation with two[3]. How then is this shewn[4]? Inasmuch as our Rabbis have taught, "For ask thou now of the days that are past." It is one person who asks, not two who ask. One might have thought that it possibly means that a man should ask about things that were before the world was created. No, for the teaching says, "since the day that God created man upon the earth." One might have thought that it possibly means that a man should not ask about the six days of creation. No, for the teaching says, "of the days that are past, which were before thee[5]." One might have thought that it possibly means that a man should ask about what is above and what is below, what is before and what is after. No, for the teaching says, "and from the one end of heaven unto the other." From the one end of heaven unto the other thou mayest ask, but thou mayest not ask about what is above, what is below, what is before, what is after. Now seeing that this is deduced[6] from the words,

---

[1] Lit., is weighing and giving, a Rabbinic phrase which means, doing business, earnestly discussing.
[2] In their ignorance, arising from this lack of attention to his teaching.
[3] See p. 55.
[4] מנא הני מילי, lit., Whence are these words?
[5] Therefore, though man was not created till the sixth day, he may discuss the things which came into existence on the earlier days of the week of creation.
[6] Lit., springs out for itself.

12 a, l. 1. Deut. iv. 32.	"from the one end of heaven unto the other," to what purpose are there given me the words, "since the day that God created man upon
ibid.	the earth"? They are to agree[1] with the words of R. El'azar;

for R. El'azar said, The first man extended from the earth to the firmament[2], for it is said, "from the day that God created man upon the earth," and inasmuch as he sinned[3], the Holy One, blessed be He, placed His hand upon him, and made him small, as it is
Ps. cxxxix. 5. said, "Thou hast fashioned me after and before[4], and laid thine hand upon me." R. Jehudah said that Rab said, The first man extended from one end of the world to the other, for it is
Deut. iv. 32. said, "since the day that God created man upon the earth," and from one end of heaven unto the other. Inasmuch as he sinned[5], the Holy One, blessed be He, placed His hand upon him and made
Ps. cxxxix. 5. him small, as it is said, "and laid thine hand upon me." If so, the passages are difficult to reconcile. No, for both are of the same dimensions[6].

And R. Jehudah said that Rab said, Ten things were created on the first day, and they are these; heaven and earth, chaos and desolation, light and darkness, wind and waters, the measure of the day and the measure of the night: heaven and earth; for it is
Gen. i. 1. written, "In the beginning God created the heaven and the earth;"
Gen. i. 2. chaos and desolation; for it is written, "And the earth was chaos and desolation;" light and darkness; darkness, for it is written,
ibid. "and darkness was upon the face of the deep," light, for it is
Gen. i. 3. written, "And God said, Let there be light;" wind and water; for
Gen. i. 2. it is written, "and the wind[7] of God was brooding upon the face of the waters;" the measure of the day and the measure of the
Gen. i. 5. night; for it is written, "And there was evening and there was morning, one day." There is a Baraitha, Chaos is a green line

---

[1] By anticipation.

[2] The word "upon" (עַל) in the passage under discussion is supposed to indicate this.

[3] Lit., became of evil odour.

[4] Thus marking two distinct acts of fashioning.

[5] See note 3.

[6] The distance from earth to heaven (= to God), which is equal to the distance from one end of heaven to the other, is thus calculated by the Rabbis. שַׁדַּי (Almighty, Gen. xvii. 1) is composed of (שׁ + ד + י =) שִׁין + דָּלֶת + יוּד. Omitting from each of these words the first letter, we get

ו + י + ת + ל + ד + ו = 50 + 10 + 400 + 30 + 4 + 6 = 500 (years' journey).

[7] Breath, spirit.

encompassing all the world, and from it darkness springs, as it is 12a, 1.25. said, "He made darkness his hiding place round about him." Ps. xviii. 12; E.V. 11. Desolation—this means the stones covered with mud¹, which are sunk in the deep, from which waters come forth, as it is said, "and he shall stretch upon it the line of chaos and the stones Is. xxxiv. 11. of desolation." And was light created on the first day? But there is against this view the passage, "and God set them in the Gen. i. 17. firmament of the heaven," and the passage, "and there was evening Gen. i. 19. and there was morning, a fourth day." But it is as R. El'azar says; for R. El'azar said, The light which the Holy One created on the first day, Adam saw by its means from one end of the world to the other. When the Holy One considered the generation of the Flood and the generation of the Dispersion², and saw that their works were vain, He stood up and took it from them, as it is said, "and from the wicked their light is withholden." And for Job whom did He take it away? For the righteous of the time to xxxviii.15. come, as it is said, "And God saw the light, that it was good," and Gen. i. 4. there is nothing good but a righteous man, as it is said, "Say ye of Is. iii. 10. a righteous man, that he is good." When He saw that He had taken away the light for the righteous, He rejoiced, as it is said, "He rejoiceth at the light of the righteous." And this is in ac- Prov. xiii. 9. cordance with the Baraitha which says, The light which the Holy One, blessed be He, created on the first day, Adam observed and saw by its means from one end of the world to the other. These are the words of R. Jacob³. But wise men⁴ say, These⁵ are the luminaries, which were created on the first day, but were not hung up until the fourth day.

R. Zot'ra bar Tobiah⁶ said that Rab said, By ten things⁷ the world was created, by wisdom⁸ and by understanding⁹ and by knowledge¹⁰,

¹ מפולמות, according to Levy (s. v.) Pu'al part. of פָּלַם, formed from פלומא = πήλωμα. But Buxt. (s. v.) explains, Id quod recens et humidum est. The word may possibly be a form of the Greek πλή(σ)μη (πλημμυρίς).

² The confusion of tongues.

³ Teacher of Rabbi (see p. 2, note 9), or a son of Achar's daughter. For further notices of him see Wolf, ii. 849.

⁴ Unnamed. This expression is of frequent occurrence.

⁵ i.e., the "lights" of Gen. i. 14.

⁶ A contemporary of Rabbi. See Bartolocci, Biblioth. Rabb. III. 678.

⁷ Cf. Pirḳe Aboth v. 1, with Dr C. Taylor's note there.

⁸ Knowledge derived from others (orally, or by books).

⁹ Inventive power.   ¹⁰ Contemplation.

12 a, ll. 13. and by strength¹ and by rebuke and by might², by righteousness³ and by judgment⁴, by mercy⁵ and by compassion⁶: by wisdom and by understanding; for it is written, "The Lord by wisdom founded the earth; by understanding he established the heavens," and by knowledge; for it is written, "By his knowledge the depths were broken up;" by strength and might; for it is written, "Which by his strength setteth fast the mountains, being girded about with might;" by rebuke; for it is written, "The pillars of heaven tremble, and are astonished⁷ at his rebuke;" by righteousness and judgment; for it is written, "Righteousness and judgment are the foundation of thy throne;" by mercy and compassion; for it is written, "Remember thy compassion, O Lord, and thy mercies, for they are from of old."

Margin references: Prov. iii. 19. Prov. iii. 20. Ps. lxv. 7; E.V. 6. Job xxvi. 11. Ps. lxxxix. 15; E.V. 14. Ps. xxv. 6.

And R. Jehudah said that Rab said, At the time that the Holy One, blessed be He, created the world, it went spreading on like two clews of woof and warp, until the Holy One, blessed be He, rebuked it and brought it to a standstill, as it is said, "The pillars of heaven tremble, and are astonished⁷ at his rebuke." And this is what Resh Lakish also said, What is the meaning of the words "I am God Almighty" (שדי)? It means I am He *Who* (ש) said to the world, *Enough* (די). Resh Lakish said, At the time that the Holy One, blessed be He, created the sea, it went spreading on, until the Holy One, blessed be He, rebuked it and made it dry, for it is said, "He rebuketh the sea and maketh it dry, and drieth up all the rivers."

Margin references: Job xxvi. 11. Gen. xvii. 1; xxxv. 11. Nah. i. 4.

Our Rabbis have taught thus, The house of Shammai say, The heavens were created in the beginning, and afterwards the earth was created, for it is said, "In the beginning God created the heaven and the earth." But the house of Hillel say, The earth was created in the beginning, and afterwards the heavens, for it is said, "in the day that the Lord God made earth and heaven." The house of Hillel said to the house of Shammai, According to your

Margin references: Gen. i. 1. Gen. ii. 4.

---

¹ Material power.
² Moral power.
³ Involves a touch of kindness, a transition to the sense of alms, charity, which is reproduced in the δικαιοσύνη of Mt. vi. 1.
⁴ Strict justice.
⁵ The outward act.
⁶ The feeling which prompts to action.
⁷ Lit., stiffened.

words a man builds an upper story, and afterwards builds a house: 12a, ii. 26. and the heavens are the upper story, as it is said, "It is he that Amos ix. 6. buildeth in the heavens his upper stories, and hath founded his vault upon the earth." The house of Shammai said to the house of Hillel, According to your words a man makes a footstool and afterwards makes a throne: and the heavens are a throne, as it is said, "Thus saith the Lord, The heaven is my throne and the Is. lxvi. 1. earth is my footstool." But wise men[1] say, The one and the other were created together[2], as it is said, "Yea, mine hand[3] hath Is. xlviii. laid the foundation of the earth, and my right hand[4] hath spread 13. out the heavens: when I call unto them, they stand up together." And the others[5]—what do they say of the word "together"? for[6] they cannot be separated the one from the other. The passages are difficult to reconcile[7]. Resh Lakish said, When they were created, He created the heavens, and afterwards created the earth, but when He stretched them out, He stretched out the earth, and afterwards stretched out the heavens.

What are we to say of the word "heavens"? R. Jose bar Chănina[8] said, It means the place where there is water[9]. In a Kabbalistic Mishnah[10] it is explained as equivalent to fire and water[11], thus teaching that the Holy One, blessed be He, brought them and mingled them one with the other, and made from them the firmament.

---

[1] See p. 59, note 4.
[2] See Dr C. Taylor, *Sayings etc.*, p. 107, note 40, where he points out that "the Hillelite theory corresponds to 1 Cor. xv. 46," and that "the three views" (of Shammai, Hillel, and the "wise men") may be taken as texts for three philosophies, viz., *idealism, evolutionism*, and *dualism*.
[3] i.e., the left hand.
[4] At the same time.
[5] Shammai and Hillel.
[6] If it is a case of "together" (יַחְדָּיו).
[7] For both passages separate them, while putting them in a different order.
[8] A contemporary of Jonathan. See p. 76, note 8.
[9] i.e., the word שָׁמַיִם ("heavens"), according to that Rabbi, is compounded of שָׁ (there) and מַיִם (water).
[10] Extra-canonical. For the Heb. word here used see Glossary, under MISHNAH.
[11] i.e., the word, according to that Mishnah, is compounded of אֵשׁ (fire) and מַיִם.

12 a, ii. 35. R. Ishmael questioned R. Akiba, when they were walking on the road. He said to him, Thou art one who hast served for twenty-two years Nachum, the man surnamed Gamzu¹, the man who expounded the meaning of all the particles *eth*² which are in the Law. "*Eth ha-shamayim v'eth ha-aretz*"—what was his exposition of these³? He said to him, If the words had been simply *shamayim v'eretz*, I should have said, *shamayim* is the name of the Holy One, blessed be He⁴. But now that the words are *eth ha-shamayim v'eth ha-aretz*, *shamayim* means the literal heaven, and *eretz* the literal earth. And why do I find the expression, *v'eth ha-*

12 b *aretz?* To shew that the heaven preceded⁵ the earth. "And
Gen. i. 2. the earth was chaos and desolation." Assuredly He began with heaven at first. What reason then was there for His considering the affairs of the earth? The house of R. Ishmael teaches thus⁶, He is like a king of flesh and blood, who saith to his servants, Rise up early and come to my door. He himself rises early, and finds women⁷ and men. Whom does he praise? Him⁸ who was under no obligation to rise early, yet did rise early⁹.

---

¹ His surname was fancifully explained by the story that, when deprived of goods, of feet, of hands, etc., his invariable remark was גַּם זוּ לְטוֹבָה, *this also* (Gamzu) is well. (See for other references to him Ta'ănith, 21 *a*, ii. 1, Sanhedrin, 108 *b*, ii. 35). He was really surnamed after the place from which he came, Gimzo. For the union of discipleship and service indicated in this passage cf. Mt. x. 24, and the remark in *B'rakhoth* 7*b*, ii. 28, גדולה שמושה יותר מלמודה, *service is better than study*, and in *Pirķe Aboth*, i. 18, לא המדרש הוא העיקר אלא חמעשה, *not learning, but doing is the groundwork*.

² אֶת in Heb. is sometimes (as in Gen. i. 1) the mark of the object of the verb, and sometimes the equivalent of *with*. Nachum asserted that it always meant the latter. Cf. Aquila in his Greek version of the O.T. (see *Dict. Chr. Biog.* iii. 17, sq.).

³ i.e., of the word את, as occurring twice in that verse.

⁴ So that (according to him) את is necessary to prevent us from thinking that the sense is, In the beginning the Holy One created God and the earth.

⁵ Lit., to cause the heaven to precede.

⁶ Lit., (The teacher) of the house of R. Ishmael teaches (thus).

⁷ He naturally expected to find men only.

⁸ Meaning really, *her*.

⁹ Rashi's explanation is, The earth is under no obligation to rise early, and besides, all the work of the earth is slow, while the work of the heavens is quick [as revolving round the earth, according to the belief of Rashi's day]. Yet the earth attained a pace commensurate with the heavens at the time of their creation, and thus she is to be commended.

There is a Baraitha of R. Jose, which says, Woe to the creatures 12 b, l. 9. which see and know not what they see, which stand and know not upon what they stand. Upon what does the earth stand? Upon the pillars, as it is said, "Who shaketh the earth out of her place, Job ix. 6. and the pillars thereof tremble." The pillars stand upon the waters, as it is said, "To him that spread forth the earth upon the waters;" Ps. cxxxvi. 6. the waters upon the mountains, as it is said, "the waters stood Ps. civ. 6. above the mountains"; the mountains upon the wind, as it is said, Amos iv. 13. "For lo he that formeth the mountains and createth wind;" the wind upon the storm, as it is said, "Storm making the substance Ps. cxlviii. 8. of the wind[1];" the storm is suspended upon the arm of the Holy One, blessed be He, as it is said, "underneath are the everlasting Deut. xxxiii. 27. arms." And wise men[2] say, It stands upon twelve pillars, as it is said, "He set the bounds of the peoples according to the number Deut. xxiii. 8. of the children of Israel." And there are some who say, Seven pillars, as it is said, "she hath hewn out her seven pillars." R. Prov. ix. 1. El'azar ben Shammua'[3] says, Upon one pillar, and its name is The Righteous[4], as it is said, "but the righteous is the foundation of the Prov. x. 25. world."

R. Jehudah said, There are two firmaments, as it is said, "Be- Deut. x. 14. hold, unto the Lord thy God belong the heaven and the heaven of heavens." Resh Laḳish said, There are seven[5], and these be they, Vilon[6], Raḳia', Sh'chaḳim, Z'bul, Ma'on, Makhon, Araboth. Vilon serves no purpose whatever save this, that it enters in in the morning, and goes forth in the evening[7], and renews every day the work of Creation, as it is said, "That stretcheth out the Is. xl. 22. heavens as a curtain, and spreadeth them out as a tent to dwell in." Raḳia' is that in which are set sun and moon, stars and constellations, as it is said, "and God set them in the firmament Gen. i. 17.

---

[1] So Rashi explains the verse in its application here. The correct rendering is doubtless the ordinary one, "stormy wind, fulfilling His word."

[2] See p. 59, note 4.

[3] Teacher of Rabbi, and one of the הָרוּגֵי מַלְכוּת. See p. 15, note 8, and Wolf, ii. 813, 868.

[4] i.e., God.   [5] Cf. Test. xii. Patr. Levi, 3.

[6] = velum, a curtain.

[7] An ambiguous expression, as to the meaning of which Rashi and the authors of the Tosaphoth (see Glossary, TOSIPHTA) differ. Rashi says, In the *absence* of Vilon the light (of day) is seen. The others say, Vilon is *present* by day, and withdraws at night; otherwise the stars would not then be visible.

(Raḳia‘) of the heaven¹." Sh'chakim is that in which the millstones stand and grind manna for the righteous, as it is said, "Yet he commanded the clouds (Sh'chakim) above and opened the doors of heaven; and he rained down manna upon them to eat, etc." Z'bul is that in which is the heavenly Jerusalem² and the Temple, and the altar is built there, and Michael the great prince stands and offers upon it an offering, as it is said, "I have surely built thee an house of habitation (Z'bul), a place for thee to dwell in for ever." And whence do we get it that it is called heaven? Because it is written, "Look down from heaven and behold from the habitation (Z'bul) of thy holiness and thy glory." Ma‘on is that in which are companies of ministering angels, who utter His song in the night and are silent in the day for the sake of the glory of Israel,³ as it is said, "By day the Lord gives His merciful command⁴ and by night His song is with me."

Resh Laḳish said, Every one who studies in the Law by night,— the Holy One, blessed be He, draws over him the thread of grace by day, as it is said, "By day the Lord gives his merciful command." And what is the reason that by day the Lord gives his merciful command? Because of what follows, viz., "and by night his song is with me." And there are some who say that Resh Laḳish said, Everyone who studieth in the Law in this world which is like the night, the Holy One, blessed be He, stretches over him the thread of grace for the future world which is like the day, as it is said, "By day the Lord gives his merciful command, and by night his song is with me."

R. Levi said, Every one that leaveth off the words of the Law, and studieth the words of idle talk, coals of broom devour him, as it is said, "who cut up mallows over idle talk, and the root of the broom eateth them⁵."

And whence do we get it that it⁶ is called heaven? As it is said, "Look down from thy holy habitation (Ma‘on), from heaven." Makhon is that in which are the treasures of snow and the treasures

---

¹ Therefore there must have been heavens before.
² Cf. Heb. xii. 22, Apoc. xxi. 10 sqq.
³ That Israel's songs of praise, as uttered by day, may have the opportunity of being heard.
⁴ He shews mercy to Israel, by commanding His angels to keep silence.
⁵ Reading apparently (against the Mas. pointing) לְחָמָם.
⁶ Ma‘on.

of hail, and the high dwelling-place of harmful dews, and the high dwelling-place of round drops[1], and the chamber of the whirlwind and of the storm, and the retreat of noisome vapour, and their doors are made of fire, as it is said, "The LORD shall open unto thee his good treasure[2]." But are not these in the firmament? [12 b, ll. 16. Deut. xxviii. 12.]

Nay, they are in the earth, as it is written, "Praise the LORD from the earth, ye dragons and all deeps; fire and hail, snow and vapour; storm making the substance of the wind[3]." R. Jehudah said that Rab said, David besought the Merciful One[4] for them, and He sent them down to the earth. He said before Him, O Lord of the world, "Thou art not a God that hath pleasure in wickedness; evil shall not sojourn with thee" in thy dwelling[5]. Righteous art thou, O Lord; evil shall not sojourn in thy dwelling. And whence do we get it that it[6] is called heaven? Because it is written, "And hear thou in heaven, the habitation (Makhon) of thy dwelling." [Ps. cxlviii. 7, 8. Ps. v. 5; E.V. 4. 1 Kings viii. 39, 43, 49.]

Araboth is that in which are righteousness and judgment and grace[7], the treasures of life and the treasures of peace and the treasures of blessing, and the souls of the righteous, and the spirits[8] and souls which are about to be created[9], and the dew with which the Holy One, blessed be He, is about to quicken mortals: righteousness and judgment; for it is written, "Righteousness and judgment are the foundation of thy throne:" grace; for it is written, "And he put on grace as a coat of mail:" the treasures of life; for it is written, "For with thee is the fountain of life:" and the treasures of peace; for it is written, "and called it, The LORD is peace:" and the treasures of blessing; for it is written, "He shall receive a blessing from the LORD:" the souls of the righteous; for it is written, "Yet the soul of my lord shall be bound in the bundle of life with the LORD thy God:" the spirits and souls which are about to be created; for it is written, "For the spirit before me shall join [Ps. lxxxix. 15; E.V. 14. Is. lix. 17. Ps. xxxvi. 9. Jud. vi. 24. Ps. xxiv. 5. 1 Sam. xxv. 29. Is. lvii. 16.]

[1] Such as are found on plants.
[2] Shewing that there must be somewhere a treasure of bad things as well.
[3] See p. 63, note 1.   [4] Lit., Compassion.
[5] The expression, "in thy dwelling," is not now found in this passage, and is probably a spurious addition.
[6] Makhon.
[7] The righteousness, which involves a touch of kindness. See p. 60, note 3.
[8] The spirit (רוּחַ) perishes at death; not so the soul (נֶפֶשׁ).
[9] This refers to bad souls, e.g., Korah, which are created from time to time. All good ones were created from the beginning.

itself to a body[1], and the souls which I have made:" and the dew with which the Holy One, blessed be He, is about to quicken mortals; for it is written, "Thou, O God, didst send a plentiful rain, thou didst confirm thine inheritance when it was weary." There there are celestials[2] and seraphs and holy beings and ministering angels, and the throne of glory, and the King, the Living God, high and lifted up, sitting over them among the clouds[3], as it is said, "Cast up a highway for him that rideth upon the clouds (Araboth); his name is Jah." And whence do we get it that they[3] are called heaven? Because mention of riding occurs in two passages[4]. It is written in one place, "Cast up a highway for him that *rideth* upon the clouds," and it is written in another, "who *rideth* upon the heaven for thy help." And darkness and cloud and thick darkness surround Him, as it is said, "He made darkness his hiding place, his pavilion round about him; darkness of waters, thick clouds." And how is there darkness in the presence of the Lord? For against this, there is the passage, "He revealeth[5] the deep and secret things; he knoweth what is in the darkness and the light dwelleth with him." There is no difficulty. The one refers to that which is within, the other to that which is without. And R. Acha bar Jacob[6] said, There is again a firmament above the heads of the living creatures, for it is written, "And over the heads of the living creatures there was the likeness of a firmament, like the colour of the terrible crystal." So far thou hast permission to speak. Thenceforward thou hast not permission to speak. For thus it is written in the Book of Ben Sira[7], "Seek not out the things that are too

(margin references: 12 b, ii. 33; Ps. lxviii. 10; E.V. 9; Ps. lxviii. 4; Deut. xxxiii. 26; Ps. xviii. 12; E.V. 11; Dan. ii. 22; 13 a; Ezek. i. 22; Ecclus. iii. 21, 22.)

---

[1] See Rosenmüller's *Scholia* on Isaiah *in loc.* for a discussion of this sense, which is favoured by the Chaldee paraphrase and adopted by Ḳimchi.

[2] Lit., wheels, for by them the Divine Chariot (see p. 55, note 4) is moved and guided. Ezek. i. 15 sqq.

[3] Araboth.   [4] Lit., There comes riding, riding.

[5] גלי. But גלא is the form in the Massoretic text of Daniel, and is accordingly adopted in the margin of the Lemberg edition.

[6] A contemporary of R. Papa (see p. 12, note 3). He spoke in the name of R. Jochanan (see p. 11, note 7). He is apparently quoted under the name of Papa bar Jacob, p. 79, where see note 5.

[7] The work of Joshua ben Sira ben Eliezer, a priest at Jerusalem, who composed the book about B.C. 190. Of the original Hebrew we have only fragments. The book survives in several versions, viz., the following: (1) Syriac and Greek (primary), (2) Latin (also to a certain extent primary), (3) Armenian,

hard for thee, and into the things that are hidden from thee en- 13 a, l. 8.
quire thou not. In what is permitted to thee instruct thyself;
thou hast no business with secret things¹."

There is a Baraitha, viz., Rabban Jochanan ben Zakkai said,
What answer did the Bath-Kol² make to that wicked man³ at
the time when he said, "I will ascend above the heights of the Is. xiv. 14.
clouds; I will be like the Most High"? The Bath-Kol went forth
and said to him, Thou wicked man, son of a wicked man, grandson
of Nimrod the wicked⁴, who led all the world to rebel against Him
in his⁵ kingdom, how many are the years of a man? Seventy
years, as it is said, "The days of our years are threescore years and Ps. xc. 10.
ten, or even by reason of strength fourscore years." And is it
not from the earth to the firmament a journey of five hundred
years⁶? And the thickness of the firmament is itself equal to a
journey of five hundred years, and so too the interspaces of the

Aethiopic, Sahidic and Syro-Hexaplaric (secondary, from the Greek), (4) Arabic
(secondary, from the Syriac). The Greek version (whence our Auth. Vers. is
taken) was made by Ben Sira's grandson, circ. B.C. 130. See further in Dr
Westcott's Article, *Dict. of Bible*, and in Prof. Margoliouth's *Place of Eccl. etc.*,
Oxford, 1890.

¹ "The fullest recension of [this passage] is in Ber. R. 8 (ed. Warsh. 17 a)
where v. 21 and the substance of v. 22 are quoted as follows: 'Rabbi Elazar
said in the name of Ben Sira (so also in Jer. Chag. 77 c), What is too great for
thee, seek not out, into what is too strong (powerful) for thee, search not; what
is too high for thee seek not to know; into what is hidden from thee inquire
not; what is within thy power (that which is within thy reach, that which is
practically before thee), consider, and busy not thyself with secret things.' The
same saying is quoted with slightly different wording, in the Jer. Talmud
(Chag. 77 c)...but [as in the Bab. Tal. text above] without the first two clauses
given in Ber. R. 8." Edersheim, *Speaker's Comm. in loc.*

² So called as being similar, yet inferior, to (lit., the daughter of the voice of)
the actual prophetic utterance.

³ Nebuchadnezzar, but suggesting to Jochanan's contemporaries Titus, as
the then enemy of the Jews.

⁴ Nebuchadnezzar is spoken of as descended from Nimrod, not in a
literal sense, but (cf. John viii. 41) because of his similarity in place of
origin, and on account of his character and deeds. Jewish tradition, however, gives this further link between them that, while Nimrod was a
descendant of Ham (Gen. x. 6—8), Nebuchadnezzar was sprung from one
of Solomon's wives ("strange women, together with the daughter of Pharaoh."
1 Kings xi. 1).

⁵ Nimrod's.

⁶ Compare the Rabbinical saying, that Jacob's ladder had so many steps
that it would take five hundred years to mount.

13 a, l. 19. firmaments[1]. Above there are the holy living creatures. The feet of the living creatures are of corresponding measure to all the things mentioned above, the ankles of the living creatures are of corresponding measure, the legs of the living creatures are of corresponding measure, the knees of the living creatures are of corresponding measure, the thighs of the living creatures are of corresponding measure, the bodies of the living creatures are of corresponding measure, the necks of the living creatures are of corresponding measure, the heads of the living creatures are of corresponding measure, the horns of the living creatures are of corresponding measure. Above them is the throne of glory. The feet of the throne of glory are of corresponding measure. The throne of glory is of corresponding measure. The King, the Living and Eternal[2] God, high, and lifted up, sitteth upon them[3]. And thou didst say, "I will ascend above
Is. xiv. 15. the heights of the clouds; I will be like the Most High." "Yet thou shalt be brought down to hell, to the uttermost parts of the pit."

Nor the Chariot with one[4]. R. Chia teaches, But you may impart to him the heads of the divisions[5].   R. Zera said, You may only impart the heads of the divisions to the chief of a college, and to every one whose heart within him yearns for knowledge.   There are others who say, Even to him[6] you are to impart these, only if his heart within him yearns for knowledge.

R. Ami said, You may impart the secret things of the Law
Is. iii. 3. only to one in whom are five requisites, as follows, viz., "The captain of fifty[7], and the man of influence, and the counsellor[8], and the wise among artificers[9], and the instructed whisperer[10]." And R. Ami

---

[1] The firmaments are seven in number. See p. 63.
[2] Lit., established.
[3] Cf. Eph. iv. 13.   [4] See p. 55.
[5] A summary or synopsis of the teaching, not meaning a table of contents or headings of sections, but a sketch (ἐκτύπωσις) in words which shall give the key, as φωνᾶντα συνετοῖσιν.
[6] The chief of a college.
[7] A man fifty years of age, so as to be qualified to give interpretations publicly.
[8] One who understands how to intercalate years, so as to fix the dates of successive Passovers.
[9] חָרָשׁ is an artificer, and is no doubt the right word in this passage. But the Rabbinic interpretation is, one who makes the whole world deaf (חֵרֵשׁ) by his oratorical power.
[10] The Rabbinic explanation is, one who whispers (לחש) Kabbalistic secrets into the ear.

said, You must not impart the words of the Law to a Cuthite[1], 13 a, ll. 3. for it is said, "He hath not dealt so with any nation (גו), and as for his judgments, they have not known them." Ps. cxlvii. 20.

R. Jochanan[2] said to R. El'azar, Come, I will fully instruct[3] thee in the subject of the Chariot. He said to him, I am not old enough. When he was old enough, R. Jochanan's soul had passed away[4]. R. Asi said to him, Come, and I will fully instruct thee in the subject of the Chariot. He said to him, If I had been worthy, I should have received full instruction from R. Jochanan thy teacher. R. Joseph was giving full instruction in the subject of the Chariot. The wise men of Pumbeditha[5] were teaching the subject of Creation. They said to him, Would that our lord would instruct us fully in the subject of the Chariot. He said to them, Instruct me fully in the subject of Creation. After they had instructed him fully, they said to him, Would that our lord would instruct us fully in the subject of the Chariot. He said to them, There is a Baraitha with reference to these things which says, "Honey and milk are under thy tongue[6]." Let words sweeter Cant. iv. 11.

[1] The older reading, גוי, obviously required by the words which follow, must have been altered from fear of the Christians. Such changes or omissions, caused by the "censorship," are tolerably frequent in the Talmud. See *Introd*.

[2] See . 11.

[3] Cf. the use of πληροῦν in N.T., e.g., Mt. v. 17.

[4] Lit., was at rest. Cf. Is. lvii. 2 (according to the Jewish interpretation). So John xi. 11.

[5] Called also Golah, "the abode of the *captivity*" (exiles), twenty-two parasangs N. of Sora, probably at the mouth (Pum) of a canal called Beditha. It was the residence of the chief Jewish families of Babylonia, but as the seat of an Academy it was later than Nehardea and Sora, while on the other hand its school was more permanent and of more influential character than even the latter of these. See p. 6, note 1. The people of the place had an evil reputation for theft and fraud. The Academy was famed for its subtleties of exposition, whence the proverb (*Talm. Bab., Baba Metzi'a*, 38 *b*), "Thou art of Pumbeditha; then thou canst make an elephant pass through the eye of a needle." (Neubauer's *Géog. du Talmud*, p. 349). Here follow the earlier heads of the Academy at Pumbeditha, with the dates of their accession to office: Jehudah bar Jecheziel, A.D. 250; Hunna bar Chia, A.D. 292; Rabba bar Nachman, A.D. 297; Joseph bar Chia, A.D. 309; Abai Nachmani bar Chalil ha-Cohen, A.D. 322; Rabba bar Joseph bar Chama (who however resided at Machusa), A.D. 337; Nachman bar Isaac, A.D. 351; Chama bar Tobiah, A.D. 355—376. See Etheridge, pp. 161—172.

[6] There the bridegroom says it to the bride, and so God to Israel. Therefore such things, sweet though they be, cannot be made the subjects of teaching.

than honey and milk be under thy tongue. R. Abohu¹ said, It² is drawn from this passage, viz., "things to be concealed under thy clothes³," that is to say, things which are the secrets of the world shall be under thy clothes. They said to him, We have worked in them as far as the words, "And he said unto me, Son of man⁴." He said to them, But this is the subject of the Chariot⁵. Some one puts a difficulty. How far does the subject of the Chariot reach? Rab says, It reaches to the last occurrence of the expression, "I saw." R. Isaac says, It reaches to the Chashmal⁶. We instruct fully to the words, "and I saw;" thenceforward we only impart the heads of the divisions.

There are others who say, As far as, "and I saw," we impart the heads of the divisions; thenceforward, if the man be wise and of ready intelligence, Yes; if not, No. And how are we to expound in Chashmal? For there is the story of the child, who was studying⁷ in Chashmal, and there came out a fire and consumed him. The case of the child is different, for he had not reached the fitting age.

R. Jehudah said, Of a truth remember thou that man for good⁸, and Chănaniah son of Hezekiah was his name⁹. But for him the Book of Ezekiel would have been withdrawn¹⁰, for its words were

---

¹ Of Cæsarea; a 3rd century teacher.

² viz., the duty of reticence on the subject of the Chariot.

³ But the Eng. Vers. renders, and no doubt correctly, "The lambs are for thy clothing."

⁴ Maimonides (*Moreh Nev.* iii. 5) says, Wise men say, You may teach the first two sections (beginning i. 4 and i. 15), but not the third (beginning i. 27), which is *Chashmal* and its belongings, save only under general heads. But Rabbi (see p. 2, note 9) says, that all these are "the Chariot," and that in the case of any of them the general heads only are to be taught.

⁵ i.e., If you understood this, you would not come to me to teach you "the Chariot."

⁶ The "amber," not meaning, to the place where this word first occurs, but as far as the passage called by this name. Cf. "Elias" (Rom. xi. 2), "the bush" (Mk. xii. 26), in N.T. as designations of particular sections of the Scriptures.

⁷ Lit., expounding. Hottinger (*De Incestu etc.*, p. 54), takes the story to refer to one who was a child not in years but in knowledge of the Talmud. Cf. Hebrews v. 13.

⁸ Cf. Neh. v. 19 (Lk. xxiii. 42), but cf. for a somewhat different aspect of the same Heb. phrase, Mishnah of *B'rakhoth*, v. 3.

⁹ He lived before the destruction of the second Temple. See *Juch.* p. 65 *b*.

¹⁰ The Apocryphal Books were called גנוזים, hidden.

opposed to the words of the Law¹. What did they do? They [13 a, ii. 33.] brought up for him three hundred measures of oil, and he sat in an upper chamber and expounded it.

Our Rabbis have taught, There is a story of a certain child who was reading in his teacher's house in the Book of Ezekiel, and he was pondering over Chashmal, and there came out fire from Chashmal and burnt him, and they sought in consequence to withdraw the Book of Ezekiel. Chănaniah ben Hezekiah² said to them, If he³ was wise, are all wise⁴?

What is the meaning of Chashmal? R. Jehudah said, Fiery beings [13 b] who speak⁵. In a Kabbalistic Mishnah⁶ we are taught that it means, At times they are silent and at times they speak⁷; at the time that the utterance goeth forth from the mouth of the Holy One, blessed be He, they are silent, and at the time that the utterance goeth not forth from the mouth of the Holy One, blessed be He, they speak. "And the living creatures ran and re- [Ezek. i. 14.] turned as the appearance of a flash of lightning." What is the meaning of "ran and returned?" R. Jehudah said, As the light which goeth forth from the mouth of the furnace. What is the meaning of "as the appearance of a flash of lightning?" R. Jose bar Chănina said, Like the flame that goeth forth from

---

¹ Tradition said that there were 250 points of difference between the Law and Ezekiel. Two instances are given by Rashi in his commentary on this passage. 1⁰. From Ezekiel (xliv. 31) it might be thought that Israelites generally might eat "anything that dieth of itself or is torn," though it was forbidden to the priests, while in Leviticus (xxii. 8) such food is forbidden to all. 2⁰. The Law mentions no sacrifice on the 7th day of the 1st month, such as is prescribed in Ezekiel (xlv. 20). Again Ezekiel (xliv. 22) allowed a widow to marry, if, being the widow of a priest, she took a priest; not so the Law (Lev. xxi. 14). The reconciliation in this last case is, that a widow in the specially honourable sense of the word, viz., one who has not been (a) divorced, or (b) twice married, or (c) the subject of a levirate marriage, may be married to an ordinary priest, but not to the high-priest. One who is not a widow in this special sense cannot marry any kind of priest.

² Flourished in the time of the 2nd Temple. See Bartolocci, *Biblioth. Rabb.* ii. 847.

³ The child.

⁴ The answer is, No, and therefore it is not needful to withdraw the Book, as there is no fear that any considerable number of persons will meet the child's fate by an appreciative study of its contents.

⁵ חשמל=חיות אש ממללות.

⁶ See p. 61, note 10.

⁷ עתים חשות עתים ממללות.

13 b, i. 10. between the potsherds.   "And I looked, and, behold, a stormy
Ezek. i. 4. wind came out of the north, a great cloud, with a fire infolding
itself, and a brightness round about it, and out of the midst thereof
as the colour of amber, out of the midst of the fire." Whither did
it[1] go?   R. Jehudah said that Rab said, It went forth to sub-
due the whole world under the wicked Nebuchadnezzar.   And
wherefore was all this done?   That the peoples of the world
might not say, The Holy One, blessed be He, delivered His children
into the hand of a mean people[2]. The Holy One, blessed be He,
said, What forced me to minister to worshippers of carved images?
The iniquities of Israel, they forced me.

Ezek. i. 15.   "Now as I beheld the living creatures, behold one wheel
upon the earth beside the living creatures." R. El'azar said, It
means a certain angel, who stands upon the earth and his head
reaches to the level of the living creatures.   In a Kabbalistic
Mishnah we are taught that his name is Sandalphon[3], who is
higher than his fellows by the space of a journey of five hundred
years, and he stands behind the chariot and binds crowns for his
Ezek. iii. 12. Maker[4].   Is it so? But there is the passage, "Blessed be
the glory of the LORD from his place[5]."   Strictly speaking,
His place it is impossible to know[6], but he[7] utters the Name over
the wreath and thereupon it goes and rests by His head.

[1] The storm.

[2] Cf. "The land of the Chaldæans; this people has come to nothing," a possible, or even probable, rendering of Is. xxiii. 13. See Delitzsch and Cheyne *in loc.*

[3] Perhaps συνάδελφος. For the Messianic side of the thought suggested by his name cf. Deut. xviii. 18, Ps. xxii. 22, Rom. viii. 29, Heb. ii. 11, 12, 17.

[4] i.e., offers the prayers of the righteous. Cf. Heb. vii. 25, Apoc. viii. 3, 4. For "his Maker" cf. Prov. viii. 22 (קָנָנִי, He formed me). "In the Liturgy for the Feast of Tabernacles it is said that Sandalphon gathers in his hands the prayers of Israel, and, forming a wreath of them, he adjures it to ascend as an orb for the head of the supreme King of kings." Hershon, *A Talmudic Miscellany*, p. 250. Cf. Longfellow, *Sandalphon*.

"Erect, at the outermost gates
Of the City Celestial he waits,
    *   *   *   *
And he gathers the prayers as he stands,
And they change into flowers in his hands."

[5] Which expression from its vagueness is taken to imply that God's "place" is unknown and so unapproachable even by Sandalphon.

[6] No one knows God's place, for He always rises higher than any fixed place.   [7] Sandalphon.

Rabba said, All which Ezekiel saw, Isaiah saw[1]. To what is Ezekiel like? He is like a rustic who has seen the king. And to what is Isaiah like? He is like a townsman[2] who has seen the king.

Resh Laḳish said, What is the meaning of the passage "I will sing unto the LORD, for he is highly exalted[3]"? It means a song to Him who takes His place proudly above the high, as the Mishnah teacher said, The king among living creatures is a lion, the king among domestic beasts is an ox, the king among birds is an eagle, but man takes his place proudly above them, and the Holy One, blessed be He, takes His place proudly above them all, and above the whole world in its entirety.

A certain passage says, "And as for the likeness of their faces, they had the face of a man; and they four had the face of a lion on the right side; and they four had the face of an ox on the left side, etc." and it is written, "And every one had four faces: the first face was the face of the cherub, and the second face was the face of a man, and the third the face of a lion, and the fourth the face of an eagle." And lo, the ox is not reckoned in[4]. Resh Laḳish said, Ezekiel besought the Merciful One with regard to him, and He changed him into a cherub. He addressed Him thus, Lord of the Universe, shall an accuser become an advocate[5]? What is the meaning of cherub? R. Abohu

---

[1] The difficulty to which Rabba is alluding is the discrepancies between Isaiah and Ezekiel, e.g., in their visions of God's glory, wherein Isaiah saw six wings, while Ezekiel saw but four.

[2] And therefore is cultured and polished. Thus, being less impressed by the glory, he does not relate the vision at such length as the countryman Ezekiel, who gives us an account of the vision of God four times (i. viii. x. xliii. 3) while Isaiah gives it but once (vi.). Other reasons which have been suggested for the contrast here noticed between them are, (1º) It was needful for Ezekiel to be very explicit in order to meet the Jewish belief that no visions of God would be granted outside Canaan (so Abarbanel, Comm. on Ezek. i.), or, (2º) The men of the Captivity (unlike those of Isaiah's time, who were familiar with such visions) had need of special details to support them in their trials.

[3] Lit., He has proudly shewn forth His superiority (not merely to the animals, but) to the proud (themselves).

[4] Hottinger (De Incestu etc. in loc.) however suggests that כְּרוּב in this passage may mean an ox. Cf. the Chaldee and Syriac root כרב, to plough.

[5] i.e., Can a calf (= ox), as long as he remains a calf, from being our enemy (as always from the days of the golden calf), become a friend? No, not till he

13 b, l. 37.	said, It is equivalent to a growing child¹. For so in Babylon a young child is called Rabya. R. Papa said to Abohu², But, as it is
Ezek. x. 14.	written, "The first face was the face of the cherub, and the second face was the face of a man, and the third the face of a lion, and the fourth the face of an eagle," this shews that the face of a cherub is the same thing as the face of a man³. There are large faces and there are small faces⁴.
Is. vi. 2 Ezek. i. 6.	There is a passage which says, "each one had six wings," and there is a passage which says, "And every one had four faces, and every one of them had four wings." There is no difficulty. The one case was at the time when the Holy House was standing, the other at the time when the Holy House was not standing. As if it were possible⁵ to say which two of the wings of the living creatures were taken away. Which of them were taken away? R. Chănaneel⁶ said, that Rab said, Those with which
Is. vi. 2, 3. Prov. xxiii. 5.	they utter their song. It is written thus, "And with twain he did fly. And one cried to another and said," and it is written, "Wilt thou set thine eyes upon it? But it is gone." But our Rabbis say,
Ezek. i. 7.	Those with which they cover their feet, as it is said, "And their feet were as a straight foot⁷." And if none had been taken away, how would he have known⁸? Perhaps it was uncovered, and he saw it. But if thou sayest, Not so, then I may argue thus: "And as for the likeness of their faces, they had the face of a man," and I may argue that in this case also they were taken away. But when you reply that in this case⁹ it was uncovered and he saw it, then I rejoin that in this case also¹⁰ it was uncovered and he saw

is changed into a man. Ezekiel was seeking intercessions on behalf of men. Those of an ox, as being man's foe, could not be sincere, and hence the prophet's prayer.

¹ As though בְּרוּגְ were made up of the element כ and רוב from the same root as רביה of the text.

² אבי of the Heb. text is obviously an error.

³ And thus disproves the notion that it means a *boy's* face.

⁴ The large face represents God as He is, the small, God as manifested to us. The ancient of days (Dan. vii. 9) is the Father (אַפֵּי רַבְרְבִי), the son of man (ver. 13) is the Messiah (אַפֵּי זוּטְרֵי). Such was the belief of many Jews in Christ's time. They illustrated by reflection in a large and a small looking-glass.

⁵ i.e., Surely it would not be possible etc.

⁶ A disciple of Rab, but nothing beyond this is known of him.

⁷ See p. 85, note 2.   ⁸ That it was a straight foot.

⁹ viz., of the face.   ¹⁰ viz., of the feet.

it. But no[1], for in this case, even granting that the face is customarily uncovered before one's teacher, the legs are not customarily uncovered before one's teacher[2]. [13 b, ll. 23.]

There is a certain passage which says, "Thousand thousands ministered unto him, and ten thousand times ten thousand stood before him," and there is a certain passage which says, "Is there any number of his armies?" There is no difficulty. The one was at the time when the Holy House was standing, and the other was at the time when the Holy House was not standing. [Dan. vii. 10.] [Job xxv. 3.]

As though it were possible to say[3] that the family[4] of the Most High was diminished. There is a Baraitha, Rabbi says in the name of Abba[5] Jose ben Dosai, "Thousand thousands ministered unto him," this is the number of one troop, but of His troops there is no number. And R. Jeremiah bar Abba[6] said, Thousand thousands ministered unto him at the fiery stream, as it is said, "A fiery stream issued and came forth from before him: thousand thousands ministered unto him, and ten thousand times ten thousand stood before him." Whence does it come forth? From the perspiration of the living creatures. And upon what is it poured? R. Zot'ra bar Tobiah said that Rab said, Upon the heads of wicked men in Gehenna, as it is said, "Behold the tempest of the LORD, even his fury, is gone forth, yea, a whirling tempest; it shall burst upon the head of the wicked." And R. Acha bar Jacob said, Upon those who were held back[7], as it is said, "Who were held back before their time, whose foundation was poured out as a stream." There is a Baraitha to the effect that R. Simeon the Holy said, These are nine hundred and seventy-four generations, which were held back from being created before the world was created, and so were not created. The Holy One, blessed be He, [Dan. vii. 10.] [Jer. xxiii. 19.] [Job xxii. 16.] [14 a]

---

[1] Your rejoinder does not apply.
[2] And therefore the two cases are not really parallel.
[3] Surely it would not be possible etc. פמליא[4].
[5] Abba is a pre-Christian title.
[6] A disciple and colleague of Rab. See *Juch.* 159 *b*; Wolf, ii. 876.
[7] 974 generations were "held back." For God's original plan was that 1000 generations (see 1 Chron. xvi. 15, Ps. cv. 8) should pass before He gave the Law. But He changed His purpose, that man might not be so long without a guide of life, and in the 26th generation (Gen. v. xi., Exod. vi. 16—20) the Law was given. The souls of the remaining generations had however been in readiness from the beginning, and so they are spread over the remainder of the world's existence, a few in each age.

stood and scattered them¹ through all the successive generations, and these are the shameless who are in a² generation. But R. Nachman bar Isaac said, They are these who are wrinkled³ for blessing. This is the meaning of that which is written, As for these disciples of the wise, who have become wrinkled over the words of the Law in this world, the Holy One, blessed be He, discloses to them the secret of the world to come, as it is said, "their foundation was overflowed with a stream⁴."

<small>Job xxii. 16.</small>

Samuel said to Chia bar Rab⁵, Thou clever fellow⁶, come, and I will tell thee something from those noble words, which thy father used to say. Every several day ministering angels are created from the fiery stream, and they utter a song and perish⁷, as it is said, "They are new every morning; great is thy faithfulness."

<small>Lam. iii. 23.</small>

But R. Samuel bar Nachmani differs in his view; for R. Samuel bar Nachmani said that R. Jonathan⁸ said, Every several utterance that goeth out of the mouth of the Holy One, blessed be He, there is created from it an angel, as it is said, "By the word of the LORD were the heavens made; and all the hosts of them by the breath of his mouth."

<small>Ps. xxxiii. 6.</small>

There is a passage which says, "His raiment was white as snow, and the hair of his head like pure wool," and yet it is written, "His locks are curling and black as a raven." There is no difficulty. The one is the case where He is engaged in session⁹, the other where He is engaged in war. For the Mishnah teacher

<small>Dan. vii. 9.</small>

<small>Cant. v. 11.</small>

---

¹ But Rashi explains שְׁתָלָן handed them over to Gehenna.

² i.e., each.

³ The Heb. root has the two senses, *to be held back*, and *to be wrinkled*.

⁴ Another way of rendering the same passage. Nachman is also here playing on the similarity of the two words יְסוֹדָם, "their foundation," and סוֹדָם, *their secret*.

⁵ Chia bar Rab was a contemporary of Hunna. Chia's mother was a shrew, and carefully did the opposite of what her husband desired. On Chia's trying to outwit her by telling her that his father desired the contrary of what he knew him to wish, Rab rebuked him for his deceit, but thanked him for the goodwill that prompted it. See *Juch.* 137 *b*.

⁶ Lit., son of a lion.

⁷   "The Angels of Wind and of Fire
      Chant only one hymn, and expire
      With the song's irresistible stress."—Longfellow, *Sandalphon.*

⁸ Believed to have been a contemporary of Akiba, and thus to be reckoned among the earliest Gemaric teachers. See *Juch.* 152 *b*; Wolf ii. 846.

⁹ i.e., teaching.

said, No one, look you, is nobler in session than an old man, and 14 a, 1. 20.
no one, look you, is nobler in war than a youth.   One passage
says, "His *throne* was fiery flames," but another says, " till *thrones* Dan. vii. 9.
were placed, and one that was ancient of days did sit."   There is Dan. vii. 9.
no difficulty, One throne is for Him and one for David[1].   As says
a Baraitha, viz., One for him and one for David.   These are the
words of R. Akiba.   R. Jose the Galilaean said to him, Akiba, how
long dost thou shew irreverence to the Shechinah[2]?   Nay, but[3] one is
for judgment and one for grace[4].   Was he convinced by him, or
was he not[5]?   Come and hear[6].   One is for judgment and one for
grace.   These are the words of R. Akiba.   R. El'azar ben Azariah
said to him, Akiba, what hast thou to do with Haggadah[7]?   Be off[8].
Thy sayings have to do with stripes and bitters[9].   But the real
meaning is that one is for a throne and one for a footstool ; a
throne that He may sit upon it, and a footstool as the resting-place
for His feet, as it is said, "The heaven is my throne and the Is. lxvi. 1.
earth is the resting-place of my feet."

When R. Dimi[10] came[11], he said, Eighteen curses did Isaiah
pronounce upon Israel, and he was not satisfied[12] until he had
spoken against them this passage, "The child shall behave himself Is. iii. 5.
proudly against the elder, and the base against the honourable."
Eighteen curses, what are they?   As it is written, " For, behold, Is. iii.
1—4.

[1] i.e., The Messiah.   Comp. Ps. cx., Ezek. xxxiv. 23, 24, xxxvii. 24, 25.

[2] Lit., make the Shechinah (God) a common (profane) thing (by thus placing the Messiah in juxtaposition with Him).

[3] Both being for God.

[4] See p. 65, note 7.

[5] Lit., Did he receive (the rebuke) from him, or did he not receive (it) from him?

[6] פָּ (א)שֶׁ(מָע) always introduces an objection intended to overthrow the whole argument.

[7] See Glossary.

[8] כַּלֵּךְ a contraction of כַּלֵּה וְלֵךְ = stop and go (elsewhere).

[9] Bitters; literally, aloes (Ps. xlv. 9; E. V. 8), but here probably with a play upon the word, as also meaning tents. The general sense is, deep doctrines, as opposed to mere points of grammar. נגעים would be misfortunes coming on a man's person or house, אהלות uncleanness by the death of a person in a tent. These involved difficult questions, and were what Akiba delighted in. Accordingly the advice here given him is *ne sutor ultra crepidam*.

[10] A disciple of Jochanan. See Wolf, ii. 870.

[11] From Palestine to Babylonia.

[12] Lit., his thought was not cooled.

14 a, l. 31. the Lord, the LORD of hosts, doth take away from Jerusalem and from Judah stay and staff, the whole stay of bread and the whole stay of water; the mighty man and the man of war; the judge and the prophet and the diviner and the elder; the captain of fifty and the man of influence, and the counsellor, and the wise among artificers, and the instructed whisperer. And I will give children to be their princes and suckers out[1] shall rule over them, etc." "Stay" —these are the learned in the Law[2], "staff"—these are the learned in Mishnah, e.g., R. Jehudah ben Tema[3] and his fellows. R. Papa and our Rabbis differ in respect of this. One says, there are six hundred divisions of Mishnah, and another says there are seven hundred divisions of Mishnah. "The whole stay of bread"—these
Prov. ix. 5. are the learned in Talmud[4], as it is said, "Come, eat ye of my bread, and drink of the wine which I have mingled." "And the whole stay of water"—these are the learned in Agadah, who draw out the heart of man like water by means of Agadah. "The mighty man"—this is the man learned in oral tradition[5]. "And the man of war"—this is he who knows how to handle matters[6] in the battle of the Law. "The judge"—this is a magistrate who gives true decisions faithfully. "The prophet"—this is what the word itself conveys. "The diviner"—this is a king, as it is said,
Prov. xvi. 10. "Divination is in the lips of the king." "The elder"—this is he who is worthy to sit as a teacher presiding over an Academy. "Captain of fifty"—do not read "captain of fifty," but captain of fifths. This is he who knows how to handle matters in the five sections of the Law. There is another explanation of "Captain of fifty" according to R. Abohu; for R. Abohu says, Hence we learn that an interpreter is not appointed over the congregation, who is less[7] than fifty years old. "And the man of influence"—this is he

[1] Those who drain the country of all that is valuable in it.

[2] The Law is their *support*.

[3] Probably one of the הָרוּגֵי מַלְכוּת. See p. 15, note 8.

[4] In the most general sense of the word.

[5] i.e., who can hand on accurately what has been taught him and invents nothing.

[6] Lit., to take up and to give. The expression, used primarily of buying and selling (see for this sense p. 80, note 5), then came to mean, as here, the study of the Law.

[7] פחות is connected with פֶּחָה, פַּה (e.g., Neh. v. 14), which latter means an officer *less* than (subordinate to) the king. For this passage see also notes on p. 68.

on whose account his generation has influence above in the courts of heaven, e.g., R. Chănina ben Dosa[1], or below on earth, e.g., R. Abohu in the household of Caesar[2]. "The counsellor"—one who knows how to intercalate years and to fix months. "And the wise"—this is the disciple who makes his teachers wise. "Artificers"—at the time that he is unfolding the words of the Law, all are made like deaf men[3]. "And instructed"—this is he who draws instruction from the heart of a matter[4]. "Whisperer"—this is he to whom it is fitting to impart the words of the Law, which is given in a whisper[5]. "And I will give children to be their princes." What is the meaning of the words, "And I will give children to be their princes"? R. El'azar said, These are the children of men who are empty of good works. "And suckers out shall rule over them." R. Papa[6] bar Jacob said, Foxes[7], sons of foxes. And he[6] was not satisfied[9], until he had said to them, "The child shall behave himself proudly against the elder, and the base against the honourable. These are the children of men who are empty of good works. They shall behave themselves proudly against him who is filled with good works as a pomegranate[10]. "And the base against the honourable." Let him come, to whom heavy sins are like light, and behave himself proudly against him to whom light are like heavy.

[1] He was a contemporary of Rabban Gamaliel, and saw the overthrow of Jerusalem by the Romans. See *Ta'anith* 24 *b*, ii. 30, "All the world is sustained simply for the sake of Chănina my son," and Mishnah of *B'rakhoth*, v. 5, "They said of R. Chănina ben Dosa that he used to pray over the sick, and say, This one lives, and that one dies. They said to him, Whence knowest thou? He said to them, If my prayer is fluent in my mouth (אם שגורה תפלתי בפי), I know that it is accepted, and if not, I know that it is rejected." See also *Juch.* 65 *a* ; Wolf, ii. 834.

[2] Rashi relates (referring to *Sanhedrin*, 14 *a*, ii. 7) that there came out some noble ladies (מטרוניתא) from the household of Caesar to meet and welcome him. These no doubt were proselytes to Judaism, who had been converted by him.

[3] See p. 68, note 9.
[4] Lit., understands one thing out of another.
[5] By the presiding Rabbi to the interpreter (m'thurg'man) who declares it aloud to the listeners.
[6] Apparently an error for Acha. See p. 66, note 6.
[7] Men with the intellect of children but the wickedness of full-grown men, were likened to foxes. So Hottinger (*De Incestu etc.*, p. 87).
[8] Isaiah.   [9] See p. 77, note 12.
[10] As a pomegranate, when ripe, splits and shews its seeds, so when a man has a store of good works in him, they must come to light.

14 a, ii. 24. R. Kattinah[1] said, Even at the time of the destruction of Jerusalem there did not cease from them faithful men, as it is said, Is. iii. 6. "When a man shall take hold of his brother in the house of his father, saying, Thou hast clothing, be thou our ruler." Let things which are hid from the children of men, as a garment hides, be under thy hand[2]. "And this ruin." What is the meaning of the expression "and this ruin"? Words which the children of men cannot understand, but if one tries, he stumbles over Is. iii. 7. them, they are under thy hand. "In that day shall he swear, saying, I am not an healer, for in my house is neither bread nor clothing. Ye shall not make me ruler of the people." "Shall he swear" is simply a term expressing an oath, as it is said, "Thou Exod. xx. 7. shalt not swear falsely by the name of the LORD thy God." "I am not an healer," i. e., I have not been of those that heal[3] a college. "For in my house is neither bread nor clothing," i.e., There is not in my hand either Torah or Mishnah or Gemara.

And perhaps it is different here[4]. For if he had said to them, I teach Gemara, they would have said to him, Tell us something. But no, he cannot have feared detection, for he might have said, that he had learned it but had now forgotten. What is the meaning of the words "I am not an healer"? They mean, I am not a healer at all. But, after all, behold Rabba said, Jerusalem was not laid waste till there ceased from it honest Jer. v. 1. men, as it is said, "Run ye to and fro in the streets of Jerusalem, and see now, and know, and seek in the broad places thereof, if ye can find a man, if there be any that doeth justly, that seeketh truth, and I will pardon her." There is no difficulty. The one has to do with the words of the Law, the other with common 14 b business[5]. In the words of the Law there were honest men left, in common business there were not.

Our Rabbis have taught thus: There is a matter concerning Rabban Jochanan ben Zakkai, that he was riding upon his ass and was travelling on the road, and R. El'azar ben Arakh[6] was

---

[1] Not to be confused with Zera (p. 26) who had this *sobriquet*. See *Juch.* p. 124 a. For Kattinah's son Daniel see p. 38 with note 2.

[2] i.e., Do thou teach such things. [3] i.e., rule and teach.

[4] Perhaps after all it may not be through honesty but from fear of detection that he declines.

[5] Lit., taking up and giving. See p. 78, note 6.

[6] One of the five disciples of Jochanan ben Zakkai. For Jewish opinion of him see *Pirke Aboth*, ii. 10, 11.

behind him, as driver. [El'azar] said to him, Rabbi, teach me a section on the subject of the Chariot¹. [Jochanan] said to him, Have I not taught you thus, *nor the Chariot with one, but if a man do so, he must be a wise man and one who has much knowledge of his own²?* [El'azar] said to him, Rabbi, allow me to say before thee one thing which thou hast taught me³. [Jochanan] said to him, Say on. Immediately Rabban Jochanan ben Zakkai dismounted from the ass, and wrapped himself up⁴ and seated himself upon the stone under the olive tree⁵. [El'azar] said to him, Rabbi, wherefore didst thou dismount from the ass? [Jochanan] said to him, Is it possible that thou shouldest investigate the subject of the Chariot and that the Shechinah is with us, and that the ministering angels accompany us, and that I should ride upon the ass? Immediately R. El'azar ben Arakh entered upon the subject of the Chariot and expounded, and there came down fire from heaven and encircled all the terebinth trees which were in the field. They all opened their mouths and uttered a song. What was the song which they uttered? "Praise the Lord from the earth, ye dragons and all deeps...fruitful trees and all cedars...praise ye the Lord." An angel⁶ answered from the fire and said, *This*⁷ is the subject of the Chariot⁸. R. Jochanan ben Zakkai stood up and kissed him upon his head and said, Blessed be the Lord God of Israel, who hath given to Abraham our father⁹ a son who knoweth to do wisely and to search and expound in the subject of the Chariot. There is one who expoundeth well, but doth not perform

a 14 b, 1. 6.

Ps. cxlviii. 7, 9, 14.

---

¹ See p. 55, note 4. Of the two divisions of Ḳabbala there spoken of, the Creation, and the Chariot or mode of government of the world, the latter was of special interest to the Jews, as dispersed and persecuted by the Gentile power.

² See p. 55.

³ i.e., so as to shew that I come under the above-mentioned exception to the rule.

⁴ The stricter Jews still on the Day of Atonement wrap the Tallith closely round their heads, so as the better to concentrate their thoughts.

⁵ Cf. John i. 48.

⁶ The old reading according to the Tosaphoth was מלאך המות, the angel of death.

⁷ Lit., These are—

⁸ Even the angels were eager to use any means for increasing their knowledge on the subject of the Chariot.

For boasted descent from Abraham, cf. Mt. iii. 9, Lk. xiii. 16, John viii. 33, 39, Rom. ix. 7, Heb. vii. 5.

14 b, l. 23. well. There is one who performeth well, but doth not expound well. Thou dost expound well and dost perform well. Blessed art thou, Abraham our father, from whose loins hath come forth El'azar ben Arakh.

And when these things were told to R. Joshua[1], he and R. Jose, the priest[2], were travelling on the road. They said, Let us also expound on the subject of the Chariot. R. Joshua opened his mouth and expounded. And it was the day of the summer solstice[3]. The heavens were wrapped in clouds, and there appeared the form of a bow in the cloud, and the ministering angels were assembling and coming to hearken, as the children of men assemble and come to look on at the festivities of bridegroom and bride. R. Jose the priest went forward and uttered these words before Rabban Jochanan ben Zakkai, and he[4] said, Blessed are ye, and blessed is she that bare you[5]. Blessed are mine eyes, that they have thus seen. And also in my dream I and ye were resting upon Mount Sinai, and a Bath-ḳol[6] was sent to us from heaven which said, Come up hither, come up hither. Large banqueting chambers[7] are prepared and fair coverlets are spread for you, you and your disciples and your disciples' disciples, as fitted to attain to the third[8] degree of blessedness.

Is it so? And yet there is a Baraitha to this effect. R. Jose in the name of R. Jehudah says, These are the three consecutive expositions[9]. R. Joshua explained things before his master R. Jochanan ben Zakkai; R. Aḳiba explained things before his master R. Joshua; Chănaniah ben Chăkhinai[10] explained before his master R. Aḳiba. But behold, R. El'azar ben Arakh was not thought

---

[1] J. ben Chănania. For him see p. 7, note 8.

[2] He also was a pupil of Jochanan ben Zakkai, and is the author of a poem used in the Temple Service.

[3] When the sky should be cloudless.   [4] Jochanan.

[5] Cf. Lk. xi. 27.   [6] See p. 67, note 2.

[7] Lit., reclining places, banqueting couches (τρικλίνια).

[8] i.e., the third of the seven, which (in an ascending scale) are, torches, lilies, lightning, stars, the brightness of the firmament, the moon, the sun.

[9] Lit., pleasures, or gratifications, meaning three recitals of Ḳabbala. The pupils repeated the lesson three times to their master, to ensure that they had not made any mistake in their development of doctrine from his words.

[10] A disciple of Aḳiba. He was one of five judges (variously enumerated, but always including Ben Azzai and Ben Zoma) "qui coram sapientibus judicarunt." See Wolf, ii. 834 for further particulars; also *Juch.* 65 b.

worthy of a place with the three. No, for the principle is, He who 14 b, l. 35. teaches and before whom others teach is considered worthy, while he who teaches and before whom others do not teach is not considered worthy. But what do you say then to the case of Chănaniah ben Chăkhinai? For others did not teach before him, and yet he was considered worthy. Yes, for he taught at least in the presence of one¹ who taught others.

Our Rabbis have taught, Four men went up into Paradise², and they were these, Ben Azzai³, and Ben Zoma⁴, Acher⁵, and R. Akiba. R. Akiba said to them, When ye come near to the stones of pure marble, do not say, Water, water⁶! for it is said, "He that speaketh Ps. ci. 7. falsehood shall not be established before mine eyes." Ben Azzai gazed and died. Concerning him the Scripture says, "Precious in Ps. cxvi. the sight of the Lord is the death of his saints." Ben Zoma 15. gazed and went mad, and concerning him the Scripture says, "Hast Prov. xxv. thou found honey? Eat so much as is sufficient for thee; lest thou 16.

¹ viz., his master, while El'azar ben Arakh did not.

² פרדם the Garden. This was a name borne by Kabbalistic literature, and especially by the study of the Creation as opposed to that of "The Chariot." Later, the word was applied to the perfect knowledge of the four methods of interpretation, the names of which began severally with the letters of this word, viz. (i) פשט, literal, (ii) רמז, secondary, suggestive, (iii) דרש expository, allegorical, (iv) סוד, Kabbalistic, and again, to matters relating to the five commandments enumerated by Maimonides (see Bernard's *Selections from Yad hachazakah*, p. 109, note 5). The Tosaphoth on the passage in the text says, "and they did not go up literally, but it appeared to them as if they went up."

³ His full name was Simeon ben Azzai. He was skilled in the Law and despised all other men's knowledge, as compared with his own. See Dr C. Taylor, *Sayings etc.*, p. 79, note 5, for interesting particulars regarding him, also Wolf, ii. 864. See also p. 82, note 10. He and Ben Zoma were not ordained. Hence they have not the title of Rabbi.

⁴ Simeon ben Zoma, a mystic. See Dr C. Taylor, p. 77, note 1, and Wolf, ii. 863.

⁵ אחר (lit., *another*) is Elisha ben Abuyah, whose name was suppressed on account of his dualistic (? Christian) heresies. His name stands for that of the principal character in the Hebrew rendering of Goethe's *Faust, Eine Tragödie in einer Hebräischen Umdichtung* von Dr Max Letteris, Wien, 1865. See also the substance of the Talmudic notices of Acher brought together in Hershon's *Genesis* (The Pentateuch according to the Talmud), pp. 35—37.

⁶ As the Queen of Sheba is said to have done in Solomon's Temple. So Kabbalistic students might act, as unprepared for the depths of esoteric teaching.

be filled therewith and vomit it." Acher cut the plants[1]. R. Akiba departed[2] in peace.

They asked Ben Zoma, Quid de castratione canis? He said to them, "Neither shall ye do thus in your land," meaning, All the things that are done in your land ye shall not do.

They asked Ben Zoma, In re puellae gravidae what about the high priest[3]? Shall we take into consideration that which was discussed by Samuel? For Samuel said, Quoties velim, coire sine sanguine possum. Or perhaps it may be said, This case of Samuel is not a usual thing. He (Ben Zoma) said to them, This case of Samuel is not a usual thing. But we take into consideration the possibility eam in balneo gravidam factam esse.

But against this view Samuel said, Omne semen coitus quod non velut sagitta emittitur, non generat. But this may only mean quod primo velut sagitta emissum est. Our Rabbis have taught thus, There is a story about R. Joshua ben Chănaniah, that he was standing upon a high ridge of the Temple mountain, and Ben Zoma saw him and did not stand up before him. He said to him, Whence and whither tend thy thoughts, Ben Zoma? He said to him, I was considering the interval between the upper and the lower waters[4], and there is only between the two a bare three fingers' breadth, as it is said, "And the spirit of God was brooding upon the face of the waters," like a dove which broods over her young without touching them. R. Joshua said to his disciples, Ben Zoma is certainly still out of his mind. "And the spirit of God was brooding upon the face of the waters." When was it doing so? On the first day? But the division between the upper and lower waters was on the second day, for this is what is written, "and let it divide the waters from the waters." And about what

---

[1] i.e, in some way made a bad use of his learning. It probably means either (i) that he corrupted the text of the Law, or (ii) that his heresy, according to his enemies, consisted "in assuming the separate existence of two or more co-equal Deities, instead of merely distinct Intelligences [like the branches of a plant] in the one essence." So Hershon, p. 37.

[2] i.e., came out from his contemplation.

[3] An ordinary priest might take a widow (see p. 71, note 1), the high priest not, but only a virgin out of his own people, and here again it was a matter of discussion whether these last words did not confine him to one of a priestly family.

[4] Thus shewing that he was studying the Creation and not "the Chariot."

is the interval? R. Acha bar Jacob said, About the thickness of a hair. And our Rabbis say, The interstices between closely fitting planks of a bridge. Mar Zot'ra, or, if you like, I will say Rab Asi, said, Like two cloaks that are spread out together, and there are some who say with regard to it, Like two inverted cups that are pressed together.

Acher cut the plants[1]. It is of him that the Scripture says, "Suffer not thy mouth to cause thy flesh to sin." What was the matter referred to? He saw the Metatron[2], to whom is given the permission to sit to record the merits of Israel. He[3] said, We are taught that in heaven there is no sitting down nor anger nor back[4] nor weariness. Are there—God forbid!—two First Principles[5]? They brought out the Metatron and gave him sixty strokes with a lash of fire. They said to him, What is the reason that, when thou sawest him, thou didst not rise up before him? He was given permission to strike out the merits of Acher. There came out a Bath-Kol and said, "'Return, O backsliding children,' except Acher." He said, Inasmuch as that

15 a, 1. 16.

Eccles. v. 6.

Jer. iii. 14.

---

[1] It is said that Acher's evil conduct arose either (i) from his father's having dedicated him to the study of the Law for the sake of the honour which that study would bring him, and not for the honour of God, or (ii) because shortly before his birth his mother, when passing a boarding-house, where roast pig was being cooked, desired to taste it!

[2] The derivation and meaning of the name are doubtful. The chief views are, (i) from the Chaldee נטר = custodivit, or (ii) = Greek μηνυτώρ (μηνυτής), the messenger, delegate of God, or (iii) from the Greek μετά and θρόνος, he who sits *behind the throne* of God, where his office is to record the merits of Israelites, or (iv) from the Latin *Metator,* = *praecursor,* the Angel who *went before* Israel in the wilderness (Exod. xxiii. 20, xxxii. 34, xxxiii. 2). Frequent mention is made of the Metatron in Rabbinical literature. Some identified him with Enoch, others with an Angel called שׂר הָעוֹלָם, *prince of the world,* others again (in the 3rd cent. A.D.) even with our Lord. Unlike angels, who have but one foot, and that a calf's foot (for this idea see p. 74), the Metatron has two feet, and therefore can (and is alone permitted to) *sit* in heaven, as, unlike the angels, he combines Divine with human characteristics. When the Metatron heard Acher enquire whether there were two First Principles, he ought to have risen in horror at the thought. By not doing so, he gave an occasion to err, and hence his punishment.

[3] Acher.

[4] For the angels have eyes all round them, that all may constantly see God. Cf. Ezek. i. 6.

[5] i.e., Is then Dualism the right faith?

15 a, l. 24. man¹ is excluded from yonder world², let him go and enjoy himself in this world. Acher went forth into evil courses³. He went forth and met a loose woman. He solicited her⁴. She said to him, Art not thou Elisha ben Abuyah? He pulled up a radish from the garden on the Sabbath and gave it to her. She said, He is another⁵.

Acher asked this question of R. Meir⁶, after he (Acher) had gone forth into evil courses, and said to him, What is the meaning
Eccles. vii. 14. of the passage, "God hath even made the one side by side with the other?" He said to him, Every thing which the Holy One, blessed be He, created, He created with its counterpart. He created mountains, He created hills. He created seas, He created rivers. He said to him, R. Akiba thy teacher did not say so⁷, but he explained it as meaning that He created righteous, He created sinners. He created the garden of Eden, He created Gehenna. To every individual belong two shares, one in the garden of Eden, and one in Gehenna. If a man is meritorious and righteous, he receives his own portion and also the portion of his neighbour in the garden of Eden. If he has incurred guilt, and is a wicked man, he receives his own portion and also the portion of his neighbour in Gehenna. R. Mesharshia⁸ said, What
Is. lxi. 7. is the Scripture proof? As regards the righteous, it is written, "Therefore in their land⁹ they shall possess double;" as regards the
Jer. xvii. 18. wicked it is said, "And break them with a double breach."

¹ Meaning himself.

² Lit., that (i.e., the future) world.

³ Probably meaning, that he became a Christian, or joined some Gnostic or other sect, whose doctrines were more or less tinged by Christianity.

⁴ Lit. she is solicited (by him).

⁵ i.e., a changed man from what he was before. One account is that it was from this circumstance that he got the nickname of Acher (another).

⁶ A disciple of Akiba, and said to have been descended from a Roman general named Nero, who was sent to overthrow Jerusalem, but embraced Judaism. He was Vice-President of the College of Jerusalem, when Simeon, son of Gamaliel II. and father of Rabbi, was President. Such was the estimation in which he was held (see however p. 94, note 4) that he was called אוֹר הָעוֹלָם, *light of the world.* He died about A.D. 130. See further in *Juch.* 72b; Wolf, ii. 850 and iv. 410; Etheridge, pp. 79, 80.

⁷ The objection consisting in the fact that these are not, strictly speaking, opposites.

⁸ Perhaps a son of Rabba, and disciple of Abai. See Bartolocci, *Biblioth. Rabb.* III. 690.

⁹ i.e., in the world to come.

Acher asked this question of R. Meir, after he[1] had gone forth 15 a, ii. 2. into evil courses. What is the meaning of the passage, "Gold and Job xxviii. glass cannot equal it: neither shall the exchange thereof be vessels 17. of fine gold." He said to him, These are the words of the Law, which are difficult to buy as vessels of gold and vessels of pure gold, and are easily lost[2] as vessels of glass. He said to him, R. Akiba thy teacher did not say so, but he explained it as meaning that as vessels of gold and vessels of glass, although they are broken, may be mended, so a disciple of the wise, although he have sinned, may be mended. He said to him, Do thou also turn thyself back[3]. He said to him, I have already heard from behind the curtain[4], "'Return, O backsliding children,' except Acher." Jer. iii. 14.

Our Rabbis have taught thus, There is a story about Acher, that he was riding upon his horse on the sabbath[5], and R. Meir was walking behind him to learn the Law from his mouth. He said to him, Meir, turn thee backwards, for I have already measured by means of my horse's hoofs up to this point the limit of a sabbath day's journey. He said to him, Do thou also turn thyself back. He said to him, And have I not already said to thee, I have already heard from behind the curtain, "'Return, O backsliding children,' except Acher?" He[6] forced him to enter a place of instruction. He[7] said to a child, Repeat for me thy verse. He said to him, "There is no peace, saith the LORD, unto the Is. xlviii. wicked." He brought him into another synagogue. He said to a 22. child, Repeat for me thy verse. He said to him, " For though thou Jer. ii. 22. wash thee with lye, and take thee much soap, yet thine iniquity is marked before me." He brought him into another synagogue. He said to a child, Repeat for me thy verse. He said to him, "And 15 b thou, when thou art spoiled, what wilt thou do? Though thou Jer. iv. 30. clothest thyself with scarlet, though thou deckest thee with ornaments of gold, though thou enlargest thine eyes with paint, in vain dost thou make thyself fair, etc." He brought him into another synagogue, until he had brought him into thirteen[8] synagogues. They[9] all repeated to him in the same way. In the last one he said to him[10], Repeat for me thy verse. He said to him, "But unto Ps. l. 16.

---

[1] Acher.
[2] i.e., broken.
[3] i.e., amend thy ways, repent.
[4] i.e., in secret. See p. 92.
[5] A thing which was not lawful.
[6] Meir.
[7] Acher.
[8] A lucky number in Jewish estimation.
[9] The children.
[10] The child.

the wicked[1] God saith, What hast thou to do to declare my statutes, etc.?" That child was a stammerer. It sounded as if he had said to him, And to Elisha[2] said God. Some say that there was a knife by his side, and that he cut him in pieces and distributed him among the thirteen synagogues, but some say that he only *said*, If there had been a knife in my hand, I would have cut him in pieces.

When Acher died[3], they said, Let him not be brought into judgment, but let him not be admitted to the world to come. Let him not be brought into judgment, because he studied the Law; but let him not be admitted to the world to come, because he sinned. R. Meir said, It were good to bring him to judgment, but also to admit him to the world to come. Would that I might die, that I might cause smoke to go up from his grave[4]. When R. Meir died[5], smoke went up from the grave of Acher. R. Jochanan said, A mighty deed it was to consign his teacher to the flames[6]. There was one among us, and we found not a way to deliver him. If I take him by the hand, who will snatch him away from me. He also said, Would that I might die, and extinguish the smoke from his grave. When R. Jochanan died[7], the smoke ceased from the grave of Acher[8]. The public mourner uttered this expression over him, Even the keeper of the door of Gehenna[9] stood not his ground before thee, O our teacher.

A daughter of Acher came to Rabbi. She said to him, Rabbi, give me some food. He said to her, Whose daughter art thou? She said to him, I am the daughter of Acher. He said to her, Is there still of his seed in the world? And yet it is written, "He shall have neither son nor son's son among his people, nor any remaining where he sojourned." She said to him, Remember his study of the Law, and remember not his deeds. Immediately there came down fire, and consumed the seat of Rabbi. Rabbi wept and said, And if those who disgrace themselves through it[10]

---

[1] וְלָרָשָׁע.   [2] וְלֶאֱלִישָׁע.

[3] Lit., when the soul of Acher was at rest.

[4] In token that he is in course of purification from sin.

[5] Lit., when the soul of R. Meir was at rest.

[6] Ironically. The meaning is, Anyone could do that, but who shall be able to deliver him?

[7] See notes 3 and 5.

[8] Thus showing that his purification from sin had been accomplished.

[9] Satan.   [10] The Law.

are honoured thus, how much more those who obtain praise through their use of it? 15 b, l. 24.

And R. Meir thus explained the Law from the mouth of Acher, viz., And behold Rabbah bar bar-Channah[1] said that R. Jochanan said, What is the meaning of the passage, "For the priest's lips should keep knowledge, and they should seek the law at his mouth, when he is the messenger of the Lord of hosts." It means, if the teacher be like the messenger of the Lord of hosts, let them seek the Law at his mouth, and if not, let them not seek the Law at his mouth. Mal. ii. 7.

Resh Lakish said, R. Meir was reading the Scriptures. He came upon this passage and expounded thus, "Incline thine ear, and hear the words of the wise, and apply thine heart unto my knowledge." It is not said, unto their knowledge, but "unto my knowledge[2]." R. Chănina[3] said, From this passage we learn it, "Hearken, O daughter, and consider, and incline thine ear; forget[4] also thine own people and thy father's house, etc." It would appear that the passages[5] are difficult to reconcile. But no, there is no difficulty. The one is the case of an adult, the other of a young person. Prov. xxii. 17. Ps. xlv. 10.

When R. Dimi came, he said, They say in the West[6], R. Meir was eating a date and threw away the stone. Rabba expounded the meaning of the passage, "I went down into the garden of nuts, to see the green plants of the valley, etc." Why are the disciples of wise men likened to a nut? It is to tell thee that, just as, although this nut be soiled with mud and dirt, what is in the heart of it is not therefore rejected, so also, although a disciple of a wise man has sinned, his study of the Law is not rejected. Cant. vi. 11.

Rabbah bar Shela met Elijah and said to him, What is the Holy One, blessed be He, doing? He said to him, He hath uttered doctrine in the name of all our other Rabbis, but in the name of R. Meir He hath not uttered. He said to him, Why? He answered him, Because he learned doctrine from the mouth of Acher.

---

[1] This Rabbah was a contemporary of Rab. He told wonderful tales, with assonances, in the style of the Arabian nights. See Wolf, ii. 880.

[2] The point of the remark is the same as in Mt. xxiii. 3.

[3] A contemporary of R. Ashi. See p. 6, note 1.

[4] i.e., *listen but* forget.

[5] viz., the two just quoted, as compared with Mal. ii. 7.

[6] In Palestine, as opposed to Babylonia.

15 b, ii. 4. He said to him, Why? R. Meir found a pomegranate. He ate its inside, and cast away its husk. He[1] said to him, He[2] is at this moment saying, Meir my son is speaking and says, At the time that men were afflicted, what language did the Shechinah use? I have a lightness[3] in my head. I have a lightness in my arms. If the Holy One, blessed be He, is thus grieved, when the blood of wicked men is poured out, how much more, when the blood of righteous men is poured out.

Samuel came upon R. Jehudah, who was swinging upon the bolt of a door[4], and weeping. He[5] said to him, Oh, clever one[6], why weepest thou? He said to him, Is it a small thing that is written concerning our Rabbis[7], "Where is he that counted, where is he that weighed, where is he that counted the towers?" "Where is he that counted?" for they counted all the letters that are in the Books of the Law. "Where is he that weighed?" for they weighed the light and the heavy things which are in the Law. "Where is he that counted the towers?" for they taught three hundred doctrines concerning the tower which flies in the air[8]. And R. Ami said, Three hundred questions were treated by Doeg and Ahithophel[9] concerning the tower which flies in the air. And there is a canonical Mishnah. Three kings[10] and four private persons[11] have no position in the world to come, and we—what will there be for us? He said to him, Oh, clever one, there was uncleanness[12] in their hearts.

Is. xxxiii. 18.

Sanhedrin, 90a, ii. 22.

What of Acher[13]? Greek melody[14] ceased not from his mouth.

[1] Elijah.   [2] The Holy One.
[3] A euphemism for heaviness.
[4] As the Rabbis were wont to do by way of exercise.
[5] Samuel.
[6] Lit., long-(sharp-)toothed one.
[7] i.e., about those of them who, like Acher, go into evil courses.
[8] A very obscure expression. It is conjectured to mean a balloon, and that the question to which allusion is here made is whether it came under the same rules as a tower as regards contracting uncleanness. Rashi however understands it to be a tent.
[9] In 1 Sam. xxi. 8 (E. V. 7) Doeg is called אַבִּיר הָרֹעִים, an expression explained by the Rabbis to mean (Saul's) chief Rabbi. For the reason why Ahithophel bears with the Rabbis a similar character, see 2 Sam. xvi. 23.
[10] Jeroboam I., Ahab, Manasseh.
[11] Balaam, Doeg, Ahithophel, Gehazi.   [12] Lit., clay.
[13] i.e., How did he fall from grace?
[14] Perhaps, Christian hymns.

They said about Acher, that at the time when he stood up to go 15 b, ll. 23.
out of the college, many heretical[1] books used to fall from his lap.

Nimus the weaver[2] asked R. Meir this question, Does all wool which goes down to the dyeing vat come up with the right colour[3]? He said to him, All which was clean while on its mother's[4] back does so come up: all which was not clean while on its mother's back does not so come up.

R. Akiba went in to Paradise in peace and came down from it in peace. And it is of him that the Scripture says, "Draw me; Cant. i. 4. we will run after thee." And also the angels of the ministry sought to thrust away R. Akiba[5]. The Holy One, blessed be He, said to them, Leave this elder, for he is worthy to avail himself of my glory.

What did he[6] expound? Rabbah bar bar-Channah said that 16 a R. Jochanan said, "And he[7] came[8] from the ten thousands of holy Deut. ones." He is clearly marked[9] among His ten thousand. And R. xxxiii. 2. Abohu said, "The chiefest[10] among ten thousand." He is a sign[11] Cant. v.10. among His ten thousand. And Resh Lakish said, "The LORD of Is. xlviii. hosts is His name." He is LORD amid His host. And R. Chia bar 2. Abba[12] said that R. Jochanan said, "The LORD was not in the wind: 1 Kings and after the wind an earthquake; but the LORD was not in the xix. 11, 12.

---

[1] Lit., books of the wanderers (from the truth).

[2] At no time was it a disgrace to the most learned Jew to practise a trade.

See note on R. Isaac Naphcha, p. 115, note 2. R. Jochanan was called הסנדלר, the sandal-(shoe-)maker. Cf. Acts xviii. 3.

[3] i.e., Do all who study the Law gain piety therefrom? The reference is still to the case of Acher.

[4] The sheep's.

[5] On the principle, *Noscitur a sociis*.

[6] Akiba.

[7] The LORD.

[8] The Talmud makes a play on the word for, *And he came* (וְאָתָא), as though it was equivalent to *And his sign* (וְאוֹתוֹ).

[9] Lit., He is a sign. This, recognised as it was by Akiba when he entered Paradise, might therefore, it is hinted, have been perceived by Acher on a similar occasion, who would not then have fallen into the grievous error of thinking, when he saw the Metatron sitting, that he was a second God.

[10] דָּגוּל, *dâgûl*.

[11] דֻּגְמָא, *dúgma* (δεῖγμα), a further play on words.

[12] A contemporary of Rabbi. See interesting notices of him in Etheridge, p. 89, and a list of his works, *ibid.*, p. 142.

16 a, l. 9. earthquake: and after the earthquake a fire; but the LORD was not in the fire: and after the fire a still small voice. And behold, the LORD passed by."

Our Rabbis have taught thus, Six things are said with regard to demons, three in which they are like the angels of the ministry, and three in which they are like the children of men: three like the angels of the ministry, viz., they have wings like the angels of the ministry, and they float from one end of the world to the other like the angels of the ministry, and they know what is about to be, as the angels of the ministry know it.   *Know*—thou mightest think, This cannot be.   Yes, but they hear behind the curtain[1] like the angels of the ministry. And three in which they are like the children of men, viz., they eat and drink like the children of men, they are fruitful and multiply like the children of men, and they are mortal like the children of men.

Six things are said with regard to the children of men, three in which they are like the angels of the ministry, and three in which they are like beasts: three like the angels of the ministry, viz., they have knowledge like the angels of the ministry, and they go with stature erect like the angels of the ministry, and they speak in the sacred tongue[2] like the angels of the ministry; three like the beasts, viz., they eat and drink like the beasts, and they are fruitful and multiply like the beasts, and they relieve nature like the beasts.

Everyone who gazes into four things, it were a mercy for him, had he not come into the world at all.   It is all right as regards what is above and what is beneath, and what is afterwards. This is all well and good, but before—what was, was[3].

R. Jochanan and R. Eliezer say, both of them[4], There is a parable concerning a king of flesh and blood, who said to his servants, Build me a great palace[5] upon the dunghill. They went

---

[1] See p. 87.

[2] Hebrew, thus identifying "the children of men" with Israel.

[3] i.e., It is easy to see why it is forbidden to speculate upon what is above (=God), what is beneath (=Gehenna), what is afterwards (i.e., after this world has ceased to exist), for in all such speculations as these men may easily fall into impiety; but why should that which happened before the world was, be objected to, for in this case, unlike the others, we are dealing with *facts?*

[4] When these two Rabbis agreed—which was seldom the case—the matter might be considered as established.

[5] פלטרין i.e., palatia.

and built it for him. It was not thenceforward the king's pleasure, 16 a, l. 27. to remember the dunghill which had been there[1].

Everyone, who does not respect the glory of his Maker, it would have been a mercy for him that he had not come into the world. What is the case here meant? R. Abba said, This is the man who gazes into the rainbow[2]. R. Joseph said, This is the man who commits a transgression secretly. In support of the explanation that it means the man who gazes into the rainbow, it is written, "As the appearance of the bow that is in the cloud in the day of Ezek. i. rain, so was the appearance of the brightness round about." This 28. is the appearance of the likeness of the glory of the LORD. R. Joseph said, The explanation that this is the man who commits a transgression secretly, agrees with the view of R. Isaac, for R. Isaac said, Every one who committeth a transgression secretly is as though he jarred the feet of the Shechinah, as it is said, "Thus Is. lxvi. 1. saith the LORD, the heaven is my throne, and the earth is my footstool[3]." Is it so? and yet R. El'a the elder[4] said, If a man sees that his evil nature is mastering him, let him go to a place where they do not know him, and let him put on black garments, and cover himself with black, and do what his heart desireth, but let him not profane the name of God openly. There is no difficulty. The one is the case of a man who has found a means of checking[5] his evil nature, the other of a man who has not found a means of checking his evil nature.

R. Jehudah in the name of R. Nachmani the interpreter of Resh Laḳish expounded the saying, Every one who gazes upon three things, his eyes grow weak, viz., upon the bow, and the prince, and the priests: upon the bow, for it is written, "As the appear- Ezek. i. ance of the bow that is in the cloud in the day of rain, so was... 28. the appearance of the likeness of the glory of the LORD;" upon the prince, for it is written, "And thou shalt put[6] of thine honour Numb. xxvii. 20.

---

[1] Meaning that God is willing to forget the sinful nature which is found at bottom in the hearts of even the most pious of His servants.

[2] The rainbow, as representing the glory of God, was not to be regarded too closely.

[3] Therefore to go to any dark place of the earth in order to commit sin, is to dishonour God's footstool.

[4] A contemporary of R. Jonathan (see *Juch.* 111 a), for whom see p. 76, note 8.

[5] The Heb. verb is connected with כַּף, the hollow of the hand.

[6] The Heb. has וְנָתַן, thus supplying an instance of a minute variation of reading, as compared with the Massoretic text וְנָתַתָּה.

upon him." He that gazeth upon the priests—this has to do with the time that the House of the Sanctuary was in existence, when they stood upon their platform and blessed Israel in the Ineffable Name[1].

R. Jehudah in the name of R. Nachmani the interpreter of Resh Lakish expounded this question, viz., What is the meaning of that which is written, "Trust ye not in an evil one[2], put ye not confidence in a guide?" It means, if the evil imagination say to thee, Do thou sin and the Lord will forgive, be not persuaded, as it is said, "Thou shalt not trust in an evil one," and "an evil one" is nothing but the evil imagination, as it is said, "for that the imagination of man's heart is evil," and there is no "guide" but the Lord, as it is said, "Thou art the guide of my youth." Perhaps thou wilt say, Who witnesseth against me? The stones of a man's house and the timbers of his house, these witness against him, as it is said, "For the stone shall cry out of the wall, and the beam out of the timber shall answer it." And wise men[3] say, The spirit of a man witnesseth against him, as it is said, "Keep the doors of thy mouth from her that lieth in thy bosom." What is this that lieth in a man's bosom? One says, This is his spirit; R. Zarika[4] says, The two angels of the ministry which lead him, these witness against him, as it is said, "For he shall give his angels charge of thee, to keep thee in all thy ways." And wise men say, A man's limbs testify against him, as it is said, "Therefore ye[5] are my witnesses, saith the LORD, and I am God."

[1] Cf. the following: "In what way is the sacerdotal blessing performed?...In the temple they say the Name, as it is written [i.e. the τετραγράμματον], in the provinces with the substituted name [i.e. Adonai]. *Mishn. Sota*, vii. 6." Taken from Dr Sinker's Art. Benedictions, *Dict. Chr. Ant.* i. 198.

[2] Reading רָע, *evil*, for רֵעַ, *a friend*. The latter reading is of course the correct one, as shewn by the parallelism of the clauses.

[3] For וחכ"א, the margin of the Lemberg text reads יש אומרים, *and there are who say*, an expression which in the Talmud signifies R. Nathan, who flourished A.D. 121, as the contemporary of Simeon ben Gamaliel II., just as אחרים, others, is used to designate R. Meir, who flourished at the same time. See p. 86, note 6. The omission of the names of these two celebrated Rabbis was, according to Jewish tradition (Tal. Bab. *Horaioth*, 13 b, ii. 29), a penalty for their hostility to the above-mentioned Simeon, president of the Academy. See the story as given by Wolf, iv. 419.

[4] A disciple of Jochanan.

[5] Ye, that is, your whole bodies, including therefore the limbs.

MISHNAH.

II. (2) Jose ben Joezer says[1] that a man is not to lay on his hand[2], but Joseph ben Jochanan says that a man is to lay it; Joshua ben P'rachyah[3] says that a man is not to lay it, but Mattai[4] the Arbelite[5] says that a man is to lay it. Jehudah ben Tabbai[6] says that a man is not to lay it, but Simeon ben Shetach[7] says that a man is to lay it. Shemaiah[8] says that a man is to lay it, but Abtalion[9] says that a man is not to lay it. Hillel

---

[1] Jose (margin, Joseph) ben Joezer and Joseph ben Jochanan formed the first of five pairs who successively carried on the tradition from the time of Antigonus of Socho (B.C. 190) to that of our Lord. "Their chronology cannot be precisely determined. Herzfeld (*Gesch.* II. 140) gives their dates B.C. as follows: (α) the two Josephs, 170; (β) Jehoshua and Matthai, 140—110; (γ) Jehudah, 100; Shimeʻon, 90; (δ) Shemaʻiah and Abtalion, 65—35; (ε) Hillel, 30. The last date (=100 years before the destruction of the temple) is given in Shabbath 15 a [ii. 24]." Taylor, p. 28, note 9. See the rest of that note and the two that follow it for particulars as to Joezer. When there was a disagreement among the Mishnic teachers, the decision of Joezer was ruled by the Rabbis that followed as the one which should prevail. It was said that until after Joezer's time (cf. Introd. pp. vii, viii,) disputations as to the meaning of the Law were unknown. See note by M. Wolkenberg in Hershon's *Genesis* (The Pentateuch according to the Talmud), p. 373, § 120. See also Wolf, ii. 847, and a long notice of Joezer in iv. 362—6.

[2] Upon a sacrifice. This depends on the principle that upon a festival a man must not use the services of any living thing.

[3] The Rabbinic story (see *Sanhedrin*, 107 b, a passage omitted however in expurgated editions) is that he was a sorcerer and fled with the infant Christ to Egypt, and that Christ brought back from Egypt beneath His skin magical powers thus procured. See also the story in Wagenseil's *Tela ignea Satanae*, *Toldos Jeschu*, p. 7; Wolf, ii. 843, iv. 366—370; Eth. p. 29.

[4] This is an emendation from Nittai (נתאי) of the Talmud texts. See Wolf, ii. 855.

[5] The Palestinian Arbela, here referred to, now called *Irbid*, was on the borders of the lake of Galilee, W. of Mejdjel. See Neub. *Géog. du Talmud*, p. 220.

[6] See Wolf, ii. 839, and (for him and Simeon) iv. 371—7.

[7] He received some Greek culture through a sojourn in Alexandria. See notices of him in Dr C. Taylor, *Sayings etc.*, p. 31, note 19, and in Eth. pp. 29, 30. See also Wolf, ii. 865.

[8] See Wolf, ii. 865, and for him and Abtalion, Wolf, iv. 377—8; Taylor, p. 32, note 21; Eth. p. 32. The fathers of Shemaiah and Abtalion were proselytes.

[9] See (besides the above references) Wolf, ii. 809.

and Menahem[1] did not differ. Menahem went out[2]. Shammai entered in. Shammai says that a man is not to lay it. Hillel says that a man is to lay it. The first of these several pairs were prince-presidents, and those second to them were vice-presidents[3].

GEMARA.

Our Rabbis have taught, In the three former pairs, which say that a man is not to lay[4], and in the two latter pairs which say that a man is to lay, the first were prince-presidents and the second vice-presidents. These are the words of R. Meir. But wise men say, Jehudah ben Tabbai was vice-president, and Simeon ben Shetach was prince-president. Who is the author of that teaching? For the converse would appear to be the case, because our Rabbis have taught thus, viz., that R. Jehudah ben Tabbai said, May I see[5] the consolation of Israel[6], if I have not slain a false[7] witness so as to oppose the Sadducees[8], when they say, False witnesses are not put to death, until the condemned person shall have been put to death. Simeon ben Shetach said to him, May I see[9] the consolation of Israel, if thou hast not shed innocent blood;

---

[1] See Wolf, ii. 851.

[2] i.e., left the Sanhedrin because he thought it would be more profitable to enter the king's service. See below, p. 98, note 1.

[3] This part of the Mishnah is corrupt, and not even grammatical (אב for אבות). For the prince-presidents (נשיאים) and the vice-presidents (אבות בית דין) see Glossary.

[4] They say it, inasmuch as the superior in each pair says it.

[5] Meaning the reverse. For the euphemism, cf. Rashi's interpretation of the last clause of Exod. i. 10, viz., "and *drive us* out of the land."

[6] Cf. Lk. ii. 25.

[7] This sense of the verb זמם is taken from its use in Deut. xix. 19 ("he had *thought* to do etc.") and the Rabbis argued, that when the Scripture seemed in that passage to speak of one, it really meant two witnesses, for it required two to put a man to death. If Jehudah ben Tabbai had killed two false witnesses, he would have been so far right.

[8] The Pharisees and Sadducees agreed that both witnesses must be proved guilty of perjury, before either of them could be visited with the punishment due to the person whom they accused, had he been guilty. On the other hand the Pharisees asserted, and the Sadducees denied, that this punishment ought to be inflicted on them, in case it had not yet been inflicted on the person wrongfully sentenced by their means.

[9] See note 5.

for behold, wise men have said, False witnesses are not to be put 16 b, i. 16.
to death, until they are both proved to be false, and they are not
beaten, until they are both proved to be false, and they do not have
to refund money, until they are both proved to be false. Forthwith
Jehudah ben Tabbai undertook that he would not teach doctrine
(Halachah) except in the presence of Simeon ben Shetach. All
the days of Jehudah ben Tabbai he used to stretch himself upon
the grave of the slain man, and his voice was heard, so that the
people wondered[1], saying that it was the voice of the slain man.
He said to them, It is my voice; know ye that tomorrow he[2] will
be dead, and his[3] voice will not be heard. R. Acha bar Rabba said
to R. Ashi, But perhaps he prayed him earnestly to forgive[4] him,
or perhaps he called him before the judgment seat. Who is the
authority for this view[5]? If thou sayest, It is all right according
to R. Meir, who said, Simeon ben Shetach was vice-president, and
R. Jehudah ben Tabbai was prince-president, this accords with his
teaching doctrine in the presence of Simeon ben Shetach, but if
thou sayest, Our Rabbis are right, who say, Jehudah ben Tabbai was
vice-president, Simeon ben Shetach was prince-president, how should
the vice-president teach doctrine in the presence of the prince-
president? No, what is the meaning of "he undertook?" He
spoke in reference not to teaching but to combination[6], Even if
men combine, yet will I not combine.

Menahem went out[7], *Shammai entered in, etc.* Whither did he
go out? Abai said, He went out to destruction[8]. Rabba said,
He went out for the service of the king. There is also a Baraitha
to this effect, that Menahem went out for the service of the king, and
there went out with him eighty pairs of disciples clothed in Syrian

---

[1] Lit., thought.   [2] i.e., I.

[3] i.e., my.

[4] פיוס, infin. Kal.

[5] viz., that Jehudah ben Tabbai undertook not to teach Halachah except in the presence of Simeon ben Shetach.

[6] Lit., in reference to those combining, i.e., combining for the purpose of outvoting a decision of Simeon ben Shetach. צרף, to purify, hence, to solder, and so, to combine.

[7] The "and" is not in the Mishnah. See p. 96.

[8] Heb. תַּרְבּוּת. The word occurs in the Bible only in Numb. xxxii. 14, "an increase (of sinful men)," A. V. and R. V. On account of this passage the word always bears a bad sense in later Hebrew.

robes¹. R. Shemen bar Abba² said that R. Jochanan said, Let the sabbath rest be by no means a light thing in thine eyes³; for lo, the laying on of the hands is only prohibited on account of the Sabbath rest, and the great men of the nation were divided upon the matter.   That is self-evident. But as this is a case of a Sabbath rest which clashes with a positive command, there was need of it⁴.   But this also is self-evident. It was to meet the objection of the person who says, In the matter of the laying on of the hands itself⁵ men are divided. We learn from this that it is in the matter of Sabbath rest that they are divided.   Ramai bar Chama said, Learn hence that we require the laying on to be done with all one's strength, for if thou dost imagine that we do not require it to be done with all one's strength, how is the idea of work involved in the laying on of the hands⁶?   Some people adduce the passage, "Speak unto the sons of Israel...and he shall lay his hand." The sons of Israel lay on their hands, but the daughters of Israel do not lay on their hands.   R. Jose and R. Ishmael say, Daughters of Israel lay on their hands by permission⁷. R. Jose said, Abba El'azar related to me the following story: Once we had a calf belonging to the sacrifices of peace-offerings, and we brought it to the court of the women, and the women laid their hands upon it, not because the laying on of the hands belongs to women, but so as to gratify the women. And if thou dost imagine we require the laying on of the hands to be done with all one's strength, dost thou mean to say that in order to gratify women we introduced work into holy things⁸? But do we not learn hence that we do not require it to be done with all one's strength? Nay, by all means I will grant you that we require it to be done⁹ with

---

¹ Whom he thus led away from a life of study. See p. 96.

² See p. 40, note 9.

³ The danger of its being held to be such lay in its being only a negative thing, the abstaining from work.

⁴ Viz., the direction telling which command should give way.

⁵ Apart from the question whether this act does or does not infringe upon sabbath rest, is the laying on to be done with all the strength, or not?

⁶ Lit., How does he work in laying on?

⁷ And not by commandment.

⁸ In other words, would we allow women to do work on a Sabbath, when *they* at least, whatever be the case with men, cannot justify this work by the plea of a divine command?

⁹ In the case of men.

all one's strength. He said to them¹, Rest² your hand upon it. 16 b, ii. 31.
If so, it was not because the laying on of the hands belongs to
women that it was done³. Thou mayest conclude that it has
nothing at all to do with the nature of the laying on of the
hand. R. Ami says, He is establishing two things⁴; one that
it has nothing at all to do with the nature of the laying on of the
hands, and the other that it was done in order to gratify the
women. Rab Papa said, Learn hence, Sides, and not the head
only, are forbidden; for if thou dost imagine that sides are allowed,
might they not lay hands on the sides? But no; learn hence that
sides are forbidden. R. Ashi said, Even if thou sayest, Sides are 17 a.
allowed⁵, yet that avails nothing, for everything which is along
the course of the back, as the sides are, is as the back⁶.

MISHNAH.

II. (3) The house of Shammai say, Men bring peace-offerings on a festival, and do not lay their hands on them⁷, but not burnt offerings⁸; but the house of Hillel say, Men bring both peace-offerings and burnt-offerings, and lay their hands on them.

(4) In the case of the day of Pentecost which falls upon the eve of a Sabbath, the house of Shammai say, The day for sacrificing is after the Sabbath, but the house of Hillel say, There is no day for sacrificing after the Sabbath⁹; but they

---

¹ i.e., El'azar said to the women.
² Lit., touch, as opposed to any considerable pressure.
³ But merely to gratify them, and as constituting (in their case) an *informal* act.
⁴ Lit., He says one thing and more.
⁵ In that they are not *formally* prohibited.
⁶ And therefore, as the back will naturally include the head, sides are already forbidden by implication.
⁷ Because in the case of peace-offerings, according to the house of Shammai (not so that of Hillel) the laying on of hands may be done before the festival commences.
⁸ Because in the case of burnt-offerings the laying on of hands must take place immediately before they are offered, and this is forbidden by the house of Shammai to be done on a festival.
⁹ This is obviously ambiguous, and may mean either (*a*) that the sacrifice is to be omitted altogether, or (*b*) that they are to sacrifice (and eat) on the festival itself (Friday). The Talmud proceeds (p. 101) to discuss which is the meaning, and decides for (*b*).

17 a, i. 9. both admit that, if it fall upon a Sabbath, the day for sacrificing is the day after the Sabbath. A high priest is not to clothe himself in his costly garments[1], but it is allowed in case of a mourning or of a fast, but this is not to confirm the words of those who say, Pentecost is after the Sabbath[2].

GEMARA.

R. El'azar said that R. Oshaia said, How is it that in regard to Pentecost offerings are transferable all seven days? It is because it is said, "In the feast of unleavened bread, and in the feast of weeks, and in the feast of tabernacles." Holy Writ compares the Feast of Weeks with the Feast of Unleavened Bread[3]. As in the Feast of Unleavened Bread offerings are transferable all seven days, so in the Feast of Weeks offerings are transferable all seven days. But, it is objected, I might say by parity of reason, Holy Writ compares it with the Feast of Tabernacles. As in the Feast of Tabernacles offerings are transferable all eight days, so in the Feast of Weeks offerings are transferable all eight days. But then the eighth day in the Feast of Tabernacles is a festival apart. Yes, they say indeed that the eighth day is a festival apart, but this only applies to matters connected with the lots, season, festival, korban, psalm, blessing[4].

Deut. xvi. 16.

---

[1] On that Sunday.

[2] i.e., his so clothing himself on a day of mourning or fasting, and thus marking that the day has at least a semi-festive character (which days of mourning or fasting are considered by the Jews to have) is not to be taken as arguing any agreement with the doctrine of the Sadducees, who said that in the passage, Lev. xxiii. 15, "Sabbath" means שבת בראשית = the ordinary 7th day of the week, and that therefore the Pentecost, as being "the morrow after the Sabbath," must fall on the 1st day of the week (Sunday).

[3] Hence it follows that whatever is true of the one is true also of the other.

[4] The Heb. expresses each of these six by the initial letter of the word only. (i) 'פ, lots (פּוּיִם, a lot) refers to the fact that on the eighth day lots were *not* drawn in connexion with the offering of bullocks for the prosperity of the heathen world. These were offered on the first seven days of the Feast (see Numb. xxix. 12—34) to the numbers consecutively of 13, 12, 11, 10, 9, 8, 7. The lots were cast to prevent confusion in the offering of sacrifices, by determining the part which each priest should take in the ceremonies connected with them. (ii) 'ז stands for the words זְמַן הַזֶּה, *this time*, which occur at the end of one of the Benedictions used on the 8th day of the Feast and which were held to imply that the time or *season* was to be regarded as a new one,

But as for the case of transferable offerings, they are transferable as from the first day. For there is a canonical Mishnah, viz., He who has not kept the Feast on the first high holiday of the festival, nevertheless keeps all the festival, even up to the last high holiday. If thou layest hold on much, thou dost not hold it, if thou layest hold on a little, thou holdest it¹. But with a view to what teaching has the All-merciful One written *the Feast of Tabernacles?*

It is in order to compare it with the Feast of Unleavened Bread. As the Feast of Unleavened Bread requires remaining over night, so the Feast of Tabernacles requires remaining over night. And whence do we get that? Because it is written, "and thou shalt turn *in the morning* and go to thy tents."

There is a canonical Mishnah, *In the case of the day of Pentecost which falls upon the eve of a Sabbath, the house of Shammai say, The day for sacrificing is after the Sabbath, but the house of Hillel say, There is no day for sacrificing*². Do you not think that it means that there is no day at all for sacrificing? No; it cannot mean that a day for sacrificing is not necessary. What then does it mean? We learn from this that we are to bring the sacrifice on its own day³? But how can this be? for they have discussed this point once already⁴, for we have a canonical Mishnah, viz., *The house of Shammai say, Men bring peace-offerings on a festival and do not lay their hands on them, but not burnt offerings; but the house of Hillel say, Men bring both peace-offerings and burnt-offerings and lay their hands on them.* I reply, No; there is no superfluity. For the passage is necessary. For, if he had let me hear only the

[right margin: 17 a, ii. 1. Chag. 9 a, i. 5, Beytsah 20 b, i. 23, Rosh ha-Shanah 4 b, ii. 13.]

[right margin: Deut. xvi. 7. 17 b Chag. 17 a, i. 6.]

[right margin: Chag. 17 a, i. 3.]

and not as a mere continuation of the seven day festival. (iii) ר for רֶגֶל, a name for *festival*. See p. 7, note 1. (iv) ק for קָרְבָּן a special *offering*. (v) ש for שִׁיר, a special *psalm* then sung. (vi) ב for בְּרָכָה, a special *blessing* used on the occasion.

¹ Therefore (the Talmud means) do not claim the right to offer heave-offering on the 8th day. Be content with the parallel of the seven days of Passover. For the proverb in the text, cf. כָּל־הַמּוֹסִיף גּוֹרֵעַ, He who does too much detracts from the whole (lit., everyone who adds, lessens), mentioned by Dr K. Kohler, *Hebraica*, Oct. 1888, p. 3; cf. also the French proverb, Qui trop embrasse mal étreint.

² The expression is ambiguous. See p. 99, note 9.

³ i.e., on the day of Pentecost, even though a Friday.

⁴ Therefore, if this were the meaning here, the passage would be superfluous, a thing which is impossible in Holy Writ.

17 b, i. 11. second paragraph[1], I should not have doubted through hearing it only, that the house of Shammai insist that men are not to sacrifice on the day of Pentecost, because it is possible to do so on the morrow, but, unless I had a distinct paragraph to the contrary, I should have said thus, They agree as regards the possibility of doing it on the morrow[2] with the house of Hillel[3]; and if he had let me hear only the first paragraph, I should not have doubted through hearing it only, that the house of Hillel say that men may sacrifice because it is impossible to do so on the morrow, but according to this I should have said, They agree as regards the impossibility of doing it on the morrow[3], with the house of Shammai. Hence the second paragraph was necessary[4].

But it may be objected[5], He who has not kept the Feast for the seven days of the Passover, and the eight days of the Feast of Tabernacles, and the first high holiday of Pentecost, he cannot afterwards keep the Feast. Do you not think, then, that the high holiday of Pentecost is not the day of sacrificing? But, if so, do we gather from it that there is but one day of sacrificing? I should rather say, *days* of sacrificing. But it may be objected, Rabba bar Samuel[6] taught, The Torah says, Number the days and sanctify the month, Number the days and sanctify the Pentecost. As the first day of the month is established by counting, so the Pentecost is established by counting. Do you not think that he has settled the matter from the analogy of the first day of the month? As the first day of the month is one day, so the Pentecost must be one day.

Rabba said, Nay, consider that thou mayest be in error. Perhaps in the case of the Pentecost men number days and do not number weeks[7]. But yet Abai said, There is a command to number days, for it is written, "Ye shall number fifty days[8]," and there is a

Lev. xxiii. 16.

[1] i.e., second in the order in which it stands in the *Gemara*.
[2] The Sabbath.
[3] Whereas the first paragraph says that with the house of Shammai it is "the day after the Sabbath."
[4] As shewing that even on a festival (e.g., the Sabbath) according to the house of Hillel "men may bring etc."
[5] Lit., Come, hear. See p. 77, note 6.
[6] A contemporary of Shesheth, for whom see above, p. 38, note 6.
[7] This, put as a question, is followed by Abai's disproof of such a supposition. The Pentecost, he points out, is not an analogous case to that of the 1st day of the month, for the former, unlike the latter, is calculated not by days only, but by weeks as well.
[8] It may be noted in this connexion that the words ἐν τῷ συμπληροῦσθαι

command to number weeks, for it is written, "Seven weeks shalt 17 b, ii. 8. thou number unto thee," and again the expression Feast of Weeks Deut. xvi. is found. 9.

A member[1] of the house of R. Eliezer ben Jacob[2] taught thus, Lev. xxiii. Holy Writ says, "And ye shall make proclamation," "and when ye 21, 22. reap." What is this Feast in which thou makest proclamation and reapest? Thou must reply, This is the Feast of Pentecost. When is it? If I am to say, On the high holiday, how is reaping lawful on a high holiday? But dost thou not think that it means as well on the subsequent days[3]? And although this has been said already by R. El'azar quoting R. Oshaia, nevertheless what R. Eliezer ben Jacob said was necessary[4]. If I had only the words of R. El'azar quoting R. Oshaia, I should say, As on the subsequent days of the Feast of Unleavened Bread the doing of work is prohibited, so on the subsequent days of the Feast of Pentecost also the doing of work is prohibited.

We learn the truth about this from R. Eliezer ben Jacob[5]. And if I had only the words of R. Eliezer ben Jacob, I should not have known how many days were meant[6]. We learn the truth about this 18 a from R. El'azar quoting R. Oshaia.

And Resh Lakish said, "And the feast of the harvest,"—what Exod. is this Feast on which thou feastest and reapest? Thou xxiii. 16.

("was fully come" A.V.; not so R.V.), used of Pentecost in Acts ii. 1 (cf. the use of the same expression in Luke ix. 51), have been supposed by some to refer to the Jewish custom (derived from the use of the word תְּמִימֹת in Lev. xxiii. 15 in reference to this feast), that in the case of Pentecost the festival was not considered to have begun till the *completion* of the previous day, in this case the 49th from the Passover. In the case of all other holidays (the weekly Sabbath included) the festival begins to be kept half an hour or more before sunset.

[1] Meaning one who acted as his private chaplain or confessor, and whose duty it was to tell him daily of his shortcomings. R. Solomon ben Loria was the last who kept such a member of his household. See a reference to Baybi as discharging this duty for Nachman, p. 124.

[2] He saw the second Temple, and died at the age of 80 years, about A.D. 130. See *Juch.* 57 a; Wolf, ii. 809.

[3] Lit., (days for) postponed payments, i.e., sacrifices deferred from the first till a later day of the festival.

[4] And thus is not superfluous.

[5] Inasmuch as he shews us that in some respects, e.g., reaping, they are ordinary days.

[6] For he only tells us that they are days when we reap, but not their number.

must reply, This is the Pentecost. When is it? If I am to say, On the high holiday, how is reaping lawful on a high holiday? But dost thou not think that it means as well on the subsequent days? R. Jochanan said, But regard it thus. The Feast of Ingathering—what is this Feast in which there is an ingathering? Thou must say, This is the Feast of Tabernacles. When is it? If I am to say, On the high holiday, how is work lawful on a high holiday? But if I am to say, On one of the ordinary middle holidays, how is work lawful on one of the ordinary middle holidays? But it means the Feast which comes at the *season* of ingathering; and so in this case also the Feast which comes at the *season* of harvest. Consequently both are of opinion that on the ordinary middle holidays the doing of work is forbidden. Whence do we obtain these statements[1]? Because our Rabbis have taught, "The feast of unleavened bread shalt thou keep seven days." This teaches us that on the middle holidays it is forbidden to do work. These are the words of R. Jeshaiah[2]. R. Jonathan says, The above proof is not necessary. I can prove it by an argument *a fortiori*. For if on the first and seventh days of the Feast which have not got a holiday before them and after them, the doing of work is prohibited, then on ordinary middle holidays, which have a holiday before them and after them, is it not just that the doing of work should be prohibited?

But, it is replied, Let the six days of Creation[3] bear witness against this interpretation, which have a holiday before them and after them, and yet the doing of work is permitted. Nay, it is rejoined, how are the six days of Creation a parallel case? For they have no additional sacrifice as the middle holidays have. Thou mayest say in reply, In the case of an ordinary middle holiday, as it has an additional sacrifice, let the first day of the month bear testimony, for on it there is an additional sacrifice, yet the doing of work is permitted. Nay, it is rejoined, how is the first day of the month a parallel case? For it is not called a holy convocation. Thou mayest say in conclusion, In the case of an ordinary middle holiday which is called a holy convocation, seeing that it is called a holy convocation, it is only just that the doing of work should be prohibited. There is another Baraitha, "Ye shall do no servile work," that is to say, that on an ordinary middle holiday

---

[1] i.e., On what passage in Scripture can we base them?
[2] Of Osha. See p. 7, note 5. His date is uncertain.
[3] i.e., Of the ordinary week.

CHAGIGAH.   105

the doing of work is forbidden.   The following are the words 18 a, ii. 12.
of R. Jose the Galilæan.   R. Akiba says, It was not necessary[1],
for lo, He[2] says, "These are the set feasts[3] of the Lord, etc." Lev. xxiii.
With reference to what is the Scripture speaking? If to the first [4.]
day, Behold, it has been already called a sabbath-day[4]; if to the
seventh day, Behold, it has been already called a sabbath-day;
behold, the Scripture can be speaking only of an ordinary middle
holiday, to teach thee that the doing of work is forbidden thereon.

There is another Baraitha, viz., "Six days thou shalt eat blistered Deut. xvi.
cakes[5], and on the seventh day there shall be a prohibition of [8.]
work to the Lord." As on the seventh day work is prohibited, so
on the six days work is prohibited[6].   I should have thought
perhaps, as on the seventh day there is a prohibition from all work,
so on the six days there is a prohibition from all work. But no;
for the teaching says, And on the seventh day there is a prohibition,
thus indicating that on the seventh day there is a prohibition from
all work, and that on the six days there is not a prohibition from all
work. Behold, Holy Writ has communicated it only to wise men,
to tell thee which is a forbidden day and which is a lawful day,
which is forbidden work and which is lawful work.

*But it is allowed in case of a mourning or of a fast, but this is
not to confirm the words of those who say, Pentecost is after the
Sabbath[7].*   And here there is a matter told[8] as follows: And Alexis
died in Lod, and all Israel assembled to mourn him, and R. Tarphon forbad them because it was the high holiday of Pentecost.
"High holiday". Thou mightest have thought, If it was a high

---

[1] To have this discussion; for the conclusion follows from the passage which
Akiba proceeds to quote.

[2] God.

[3] The same word as that rendered middle holiday.

[4] And therefore it would be tautology to say this again.

[5] So the Jews explain מַצּוֹת, on the ground that Exod. xii. 39, by adding to
the words עֻגֹת מַצּוֹת (round blistered cakes) the words, "for it [the dough]
was not leavened," implies that it might have been so, in other words that
מַצּוֹת of itself does not necessarily imply absence of leaven.

[6] Lit., "As the seventh is prohibited, so the six are prohibited." And so
subsequently.

[7] In the Heb. there are two slight inaccuracies in the quotation of the
Mishnah, for which see p. 100.

[8] Or, according to the margin of the Heb. text, And lo, there is a Baraitha,
a matter.

18 a, ii. 29. holiday, how could the people have come? But I will tell you. It was because it was the day of sacrificing. There is no difficulty. The one case[1] was that in which the holiday had fallen upon the first day of the week[2], the other case is that in which the holiday has fallen on the Sabbath[3].

MISHNAH.

18 b   II. (5) Men wash their hands for common[4] food and for second tithes and for heave offering, but for hallowed things[5] they dip. For the sin offering[6], if a man's hands be defiled, his whole body is defiled.

(6) If he have dipped for common food, he has credit as clean for common food, but is forbidden tithe; if he have dipped for tithe, he has credit for tithe, but is forbidden heave-offering; if he have dipped for heave-offering, he has credit for heave-offering, but is forbidden hallowed things; if he have dipped for hallowed things, he has credit for hallowed things, but is forbidden sin offering. If he have dipped for a weightier thing, he is free for a lighter thing. If he have dipped and have not got credit for it[7], it is as though he had not dipped.

(7) The garments of a common person are defiled by pressure[8] for[9] Pharisees; the garments of Pharisees are defiled by pressure for those that eat heave-offering; the garments of those that eat heave-offering are defiled by pressure for those that partake of hallowed things; the garments of those that partake of hallowed things are defiled by pressure for those that partake

---

[1] That of Alexis.

[2] Followed by the day of sacrificing, with regard to which Tarphon spoke.

[3] In which case the day of sacrificing will fall on the first day of the week, an accidental coincidence, and not to be considered as giving countenance to the view (which savoured too much of Christian customs to be acceptable) that Pentecost is to be kept on the day after the Sabbath, i.e., on Sunday.

[4] Not meaning, ceremonially unclean.

[5] See p. 115, note 6.

[6] Referring to the water of the ashes of purification, into which men dip their hands to rid themselves of sin.

[7] By his not having done it *with intention*.

[8] i.e., are looked upon as affected by uncleanness arising from pressure.

[9] i.e., as regards their use by.

of sin offering. Jose ben Joezer was pious and in the priest-hood, and yet his apron[1] was defiled by pressure for those that partake of hallowed things. Jochanan ben Gudgodah was one who ate his ordinary food all his days with observance of the laws of purification which belong to hallowed things, and yet his apron was defiled by pressure for those that partake of sin offering.

18 b, i. 9.

Gemara.

For common food and tithe how can washing of hands be needed[2]? For I can adduce against this Mishnah the following, viz., The heave offering and the firstfruits involve to one who transgresses with respect to them death and compensation to the amount of one fifth part beyond the price, and it is forbidden to strangers[3] to share in them, and these are the property of the priest and are mixed with one hundred and one things[4], and they are subject to the washing of hands and waiting till the going down of the sun. Lo, this is the case with heave-offering and firstfruits, but it is not the case with tithe, much less with common food. There is a difficulty when we place tithe against tithe, and there is a difficulty when we place common food against common food[5]. It is all right in the case of tithe against tithe. It does not present a difficulty. The one opinion is that of R. Meir, and the other that of our Rabbis. For there is a canonical Mishnah, Everything which is subject to the duty of going to the water, as far as the scribes have taught[6], defiles hallowed things, but only disqualifies[7] heave-offering and

Bikkurim,
ii. 1, and
elsewhere.

Chullin
33 b, i. 1,
Sota 30 a,
ii. 4.

---

[1] For wiping his hands after washing.

[2] Lit., Who (is there that can say that he) needs washing of hands?

[3] Not meaning Christians, or even Gentiles, but simply those not descended from Aaron.

[4] i.e., in case they are liable to be offered to God as firstfruits, they must, in order to be exempted, have become mixed with at least that number of similar objects, so as to be undistinguishable from them.

[5] The difficulty lies in the apparently contradictory directions about both tithe and common food, as gathered from the two Mishnahs.

[6] i.e., even in the cases of extra strictness which they impose by way of "a fence to the Law" (Pirke Aboth i. 1).

[7] i.e., after such touching, holy things do, but heave-offering does not, communicate the uncleanness to other things. Nevertheless the heave-offering is disqualified; i.e., the priest cannot then eat it.

18 b, ii. 5. leaves common food and tithe unaffected. These are the words of R. Meir, but wise men consider tithe affected[1].

But, you may say, there is a difficulty, where we place common food against common food. There is no difficulty. The one case[2] has to do with eating, the other[3] with touching.

R. Shimi bar Ashi deals with[4] the matter thus. Up to this point our Rabbis disagree with R. Meir only as to the eating of the tithe, but as regards the touching of the tithe and the eating of common food they do not disagree. But suppose that both the one and the other refer to eating, and still there is no difficulty. The one has to do with eating bread, the other with eating fruits. For R. Nachman[5] said, Every one who washes his hands for fruit is over scrupulous and affected[6].

Our Rabbis have taught thus, He that washes his hands—if he does it with intention[7], his hands are clean; if he does it without intention, his hands are unclean. And so he that dips his hands[8]— if he does it with intention, his hands are clean; if he does it without intention, his hands are unclean. And yet there is a Baraitha, Whether he does it with intention or not, his hands are clean.

R. Nachman said, There is no difficulty. The one[9] has to do with common food, the other[10] with tithe.

And what is your authority for saying[11] that common food[12] does not want intention? Because there is a canonical Mishnah, If a wave of water, which is let loose and contains forty seahs, falls upon a man or upon vessels, they are clean. For it teaches that a man is like vessels. As vessels have no intention, so a man has[13] no intention. But whence do you gather that he has no intention? Perhaps we are dealing with the case of a man sitting and watching

---

[1] Lit., prohibited in (the case of) tithe.
[2] Where washing of hands is required.
[3] Where it is not required.
[4] Lit., seizes.
[5] A colleague of Hunna. For the latter see p. 11, note 5.
[6] Lit., "is puffed up in spirit," and is proud of it, in a word, priggish.
[7] As a religious act.
[8] Dipping the hands implied a higher degree of purification than washing.
[9] i.e., the latter.
[10] i.e., the former.
[11] Lit., Whence dost thou say?
[12] i.e., the washing for it.
[13] i.e., need have.

when the wave shall be let loose. And [1] vessels are like a man. As a man utters his intention, so in the case of vessels persons exercise intention for them. And when thou sayest, It is the case of a man sitting and watching, what is the good of the story, for in that case he has an intention? Thou mightest have thought, It is to set a limit [2]. Perhaps otherwise he would have gone to dip himself in a collection [3] of stagnant rain-water. Thus also we limit it to the first fall, on account of the second [4] being unlawful. We learn from this that we are not to limit it. And what is your authority for saying [5] that men do not dip in the second fall? Because there is a Baraitha, viz., Men dip in the first, but do not dip in the second, that they may not dip in the air. But we also learn it [6] hence, for there is a canonical Mishnah, If fruits have fallen into the midst of a reservoir of water, and if one whose hands are unclean should reach out and lay hold of them, his hands are clean, and the fruits are clean [7]. But if he did this that he might wash his hands, his hands are clean, but the fruits are unclean [8]. *Makhshirin, iv. 7.* *19 a, i. 7.*

Rabbah put this question to R. Nachman, Thou saidst, He who dips for common food and has credit for common food, is forbidden tithe. If he claims credit, he has it; if he does not claim credit, he has it not [9]. Nay, but it means, Although he has credit for common food, he is forbidden tithe. He put this further

---

[1] Suggested as an equally probable way of explaining the collocation of "man" and "vessels" in the Mishnah just quoted.

[2] By making it necessary that he should dip himself in running water containing not less than 40 seahs.

[3] Rashi reads הרדלית. The word may be connected with ὕδωρ.

[4] The word כֵּיפִים, translated above "second," but literally *stones* (sometimes, however, *a tent* or *baldacchino*), is here explained to mean, the falling water, which after the first rush is broken up into a number of small, quickly moving drops (likened to stones), and thus not sufficient to guarantee cleansing.

[5] See p. 108, note 11.

[6] That intention is not required.

[7] On the principle that intention is not required. "Are clean:" lit., do not (come under the rule), If there shall be put (water upon fruit, it shall be unclean).

[8] As having been wet, and then drawn out by one who, while exercising intention, did not exercise it on the fruits, but only on the washing of his hands.

[9] He would say, Thus to make dipping and having credit for it to be two distinct things (as though the first were possible without the second) is at variance with the general principle that a person's own word is to be taken in such matters.

question to him, There is a Mishnah as follows, *If he have dipped and have not got credit for it, it is as though he had not dipped*[1]. Do you think it means, that it is as though he had not dipped? Certainly not, but it means that it is, as though he had not dipped for tithe. But the case supposed is that of one who has dipped for common food. He considered and brought this refutation.

He[2] went out and speculated and found that there is a Baraitha, viz., If a man have dipped and have not credit, he is forbidden tithe, but is free for common food. R. Eliezer said, If he have dipped and gone up, he may hold himself fit for any thing that he desires.

But they[3] reply, If, while he had still one foot in the water, he considered himself fit[4] for a smaller thing, he may consider himself fit for a greater thing; if he had gone up, he may not any more consider himself fit. Don't you think that this means, that he may not consider himself fit for any thing at all? No; while he had still one foot in the water, although he considered himself fit for a smaller thing only, he may consider himself fit for a greater thing; if he have gone up, then, if he did not think of himself as fit for any particular thing, he may consider himself as fit, but if he did think of himself as fit for a smaller thing, he may not consider himself as fit for a greater thing. Who is the Mishnah teacher[5] who says, While he had still one foot in the water? R. P'dath says, It is R. Jehudah, for there is a canonical Mishnah, If a collection of water is measured, and there are in it exactly forty seahs, and two men go down and dip one after the other, the first is clean, and the second is unclean. R. Jehudah said, If the feet of the first are still in contact with the water, the second also is clean. R. Nachman said that Rabbah bar Abuah said, There is a disagreement on the point among the weighty sayings of our Rabbis, but, if it is a case of passing from uncleanness to cleanness, all agree that the second also is unclean, and this is the opinion of R. P'dath. There are some who say that R. Nachman said, that Rabbah bar Abuah said, There is a disagreement as regards passing from uncleanness to cleanness, but among the weighty sayings of our Rabbis all agree that the second also is clean. And here there is a divergence from R. P'dath. Ola said,

---

[1] p. 106.   [2] The Talmudic teacher.
[3] The Gemaric teachers.   [4] Lit., had credit.
[5] For all statements, if they are to be of any value, must in the end be deduced from a Mishnah, and the Mishnah from the Bible.

They¹ asked this question of R. Jochanan, According to R. Jehudah how is it² as regards dipping needles and forks on the head of the first? Is there the case of draw and go down³ according to R. Jehudah? and is there not the case of draw and go up according to him⁴? or perhaps there is also the case of draw and go up according to him. He said to him, This is an old story. There are, suppose, three depressions in the bed of a stream, the upper and the lower and the middle one. The upper and the lower are each of the size of twenty seahs, and the middle one of forty seahs, and a collection⁵ of stagnant rain-water stretches between them⁶? R. Jehudah said, Meir used to say, A man may dip in the upper one⁷. And yet there is a Baraitha, viz., R. Jehudah says, Meir used to say, A man may dip in the upper one, but I⁸ say in the lower one and not in the upper one. He said to him, If it be a Baraitha, I withdraw my remark⁹.

*He that dips for common food and has credit for common food, etc.*¹⁰ According to whom does our Mishnah run¹¹? It is a saying of our Rabbis¹², for they make a distinction between common food and tithes. But against this view let me quote the latter part of the Mishnah, *The garments of a common person are defiled by pressure for Pharisees; the garments of Pharisees are defiled by pressure for those that eat heave-offering*¹³. This is¹⁴ in accordance

---

¹ The men of the Academy.
² The law.
³ If any one has not less than forty seahs of water falling on him, and it goes on to some one *below* him, the lower person (on Jehudah's principle that cases of "draw and go down" are valid) receives the blessing also. If "draw and go up" is valid, then in the case above adduced the needles and forks may receive the cleansing.
⁴ If "draw and go up" holds, "draw and go down" must also hold, for common experience teaches the latter to be true.
⁵ See p. 109, note 3.
⁶ The middle pool, being stagnant, cannot be used as a religious bath.
⁷ On the principle of "draw and go up."
⁸ As admitting only the principle of "draw and go down."
⁹ Lit., If it be a Baraitha, it is a Baraitha.
¹⁰ Not an accurate quotation. See for the words of the Mishnah p. 106.
¹¹ Lit., Who teach this?
¹² Unnamed, the "wise men" so often quoted. See p. 59, note 4.
¹³ We should have expected, if this part is to agree with the earlier part, that tithe would have come in (between Pharisees and heave-offering) as one term of the series. To insert it is in fact the solution of Acha bar Ada. See below.
¹⁴ Lit., They go.

with R. Meir, who says, Common food and tithe are exactly the same. Then is our conclusion to be that the former part is the teaching of our Rabbis, and the latter part that of R. Meir?

Yes, the former part is the teaching of our Rabbis, and the latter part that of R. Meir. Rab Acha bar Ada[1] teaches in the latter part five orders[2], and establishes it all according to our Rabbis.

Rab Mari said, Learn from this that common food which is treated with observance of the laws of purification belonging to hallowed things, is like hallowed things. Wherefore? Is it because he does not include it[3] among the orders? No; for perhaps this is the reason that he does not include it among the orders, that, if it were likened to heave-offering, behold, we have been already taught about heave-offering, and if it were likened to common food, behold, we have been already taught about common food, for there is a Baraitha[4], viz., common food which is treated with observance of the laws of purification belonging to hallowed things, behold, it is nevertheless as common food. R. El'azar in the name of R. Zadok says, Behold it is as heave-offering.

But observe what we learn from the latter part of the Mishnah. *Jose ben Joezer was pious and in the priesthood, and yet his apron was defiled by pressure for those that partake of hallowed things. Jochanan ben Gudyodah was one who ate his ordinary food all his days with observance of the laws of purification which belong to hallowed things, and yet his apron was defiled by pressure for those that partake of sin offering.* Of sin-offering, yes; of hallowed things, no. Wherefore he[5] considered, Common food which is treated with observance of the laws of purification belonging to hallowed things is like hallowed things. R. Jonathan ben El'azar said, A man's neckcloth has fallen from him. He says to his neighbour, Give it to me, and uncleanness is communicated[6] to him.

---

[1] A disciple of Rab, and a very old man in the time of Rabba. See *Juch.* 107 b.

[2] He in fact substitutes a different form of Mishnah, one including five (and not only four) degrees, and thus solves the difficulty. The five are, Pharisees, *those who eat tithe,* those who eat heave-offering, those who eat hallowed things, those who purify themselves with the ashes of the sin-offering.

[3] The ordinary food.

[4] חנן of the Heb. text, meaning, *There is a canonical Mishnah*, must, as the margin of the Lemberg text points out, be an error for תניא, *There is a Baraitha.*

[5] The Mishnah teacher.   [6] Lit., given.

R. Jonathan ben Amram said, A man's Sabbath clothes have been exchanged for his common clothes, and he has put them[1] on; they are unclean[2]. R. El'azar bar Zadok[3] said, There was the case of two women, companions, whose clothes were exchanged at the baths, and the matter came before R. Eliezer and he pronounced them unclean. R. Oshaia objects to him, But regard it thus. It follows that if a man stretch out his hand to a basket to take a piece of wheaten bread, and there come into his hand a piece of barley bread, in this case also he is made unclean[4]. And if thou sayest, Yes, in this case also; but yet there is a Baraitha, viz., He that guards the cask, presuming that it is wine, and it is found to be a cask of oil—it is clean so far as not to cause uncleanness.

But granting that[5], let me point out the last words[6]. But it is forbidden to be eaten. Wherefore R. Jeremiah said, This is the case of one who says, I have guarded it as regards uncleanness, but not as regards separation. And what is the meaning of this securing in a half and half way[7]? There is such a thing, and yet there is a Baraitha, If a man stretches out his hand into a basket, and the basket is upon his shoulder, and the scraper[8] is inside the basket, and it[9] is in his mind as regards the basket, but is not in his mind as regards the scraper, the basket is clean but the scraper is unclean. The basket is clean, you say. Does not the scraper make the basket unclean? No; for one vessel does not make another vessel unclean, but it may make unclean what is in the basket. Rabena said, This is the case of one who says, I have guarded it as regards its uncleanness, but not as regards its separation.

On all sides there is a difficulty. And again Rabbah bar Abuah objects, There is the case of a certain woman who went before

---

[1] The latter.
[2] Owing to the probability that they have contracted some uncleanness, from the comparative want of care which he would take of them.
[3] Flourished about A.D. 250. See Wolf, ii. 869.
[4] Because the barley bread may have been unclean. For, as he did not intend to touch it, he will not have taken proper precautions.
[5] ולטעמיך, lit., Let it be according to your taste.
[6] viz., "clean, so far as not to cause uncleanness."
[7] Lit., in part.
[8] מגרפה, a shovel, or instrument for dividing cakes of figs. But see Buxt. p. 482 for other senses.
[9] Purity.

20 a, ii. 3. R. Ishmael and said to him, Rabbi, I wove this garment in accordance with the laws of purity, but it was not in my mind to guard it in purity. But in the course of the minute enquiries which R. Ishmael was making, she said to him, Rabbi, a woman in a condition of ceremonial uncleanness pulled at the cord along with me. R. Ishmael said, How great are the words of the wise which they have spoken, viz., If it is in one's mind to guard it, it is clean; if it is not in one's mind to guard it, it is unclean. Again, there is the case of a certain woman, who went before R. Ishmael and said to him, Rabbi, I wove this cloth in accordance with the laws of purity, but it was not in my mind to guard it. But in the course of the minute enquiries which R. Ishmael was making, she said to him, Rabbi, my thread broke, and I fastened it with my mouth[1]. R. Ishmael said, How great are the words of the wise which they have spoken, viz., If it is in one's mind to guard it, it is clean; if it is not in one's mind to guard it, it is unclean.

It is all right as regards R. El'azar son of R. Zadok. For we may observe that each woman says, My neighbour is wife of a common person, and she turns her attention from her[2]. It is all right as regards R. Jonathan ben Amram also. For we may observe that inasmuch as a man pays great attention to his Sabbath clothes, he has taken his thoughts from the others[3]. But as to R. Jonathan ben El'azar, we may observe that a man will pay[4] attention to the hands of his neighbour. R. Jochanan said, It may be presumed that no man attends to what is in the hand of his

20 b neighbour? Does he not? And yet there is a Baraitha, viz., Behold, a man's[5] muleteers and his workmen are laden with clean things; although he[6] is distant from them more than a mile[7], his clean things are still clean; but if he say to them, Go and I will come after you, then when they are out of his sight[8], his clean things

---

[1] Though herself ceremonially clean, she had, or might have had, some spittle in her mouth, remaining from the time before she had cleansed herself.

[2] As hopeless; whereas, if she had thought that her neighbour might be carefully trained in purity, she would have watched her, lest either of them should contract uncleanness. The general principle is, that, if the thoughts are withdrawn from the matter, the danger of impurity at once supervenes.

[3] The common ones.

[4] נעביד is either 3rd sing. (נ for י as in Syriac), or 1st plural.

[5] Lit., his. [6] The owner.

[7] מיל, millia (passuum).

[8] Lit., when his eyes are hidden from them.

become unclean. How is the inconsistency in this Baraitha to 20 b, i. 6. be explained¹? R. Isaac Naphcha² said, The earlier part means, when he cleanses his muleteers and his workmen. Therefore, if so, the latter part should also refer to the same. No; for a common person is not careful as regards touching his neighbour. But, if so, this would hold good for the beginning also. Perhaps it may mean, when he comes to them by some by-way³. But, if so, this would hold good for the latter part also. Nay; but the true explanation is, When he said to them, Go and I will come after you, their minds were set completely at rest⁴.

May our return be to thee, "Men are not to expound, etc.⁵"

פרק ג

MISHNAH.

III. (1) Weightier rules hold in hallowed things⁶ than in a heave-offering⁷; for we may cleanse⁸ vessels in the midst of vessels for a heave-offering but not for hallowed things⁹. The outsides

---

¹ Lit., How does the beginning differ? how does the end differ?

² Naphcha, i.e., the blacksmith. For this word as title of a Rabbi see p. 11, note 7.

³ Lit., by a crooked way.

⁴ They felt that he was likely to leave them to themselves, and so became careless.

⁵ See p. 55, note 2.

⁶ Ḳodesh (קֹדֶשׁ), translated as above in Deut. xxvi. 13, is the technical name for that which is subjected to the most solemn form of dedication to God. Houses, vessels, food, etc., may be thus dedicated. In the last-named case only a priest can partake of that which is thus offered.

⁷ The heave-offering was that which the Israelite had to present from his corn to the priest, and the latter alone was allowed to partake of it. See Numb. xv. 18—21. The amount is not fixed in the Law, but the Rabbinic rule (Mishnah, T'rumoth, iv. 3) was that from the 40th to the 60th part should be paid according to the liberality of the giver. A further point of difference between heave-offering and hallowed things was that the former could be eaten throughout Palestine, the latter in Jerusalem only.

⁸ Lit., dip.

⁹ e.g., the ceremonial cleansing of cups in a basket need not in the former case, but must in the latter, be performed separately from the cleansing of the basket itself.

20 b, ii. 1. and the inside and the place for laying hold are reckoned as distinct[1] in the heave-offering but not in the hallowed things. He that takes up that which has been made unclean by pressure[2] may offer the heave-offering but not the hallowed things. The garments of those that eat the heave-offering are unclean through pressure with regard to hallowed things. The manner of the heave-offering is not as the manner of the hallowed things. For in the case of hallowed things one loosens a knot and wipes[3] and cleanses and afterwards ties up again, but in the case of a heave-offering he ties up and afterwards cleanses[4].

(2) Vessels finished in purity[5] need cleansing for hallowed things, but not for a heave-offering. The vessel includes what is within it[6] for hallowed things, but not for heave-offering.

The unclean in the fourth degree[7] in the case of hallowed things is disqualified, but in the third degree in the case of heave-offering.

And in the case of heave-offering, though one of his[8] hands be unclean, its fellow is clean; but in the case of hallowed things, both are to be cleansed; for the hand makes its fellow unclean in the case of hallowed things, but not in the case of heave-offering.

---

[1] i.e., each of the parts is for this purpose considered a separate vessel, so that, if ceremonially clean, it may be used, even if the other parts here specified be unclean.

[2] e.g., a boot worn by one who has a flux. See Lev. xv. 4, sqq.

[3] The primary sense of the original word is, to remove by the warmth of the sun's rays.

[4] In the case of hallowed things, every thing, whether garments or otherwise, between the running water and the person's body, must be removed, that the cleansing may be complete. It is not so in the case of the heave-offering.

[5] i.e., under conditions which have carefully precluded ceremonial uncleanness.

[6] i.e., If a vessel contains others within it, and has become ceremonially unclean, its uncleanness involves uncleanness to the contained vessels, when hallowed things are concerned, but not, when it is only a case of heave-offering.

[7] That which is the original source of the uncleanness is called *parent of uncleanness* (אַב הַטּוּמְאָה), that which comes next, *second as regards uncleanness* (שֵׁנִי הַטּוּמְאָה), and so on.

[8] The man's.

(3) Men may eat dry[1] food with ceremonially unclean hands in the case of heave-offering, but not in the case of hallowed things.

He who is in deep mourning[2] and he who lacks atonement[3], needs cleansing for the hallowed things, but not for the heave-offering.

Gemara.

In hallowed things. What is the reason of the prohibition? R. Ela said, Because the weight of the vessel interposes. But seeing that in a later case it is on account of the interposition, the first case cannot be on account of an interposition[4]. For we are taught in the later case, *And*[5] *the manner of the heave-offering is not as the manner of the hallowed things. For in the case of hallowed things one looses a knot and wipes and cleanses and afterwards ties up again, but in the case of a heave-offering he ties up and afterwards cleanses.* Nay, but both the earlier and later cases are because of interposition, and it was necessary that they should be separately mentioned, for if he had taught us the first only, I should say, *This* is the reason for the prohibition with reference to the hallowed things, viz., because of the vessel's weight, which actually exists. But in the latter case, where the vessel's weight is not an

---

[1] Lit., wiped (see p. 116, note 3), but the word is also used to describe such fruits as are in their nature dry, such as apples or gooseberries, as opposed to strawberries or raspberries. It should be noted that the first אכלי (אוֹכְלִין) is the participle, the second (אוּכְלִין) a substantive, *food*.

[2] The original word *Onen* (אוֹנֵן) denotes a person who has one of his seven nearest relations (father, mother, husband or wife, brother, sister, son, daughter) lying still unburied. Cf. Deut. xxvi. 14, "I have not eaten thereof [of the hallowed things, Ḳodesh, v. 13] in my *mourning*," where the Heb. has a substantive from the same root as the word in the text. An *Abel* (אָבֵל) on the other hand was one with whom this stage of mourning is passed.

[3] The person who has done all that is necessary for his cleansing, except to present his offerings. These however cannot legally be brought till the next day. During the night he is not technically unclean, nor yet clean, and the intermediate state in which he finds himself is described by the phrase above translated "lacks atonement."

[4] For otherwise there would be tautology.

[5] The "And" does not occur in the actual Mishnah. For other instances of slight deviations of this kind, see p. 15, note 1, and elsewhere.

21 a, ii. 13. clement[1], I should say, In regard to hallowed things also there is in this case no disqualifying interposition. And if he had taught us the latter only, I should say, This is the reason for the prohibition with reference to hallowed things, because a knot[2] in water is drawn 21 b tighter[3], while in the former case the water makes the vessel to swim[4], and so there is no interposition. Thus it was necessary that they should be separately mentioned.   Rabbi[5] Ela is consistent with himself[6]. For R. Ela said that R. Chănina bar Papa said, Ten degrees of superior excellence are taught here. The first five refer alike to hallowed things, and to ordinary things[7] which are treated with observance of the laws of purification belonging to hallowed things[8]; the later refer to hallowed things, but not to ordinary things, which are treated with observance of the laws of purification belonging to hallowed things. What is the reason? Because the former five involve an essential impurity arising out of the Law, our Rabbis have decided that they apply as well to hallowed things, as to ordinary things which are treated with observance of the laws of purification belonging to hallowed things. Because the later ones involve no essential impurity arising out of the Law, our Rabbis have decided that they apply to hallowed things; but to ordinary things which are treated with observance of the laws of purification belonging to hallowed things our Rabbis have decided that they do not apply.

[1] For here they are not one within another, but are strung together.

[2] קִיטְרָא. The Talmudic root קטר is equivalent to the Biblical Heb. קשר, to bind.

[3] אֲהַדּוֹקֵי מֵיהָדַק, the Ithpe'el infin. followed by the participle (= present tense) of the same voice. See Luzzatto, pp. 90, 91.

[4] אַקְפוּיֵי מָקְפוּ The Aphel infin. followed by the participle of the same voice, which part of the verb in this kind of Hebrew, often, as here, takes in the plural the termination (3rd pl. וֹ = pure Heb. וּ) of the verb and not of the noun. See Luzzatto, pp. 92, 96.

[5] The application of the title Rabbi to Ela seems at first to violate the rule that it should be confined to Western (= Palestinian) teachers (see p. 26, note 2). Ela however, although a Babylonian, had gone to Palestine and been ordained there.

[6] Lit., is according to his reason.

[7] Lit., profane.

[8] e.g., a person descended from Aaron, though only by the female line, might desire to lay upon himself and his household the same restrictions with regard to food as did a priest.

Raba[1] said, Since the later portion of the Mishnah is on account of interposition, the former is not on account of interposition. But in the former one this is the reason. It is a precaution, in order that needles and pipes should not be dipped in a vessel, the mouth of which is not of the size of the pipe of a wine-skin bottle. For there is a canonical Mishnah, viz., The communication between[2] religious baths must be as the pipe of a wine-skin as regards its thickness, and with an area of the size of two fingers making a complete revolution. He bethinks himself, This is like that which R. Nachman said that Rabbah bar Abuah said, viz., Eleven[3] features of superior excellence are taught here. The first six refer alike to hallowed things and to ordinary things which are treated with observance of the laws of purification belonging to hallowed things. The later ones refer to hallowed things, but not to ordinary things which are treated with observance of the laws of purification belonging to hallowed things.

What real difference[4] is there between what Raba and what R. Ela says? There is this difference between them. In the case of a basket and a wine-strainer which are filled with vessels and cleansed, according to the one[5] who says, The prohibition is because of interposition, there is an interposition; but according to the one[6] who says, The prohibition is for a precaution, lest haply needles and pipes should be dipped in a vessel, the mouth of which is not of the size of the pipe of a wine-skin, the answer is, there is no basket or wine-strainer the mouth of which is not of the size of the pipe of a wine-skin. And Raba has acted consistently with himself[7]; for Raba said, In the case of a basket and wine-strainer, which are filled with vessels and dipped, all are clean; but in the case of a bath, which is divided by a basket or wine-strainer, he who seeks to cleanse there—the cleansing avails

---

[1] He was a pupil of R. Joseph (for whom see p. 17, note 5) and is to be distinguished from Rabba (see p. 4, note 3). There is a long account of Raba in *Juch.* p. 182 *a*.

[2] Lit., mixings of.

[3] The clause, *The manner of the heave-offering is not as the manner of the hallowed things*, may or may not be taken as one of the "features." Hence the difference between Rabbah bar Abuah's reckoning and that of Ch'nínah bar Papa (p. 118).

[4] Those who despised Rabbinic discussions used to say contemptuously, After all their debates they have not succeeded in making it lawful to eat a raven or unlawful to eat a pigeon.

[5] viz., Ela.   [6] viz., Raba.

[7] Lit., has gone according to his reason.

22 a, i. 18. him nought, for lo, all the earth is trembling[1], and we require that there should be forty seahs of water in one place. And these words refer to a clean vessel, but in the case of an unclean vessel, seeing that the cleansing has gone up over the whole surface of the vessel, it has gone up also over the vessels which are in it[2]. For there is a canonical Mishnah, viz., Vessels which are filled with vessels and are dipped, lo, these are clean, and if they are not dipped, the mingled waters must reach that amount of mingling which takes place by means of a communication as large as the pipe of a wine-skin. How is it that it says, And if they are not dipped? This is the meaning, viz., And if it is not necessary to dip them[3], still the mingled waters must reach that amount of mingling which takes place by means of a communication as large as the pipe of a wine-skin. And lo, as regards the sayings of Raba and R. Ela, they are the subject of a Baraitha. For there is a Baraitha[4], A basket and a wine-strainer which are filled with vessels and are dipped are clean as well for hallowed things as for a heave-offering. Abba Saul[5] says, For a heave-offering, but not for hallowed things[6]. If so, then is not a heave-offering also invalid? No, for to whom are we speaking? Is it not to teachers? teachers who are possessed of knowledge? But if so, the same rule will apply to hallowed things also[7]. No, for a common person sees him and goes and dips.

Mikvaoth, vi. 2.

Then in the case of heave-offering also, a common person sees him and goes and dips[8]. We need not receive it from him.

Hallowed things also we need not receive from him. He would be angry. In the case of heave-offering also he would be angry.

He does not care, for he goes and gives it to a priest, a

---

[1] i.e., crumbling away at the edge through the action of the water.

[2] So says Rashi, but Maimonides maintains that those within the others were still unclean.

[3] Lit., it.

[4] A 1st cent. Baraitha, put forth by the Sopherim, for whom see *Introd.* p. vii.

[5] A hearer of R. Jochanan ben Zakkai. He has been erroneously identified by some with St Paul.

[6] This is the end of the 1st century Baraitha.

[7] The teacher, being a learned man in the Jewish Law, might by parity of reason *here*, as you say is the case with him in the *heave-offering*, be trusted to cleanse or not, as he saw in each that there was, or was not, a possibility that the vessels to be used were unclean.

[8] i.e., will dip unclean vessels inside another vessel, and, as not being possessed of skill in the minute points of the Law, will omit something essential, and so fail really to cleanse.

common person, his friend[1].   And what is the Baraitha to the effect that we should pay regard to the fear of such anger? It is a saying of R. Jose. For there is a Baraitha, R. Jose said, Wherefore are all believed as to the purity of wine and oil all the days of the year? It is in order that every individual may not go and build a high place for himself, and burn a red heifer for himself.

Rab Papa said, According to whom is it that we accept now-a-days the testimony of a common person? According to whom[2]? It is according to R. Jose. But let us consider the question of borrowing[3]. For there is a canonical Mishnah, viz., An earthen vessel protects everything from uncleanness[4]. These are the words of the house of Hillel.   The house of Shammai say, It only protects eatables and drinkables and every earthen vessel.   The house of Hillel said to the house of Shammai, Wherefore?   The house of Shammai said, Because it is unclean on account of the common people[5], and a vessel that is unclean does not bar.   The house of Hillel said to them, But in accordance with the rule ye have just given do ye not declare clean the eatables and drinkables that are within it[6]?   The house of Shammai said to them, When we declared clean the eatables and drinkables which are within it, it was for himself[7] that we declared them clean, but should we declare clean the vessel whose purity is a matter which relates both to thee and to him?   There is a Baraitha, viz., R. Joshua said, I am ashamed of your words, ye house of Shammai. Is it possible that if a woman be kneading in a trough, and the woman become for any reason unclean, the woman and the trough are unclean for

22 a, ii. 8.

Kelim, x. 1.

22 b.

---

[1] While the same argument does not apply to the hallowed things, because these have to be eaten on the spot and cannot be taken or given away.

[2] i.e., According to whose teaching?

[3] For (the Talmud means) it will inevitably be the case sooner or later that in some sudden emergency we shall want to borrow vessels from our neighbour. Are we to do it, if we are not certain that he has faithfully observed all the rules of cleansing?

[4] An *earthen* vessel cannot be cleansed, but, if it have incurred ceremonial defilement, e.g., through being in the room with a dead person, it must be broken. But on the other hand its *outside* cannot become unclean, and further, if placed so as to interpose between a clean and unclean thing, it bars the defilement.

[5] The owner, as not practising with knowledge and care the rules of cleansing, is virtually certain to have made it already unclean.

[6] And are ye not therefore inconsistent?

[7] viz., the owner of the house, since he might otherwise be put to much inconvenience.

22 b, i. 4. seven days, but the dough is clean? Or suppose that a bowl[1] is full of drinkables. If for any reason the bowl becomes unclean for seven days, yet are the drinkables clean?   A certain disciple, one of the disciples of the house of Shammai, joined himself to him and said to him, Shall I tell thee the reason of the house of Shammai?
He said to him, Tell me.   He said to him, Does an unclean vessel bar, or does it not bar?   He said to him, It does not bar.
Are the vessels of a common person unclean or clean[2]?   He said to him, Unclean.   But if thou sayest to him[3], It is unclean, will he care for thee at all? And not only so, but if thou sayest to him, It is unclean, he will say to thee, Mine is clean, but thine is unclean; and this is the reason of the house of Shammai. Immediately R. Joshua went and threw himself down at the graves of the house of Shammai, and said, I humble myself before you, O bones of the house of Shammai, and when your mysteries are so wonderful, how much more are your explicit teachings? They say that all his days his teeth were black by reason of his fasts.

There is a Baraitha, viz., At all events it is a matter which concerns thee as well as him; consequently we borrow them from him. But, it may be said, When we borrow them from him, we may dip them.   But if so, the house of Hillel ought to have replied[4] to the house of Shammai, When we borrow them, we dip them.

That which is unclean by reason of a dead body requires sprinkling on the third and on the seventh day. But men do not borrow a vessel for use at the end of seven days[5]. And with regard to dipping, are we not to take a man's word? And yet there is the Baraitha, The word of a common person is taken with respect to the purification of washing of that which is unclean by reason of a dead body[6].   Abai said, There is no difficulty. The one[7]

---

[1] לוגין is an error for לָגִין. See Buxt. p. 1124.

[2] כֵּלָיו... טָמֵא אוֹ טָהוֹר. Observe the breach of grammatical concord in the Hebrew.

[3] i.e., to a common person.

[4] לְיַהֲדְרוּ = גֵיהַדְרוּ, (Aphel fut.) where the לְ (=לוּ, would that) gives, as often, an optative force to the verb. See other instances of this (Syriac) use of the prefixed ל in Luzzatto, p. 91.

[5] They want it, if at all, for immediate use, and therefore there is no time to subject it to cleansing on the chance of its having in this particular way contracted defilement.

[6] How then can you say that we are not to believe him?

[7] The case which concerns the dead body.

refers to his body, the other[1] to his vessels[2]. But Raba said, 22 b, i. 25. Both the one and the other teaching refer to his vessels. And even so there is no difficulty. The one is the case of a man who says, I have never dipped vessels in the midst of vessels[3]; and the other is the case of a man who says, I have dipped, but I have not dipped in a vessel the mouth of which is not of the size of the pipe of a wine-skin[4]. And this is borne out by a Baraitha[5], viz., A common person is believed when he says, Fruits have not been rendered predisposed to defilement[6]. But he is not believed, when he says, The fruits have been rendered predisposed to defilement, but they have not been defiled[7]. And with regard to his body, is he to be believed? Surely not, For lo, there is a Baraitha, viz., In the case of a learned and observant man[8] who comes for sprinkling[9], he is to be sprinkled at once; in the case of a common person, who comes for sprinkling, he is not to be sprinkled, until he performs before us the things appertaining to the third and seventh days[10]. But Abai says, As the result of thy severity towards him at the beginning, thou dealest gently with him at the end[11].

The outsides and the inside[12]. What is the meaning of the out-

---

[1] That of dipping.

[2] He may well be too lazy to carry out the latter sort of cleansing, and yet be trusted to attend to the former.

[3] i.e., I have always dipped them separately, and thus have avoided all such risk. He is to be believed.

[4] Because in this a common person may be easily mistaken.

[5] והתני. Generally (the present case is an exception), the expression in the original denotes opposition (" And yet etc.").

[6] i.e., by washing. For example, a cabbage, as long as it is growing and thus connected with the ground, is, on general principles, not liable to defilement. After being cut and washed, the case is different, inasmuch as a wet thing is more liable than a dry to contract pollution. It is however generally easy to test whether such washing has really taken place. Hence the distinction made in the text between this and the next case.

[7] About this he can easily be mistaken. Moreover it is not easy to put to the test.

[8] See p. 141, note 1.

[9] With the ashes of the red heifer.

[10] Dipping, etc. See Numb. xix. 11, 12, 19.

[11] The sense is, that it is not really harsh treatment which in this last instance he is undergoing. For it is to his advantage to be able to point to the judicial decision of the governing body of a synagogue (a Beth-din), which can testify, if necessary, that he was properly cleansed.

[12] See p. 115.

sides and the inside? According to what is said in a canonical Mishnah, In the case of a vessel the outside of which is defiled by drinkables its outside is defiled, but its inside, its rim, and its short handles[1] and its long handles[2] are clean; but if its inside is defiled, it is all defiled.

And the place for laying hold etc. What is the place for laying hold? R. Jehudah said that R. Samuel said, The part by which he reaches it[3], and accordingly He says, "And he reached her parched corn." R. Asi said that R. Jochanan[4] said, The part of the dish of which fastidious persons lay hold[5]. R. Baybi, who stood before[6] R. Nachman[7], taught, No vessels have outsides or inside[8] whether for holy things of the sanctuary or holy things of the province[9]. He said to him, Holy things of the province, what are they? the heave-offering? But lo, there is a canonical Mishnah, viz., The outsides and inside and the place for laying hold are reckoned as distinct for the heave-offering. R. Baybi replied, Perhaps it refers to ordinary things which are treated with observance of the laws of purification belonging to hallowed things.

In what you have said you have reminded me of a saying of Rabba bar Abuah[10], viz., Eleven degrees of superior excellence are

---

[1] Lit., its ear.   [2] Lit., its hands.

[3] i.e., the part by which he holds it, when he reaches it.

[4] Jochanan lived in the middle of the third century (see p. 11, note 7) and Asi was his immediate disciple, for if there had been any one intervening, the expression would be, *said in the name of* (מִשּׁוּם), etc.

[5] i.e., a hollow in a plate (like our receptacles for gravy) for holding mustard, vinegar, oil, etc. The root צבע, here apparently used as equivalent to צבט, *to lay hold, reach*, may however have its ordinary sense, to dye, colour, e.g., with mustard. And in this connexion we may note that the phrase of the Mishnah, which is here under discussion (בית הצבטה), appears in the Jerus. Talmud, under Jochanan's editorship, as בית הצביעה.

[6] A kind of domestic chaplain, not however so much for the purpose of conducting worship, as to relieve his master Nachman (cf. Exod. xviii. 14—22) from the labour of deciding Rabbinical questions, when they arose in practice. See also p. 103, note 1, and p. 125, note 6.

[7] Jehudah and Samuel were of Babylon, Asi and Jochanan of Palestine, Baybi (to be distinguished from the B. of p. 17) and Nachman of Babylon.

[8] i.e., no distinction holds between these parts in matters connected with defilement.

[9] Lit., *of the boundaries*, but the Heb. word in its Rabbinic, as opposed to its Biblical, use is synonymous with מְדִינָה, *a province*.

[10] And, seeing that Abuah had been the teacher of Nachman, as well as of Baybi, these were silenced.

taught here. The first six refer, as well as to hallowed things, as to ordinary things which are treated with observance of the laws of purification belonging to hallowed things. The later ones refer to hallowed things, but not to ordinary things treated with the observance of the laws of purification belonging to hallowed things.

He that takes up that which has been made unclean by pressure may offer the heave-offering but not the hallowed things[1]. Why not the hallowed things?   Because of the matter that occurred. For R. Jehudah said that R. Samuel said, A matter occurred to a certain man, who was carrying a cask of consecrated wine from one place to another, and the thong of his sandal came off, and he took it up and placed it on the mouth of the cask, and it fell into the inside of the cask, and it was made unclean. In the same hour they said, He that taketh up that which has been made unclean by pressure may offer the heave-offering but not the hallowed things.   If so, the heave-offering also is forbidden.

Nay, but shall I tell you on what authority this depends[2]? This is the teaching of R. Chănaniah ben Akbia[3]; for he said, They have only made this restriction as regards Jordan or a ship, and in accordance with the matter that occurred.   What was that?   There is a Baraitha, viz., A man shall not take up the waters of sin and the ashes of sin[4], and carry them away over Jordan or in a ship, and he shall not stand on this side and throw them to the other side, and he shall not make them to swim upon the face of the waters, and he shall not ride upon the back of a beast nor upon the back of his comrade, but if he do, his feet must touch the ground; but he may bear them over a bridge, and he need not regard whether it be Jordan or any other river.   R. Chănaniah ben Akbia says, They have only made this restriction as regards Jordan and the case when the man is in a ship, and in accordance with the matter that occurred.   What was the matter that occurred?

---

[1] See p. 116.

[2] For that will shew you that the heave-offering is not included, on the principle that the Rabbis, when for any reason they have to make a new rule, restrict its operation to those cases which are absolutely similar to that which has compelled them to take action.

[3] Some read for Akbia Akiba. Chănaniah lived about A.D. 120. He was interpreter (מְתוּרְגְּמָן. see p. 79, note 5) to Jehudah ben El'ai. See *Juch.* 66 *a*, also 44 *b*.

[4] Numb. xix. 2 sqq.

23 a, i. 20. R. Jehudah said that Rab said, A matter occurred with a certain man, who was carrying the waters of sin and the ashes of sin over Jordan and in a ship, and a piece of a dead body as large as an olive[1] was found fixed in the bottom of the ship. In the same hour they said, A man shall not bear waters of sin and ashes of sin and carry them over Jordan in a ship. This question was put by them. In the case of an unclean sandal the law is clear, but what if the case be one of a clean sandal? In the case of an open cask the law is clear, but what if the case be one of a closed cask? What also if it be the case of a man who *has* passed over and borne it? R. Ela said, If he has passed over and borne it, he is unclean. R. Zera said, If he has passed over and borne it, he is clean.

Vessels finished in purity, etc.[2] Finished by whom? If a learned and observant man has finished them, why should they be dipped? but if a common person has finished them, how is it that the Mishnah calls them "finished in purity?" Rabbah bar Shela said that R. Mothnah[3] said that Samuel said, By all means, in case that a learned and observant man has finished them; yet because of a drop[4] of spittle[5] of a common person which may have fallen upon it, it is treated as unclean. "May have fallen upon it," when? If we should say, before it is completed, but lo, it is not yet a vessel[6]; or, after it is completed, but then he takes good care of it[7]. By all means in the case of the vessel before it is completed; yet perhaps at the moment that it was made, it was still liquid. It is a case for dipping, but not for the going down of the sun[8]. This Mishnic teaching[9] does not agree[10] with R. Eliezer.

---

[1] That which is dead, if it be smaller than an olive, does not render unclean.
[2] See p. 116.
[3] A pupil of Samuel (see p. 20, note 3) and colleague of Jehudah.
[4] Lit., pearl, bubble.
[5] See Lev. xv. 8.
[6] Whereas the passage in the Law (Lev. xv. 12) says a vessel.
[7] And thus there will be no risk.
[8] i.e., it is not one of the graver cases where (see p. 117, note 3) the person or thing to be purified must be plunged into water, not emerging till after sunset, while the purifying cannot be completed till the next day, by the presentation of the offerings (which cannot be made between sunset and sunrise).
[9] Of the non-canonical sort, a Baraitha.
[10] As not mentioning the case of the "pipe," with which Eliezer deals in the canonical Mishnah just about to be adduced.

For there is a canonical Mishnah, When one has cut out a pipe for the ashes of purification for sin, R. Eliezer says, Let him forthwith dip[1]. R. Joshua says, Let him be rendered unclean[2] and afterwards let him dip[3]. And we[4] discuss the question, Who is it that is cutting it out? Perhaps it is a learned and observant man, who has cut it out. But then, why should I dip? Or, a common person has cut it out. But then would R. Joshua have said, He shall be made unclean[5] and shall be dipped? Nay, for he is already unclean and continues so. And Rabbah bar Shela said that Rab Mothnah said that Samuel said, By all means let it be the case that a learned and observant man has cut it out, yet because of a drop of spittle of a common person which may have fallen upon it— When? If we should say, before he cut it out, but lo, it is not yet a vessel[6]; or after he cut it out, but then he takes good care of it. By all means it is so before he cut it out; yet perhaps at the moment that he cut it out, it was still liquid. It is all right as to what R. Joshua says, This is by way of a test[7] for Sadducees[8]. For we have a canonical Mishnah, They used to make unclean the priest who burns the heifer, in order to protest against the view of the Sadducees[9]; for they[10] used to say, This act is included among the sunset ones[11]. But thou art in accord with the teaching of R. Eliezer, if thou sayest, It is all right to say that in every case we require the sunset rule, for this is a protest against the Sadducees. But if thou sayest, In every case we do not require the sunset rule, how is it a protest against the Sadducees? Rab said, They made him as one unclean through touching a dead animal. But regard it thus. Such an unclean

---

[1] Himself and the vessel. Kal here is equivalent in sense to Hiph'il as well.
[2] Himself and the vessel.
[3] See note 1.
[4] The Talmudic teachers.
[5] No, for he is so already.
[6] We may note that a vessel ceases also to be a vessel, when a piece is broken off it, and so the laws relating to uncleanness in such a case cease to operate.
[7] Lit., a discrimination.
[8] The Sadducees said, Dipping is needless for the man who touches the ashes. The coming of sunset is enough.
[9] Lit., to bring it out (away) from the thought of the Sadducees.
[10] The Sadducees.
[11] i.e., where the coming of sunset is sufficient.

23 b, i. 2. thing will not make a man unclean[1] by touching him. Perhaps it will not, you will say. But then to what purpose is the Baraitha, viz., He that cuts it and dips it, needs dipping? Or was it that they made him as one who is unclean by touching a dead man? If so, this would require the purifications of the third and seventh days. To what purpose is the Baraitha, He that cuts it and dips it, needs dipping? Dipping, yes; but the purifications of the third and seventh days, no. But was it that they made him as one who is unclean by touching a dead man on his seventh day[2]? But lo, there is a Baraitha, viz., They absolutely refrain from making any new ordinance in the case of the heifer[3]. But Abai said, They do not say that a spade[4] makes unclean when used as a seat, according Lev. xv. 6. to the teaching, "And he that sitteth upon the vessel." I might have thought[5], If he were to turn a two gallon measure upside down, and sit upon it, or a peck measure, and sit upon it, he would be unclean. But no; I should have been wrong, for the teaching says, ibid. "And he that sitteth upon the *vessel*, upon which there sitteth—," shall be unclean. But it must mean, that which is *intended* for sitting, and the other is excepted, for if he sit upon it, he will be told, Stand up and let us do our work.

The vessel includes what is within it for hallowed things, but not for heave-offering[6]. Whence have you this utterance? R. Chanin[7] Numb. vii. said, Because the Scripture saith, "One golden spoon of ten shekels, 14 etc. full of incense." Holy Writ makes every thing which is in the spoon one. R. Kahăna[8] replies that R. Aḳiba added to the teaching, which immediately follows, the flour and the incense and the frankincense and the coals; for if the person in course of purification[9] touch the extremity of it, he disqualifies the whole.

---

[1] He that is unclean through a corpse, besides being himself unclean, defiles any one whom he touches. But if a man be unclean through a dead animal, the uncleanness does not go beyond himself.

[2] i.e., after he has completed the rites, and is just about to become clean.

[3] And therefore the last named conjecture will not hold.

[4] Which may have been used by an unclean person. Abai's point is that a spade is not naturally intended for a seat, and therefore does not come under the rule.

[5] If it were not for the word "vessel" in that passage.

[6] See p. 116.   [7] A contemporary of Ashi. See p. 6, note 1.

[8] 3rd century, a disciple of Rab and contemporary of Ashi. See *Juch*. 161 *b*.

[9] i.e., who has been dipped, and is waiting for the next day to make his offerings and so complete his cleansing.

And lo, this is the teaching of our Rabbis[1]. Whence do we learn this[2]. From the first teaching[3]; for R. Simeon ben Betheyra[4] bore testimony with reference to the ashes of the purification for sin, that, if an unclean person touch the extremity of them, he makes all of them unclean; and there is a teaching to the effect that R. Akiba added[5] this. R. Lakish said in the name of Bar Kaphra[6], The addition was only necessary for the rest of the meat-offering. For the teaching of the Law is, What stands in need of a vessel, the vessel includes it; what does not stand in need of a vessel, the vessel does not include it. But our Rabbis went farther and ordained that although a thing do not necessarily belong to a vessel, the vessel includes it. This will be all right as regards flour[7], but what is to be said about incense and frankincense[8]? R. Nachman said that Rabbah bar Abuah said, It is as though men heaped things up upon[9] a large piece of leather[10]. According to the Law if it have an inside, it includes them; if it have not an inside, it does not include them. But our Rabbis went farther and ordained that although it have no inside, it includes them[11]. And the view of R. Chanin differs from that of R. Chia bar Abba. For R. Chia bar Abba says that

---

[1] And not that of Holy Writ.

[2] viz., that it is Rabbinic only.

[3] Which, as referring to the ashes of the heifer and not to the sacrifice of the altar, is necessarily Rabbinic.

[4] He was one of three brothers, Joshua and Jehudah being the other two. They were all leading teachers in Palestine before Hillel and Shammai, and withdrew from the leadership when Hillel came from Babylonia. See Wolf, ii. 842.

[5] And so it must have been subsequent to that to which it was added.

[6] Private chaplain (see pp. 103, note 1, and 124, note 6) to Rabbi (see p. 2, note 9), and teacher of Osha'iah ben Rabba, son of Rabbi. See Wolf, ii. 879.

[7] Dough; for it can stand alone and thus need not be in a vessel, which incense and frankincense on the other hand require.

[8] Incense and frankincense, as symbolic of prayer (Ps. cxli. 2; Apoc. v. 8, viii. 3, 4), are considered of special sanctity.

[9] Lit., upon the back of.

[10] Buxtorf (s.v.) renders קרטבלא *pulvinar oblongum coriaceum*, an oblong leather cushion.

[11] And so by this Rabbinic extension of the law relating to a vessel, so that it should include the case of the piece of leather, Akiba's teaching, which he gave in the name of the Sopherim (see Introd. p. vii.) as to incense and frankincense, was justified.

24 a, i. 13. R. Jochanan says, This Mishnah is taught from the testimony of R. Akiba[1].

The unclean in the fourth degree in the case of hallowed things is disqualified[2]. There is a Baraitha, viz., R. Jose said, How is it in the case of the unclean in the fourth degree that in the matter of the hallowed things he is disqualified? But this depends on a logical argument. For look you, He who has entered on the last stage of his atonement[3], while he is free as regards heave-offering, is disqualified as regards hallowed things[4]. Is it not just, seeing that a man who is unclean in the third degree is disqualified as regards heave-offering, that he should become disqualified as regards hallowed things, if unclean in the fourth degree? But we have learned from the Law that he who is unclean in the third degree is disqualified as regards hallowed things. And that he who is unclean in the fourth degree is so, we have learned, as above, by an *a fortiori* argument.

Whence do we learn from the Law that he who is unclean in the third degree is disqualified as regards hallowed things? Because it is written, "And the flesh that toucheth any unclean thing shall not be eaten." Are we not here treating of the touching of a thing of secondary uncleanness[5]? And the Merciful One says, It "shall not be eaten." That which is unclean in the fourth degree is proved to be disqualified by the *a fortiori* argument, as we have said.

Lev. vii. 19.

And in the case of heave-offering, though one of his hands be unclean etc.[6] R. Shezbi[7] says, It is in case of contact[8] that this

---

[1] Whereas Chanin said (see p. 128) that it came from the passage, Numb. vii. 14 sqq. Akiba, as pupil of Eliezer ben Hyrkanus, is a main source of tradition.

[2] See p. 116.

[3] i.e., who is awaiting sunrise, to offer the sacrifices needful to complete his cleansing. See pp. 117, note 3, and 126, note 8.

[4] Thus then hallowed things are shewn to call for weightier observance than heave-offering.

[5] In other words, must not the expression "any unclean thing" in that passage include the unclean in the second degree?

[6] See p. 116.

[7] For him see *Juch.*, p. 189 b. He was a contemporary of Chasda (for whom see p. 21, note 1). He and Abai were Babylonian teachers, and were often engaged in discussions together.

[8] i.e., if one hand be so near the other that there is a risk that the unclean hand may touch the clean one which is in contact with the hallowed things.

teaching holds, but in case there is no contact, it does not hold¹.   24 a, ii. 1.
Abai replied to him, A wiped hand² renders its fellow unclean, so far as to make unclean for hallowed things, but not for heave-offering. These are the words of Rab. R. Jose in the name of R. Jehudah says, This is the case so far as to disqualify, but not to render unclean. If thou sayest, No doubt this is so in cases of non-contact, then here comes in the importance³ of the word "wiped;" but if thou sayest, In case of contact, yes; in case of non-contact, no; then what is the importance of the "wiped" hand⁴? It has been reported⁵ also that Resh Laḳish said, The Mishnah refers only to his own hand and not to the hand of his companion; but R. Jochanan 24 b said, Whether it be his own hand or the hand of his companion, with that same hand he may disqualify, but not render unclean. Whence did he learn this⁶? From the fact that it has been taught in the latter portion of the Mishnah, *for the hand makes its fellow unclean in the case of hallowed things, but not in the case of heave-offering*⁷.

Why am I told this again⁸? Lo, it was taught in the preceding clauses of the same Mishnah. But do you not think that one should learn from it that it is for the purpose of bringing in the hand of his companion? And moreover so powerful was it

---

¹ Thus, if it be a case of non-contact, the man, according to Shezbi, may take hold even of hallowed things. Abai replies, No, for if the point lay in the matter of contact or non-contact, the Mishnah of Rab (which he now quotes) concerning the wiped hand, would contain nothing new, a thing impossible to admit.

² As involving the risk that uncleanness may accrue in the wiping, moist things being specially liable (see p. 123, note 6) to receive and communicate uncleanness.

³ Lit., increase (of information).

⁴ If the clean hand is free for hallowed things, simply on condition of non-contact with its fellow, it can be of no importance whether that fellow-hand is wiped or not; but if on the contrary the uncleanness of that fellow-hand, irrespective of the question of *actual* contact, renders unclean or disqualifies the clean hand, by reason of the *risk* of contact involved, then it is a piece of additional information to tell us that the wiping of that fellow-hand, as involving it in the risk of receiving uncleanness from that which wipes, is held to render it (practically) unclean.

⁵ איתמר denotes a tradition of later date than either canonical or non-canonical Mishnahs.

⁶ For Jochanan was not himself a Mishnic teacher, and therefore we must shew that his teaching could be deduced from a Mishnah.

⁷ See page 116.

⁸ Lit., Lo, why again to me?

24 b, i. 8. that Resh Laḳish changed his view about it, for R. Jonah[1] said, that R. Ami said, that Resh Laḳish said, Whether it be his own hand, or the hand of his companion, with that same hand he may disqualify but not render unclean.

Yadaim, iii. 2.
And to shew that there are things which can disqualify without rendering unclean, here is a teaching[2]. For there is a canonical Mishnah, All that disqualifies for a heave-offering, renders the hands unclean, so as to be of secondary impurity. And a hand renders its fellow unclean. These are the words of R. Joshua. And other wise men[3] say, The hands themselves are only of secondary uncleanness, and that which is secondary does not produce a second[4] in the case of ordinary things. Do you think that it cannot make a second? Nay, you say, it makes a third. Or perhaps it makes neither a second nor a third. But moreover we have a Baraitha to quote on our side[5]. For there is a Baraitha, A wiped hand renders its fellow unclean, so far as to render unclean for hallowed things, but not for heave-offering. These are the words of Rabbi. R. Jose in the name of R. Jehudah says, With that same hand he may disqualify, but not render unclean.

Men may eat dry food with ceremonially unclean hands etc.[6] There is a Baraitha, viz., R. Chănina ben Antigonus[7] said, Does such a question as whether a thing be dry or wet exist as regards hallowed things? Nay, does not love for the hallowed things make men careful where they are concerned? Yea, every one will admit that it was not necessary to say this. But this is the case supposed, viz., that a man's companion put a piece of the hallowed things into his mouth, or he put it into his own mouth with a spindle or with a skewer[8], or attempted to eat along with these[9] an onion or garlic taken from unconsecrated things. Our

---

[1] A pupil of Zera. See *Juch.* p. 152 a.

[2] Meaning that it was not left for these two Rabbis to discuss it. It had been discussed already.

[3] 1st century teachers.   [4] But rather, a third.

[5] As shewing that there are things which can disqualify without rendering unclean. The last words of the Baraitha are those referred to.

[6] See p. 117.

[7] Chănina ben Antigonus was a priest, a contemporary of Aḳiba (for whom see p. 15, note 8). See Wolf, ii. 835; *Juch.* p. 85 a.

[8] A spindle and a skewer, not being either of them a vessel (inasmuch as they have no inside), cannot contract uncleanness.

[9] The hallowed things.

Rabbis decided that this should be the case for hallowed things; **24 b, ii. 4.** for the heave-offering our Rabbis decided that it should not be the case[1].

He who is in deep mourning and he who lacks atonement etc.[2] What is the reason? Seeing that hitherto they were under restrictions, our Rabbis compel them to be dipped.

MISHNAH.

III. (4) Weightier rules on the other hand hold in a heave-offering, for in Judea people are believed with regard to the purity of wine and oil all the days of the year, but, at the time of the vintage and the oil pressing[3], with regard to the heave-offering also. When the vintage and the oil pressing are over, and they bring to him[4] a cask of wine for heave-offering, he does not receive it from him, but he leaves it for the next vintage. But if he say to him, I have separated and put into the midst of it a fourth part[5] of something consecrated for hallowed things, he is believed. In the case of vessels of wine and vessels of oil which are mixed, men are believed with regard to them at the time of vintage and oil pressing and for seventy **25 a** days before the vintage[6].

[1] The object was to avoid the danger that the person with unclean hands, into whose mouth the hands of the clean person, or the spindle or skewer, were introducing the hallowed thing, might touch it afterwards with his own (unclean) hands for the purpose of pushing it in. The Rabbis decided that the man's deep reverence for hallowed things would prevent the risk of his touching it, and that therefore he might safely be allowed to have it placed thus in his mouth. To heave-offering, however, as being naturally viewed with a somewhat less degree of reverence, they held that the same reasoning did not apply.

[2] See p. 117.

[3] Lit., the wine-presses and the oil-vats.

[4] The priest.

[5] The fourth part was the smallest portion over which a blessing could be said, and thus was the smallest portion suited for a libation.

[6] The general principle is that, when hallowed things are in question, men may always be trusted to have reverence enough to make them careful, but in the case of heave-offering this will only be so at special times, when every one is on the alert and has his attention called to the subject. Further, this distinction has reference only to "the common person." The careful and observant man (חָבֵר, See p. 141, note 1) will be equally trustworthy as regards both, and that too without distinction of seasons.

GEMARA.

25 a, i. 3. In Judea, yes; but in Galilee, no. What is the reason? Resh Laḳish said, Because there is a strip of Cuthites[1] making a separation between them. But, says some one, let us bring it in a box, a chest, or a balloon[2]. Nay, what Mishnic authority is there for so doing? It is the teaching of Rabbi. For he said, A tent projected is not a real tent[3]. And there is a Baraitha, That which enters the land of the Gentiles in a box, a chest, or a balloon, Rabbi declares unclean, but R. Jose bar Jehudah[4] clean. But let one bring it in an earthenware vessel tied round with a line of thread. For R. Eliezer said, They teach in a Baraitha[5], Hallowed things are not preserved from uncleanness by a line of thread. But against this view of R. Eliezer is another Baraitha, viz., the ashes of the heifer[6] are not preserved by a line of thread. What[7]? are *they* not? Then hallowed things *are* preserved. No, says another[8], but the water destined to receive the ashes, but not yet consecrated, is preserved by a line of thread. And yet Ola said, Learned and observant men purify[9] in Galilee. Yes, but they leave the

---

[1] כות׳. Probably גוים was the original reading, inasmuch as that is the word ("Gentiles") which is used in the Baraitha immediately afterwards quoted as an authority on the question.

[2] Lit., a tower. See p. 90, note 8.

[3] Rabbi's argument is that although a balloon may in some respects resemble a tent, its similarity does not extend so far as to give it the power by which a tent, as being a partition, would intercept the contamination resulting *in transitu* from the religiously pestilential band of Cuthites.

[4] There seem to have been two of this name, the one of Babylon, the other of Jerusalem. The latter is the one here referred to. See *Juch.* p. 70 a.

[5] שונין, as an equivalent to תניא, is a somewhat unusual expression.
For "the ashes of the heifer" the Heb. has simply, *sin*.

[7] Says the teacher of the Baraitha (about the 5th century).

[8] Another teacher of about the same date, who means here that the contrast does not lie, as the former supposed, between the ashes of the heifer and hallowed things, but between the ashes of the heifer and water destined to receive the ashes but not yet consecrated.

[9] i.e., their wine, oil etc., for hallowed things. Therefore (he implies,) they cannot be affected by this band of Cuthites. The reply is, Nay, they do not attempt to send them up to Jerusalem, but wait, expecting Elijah's speedy arrival. For passover usages connected with this expectation, see *Dict. of Bible*, Art "Passover," ii. 715, note 1. "A cup of wine is poured out for him,

hallowed things alone, and when Elijah returns, then he will cleanse them.

But at the time of the vintage...[they are believed] *with regard to the heave-offering also*[1]. But against this I adduce[2] the following Baraitha, viz., He who finishes his olives shall leave aside one box and place it before the eyes[3] of the priest.   R. Nachman said, There is no difficulty. The one[4] is the case of new, the other[5] of old ones. R. Ada bar Ahaba[6] said to him, For instance things like those belonging to the house of thy father. R. Joseph said, The teaching refers to Galilee.   Abai replied to him, The other side of Jordan and Galilee, lo, these are as Judea.   Another explains, They are believed about wine at the time of wine, and oil at the time of oil, but not about wine at the time of oil, and not about oil at the time of wine.   But[7] it is perfectly clear that it is as originally explained[8].

When the vintage and the oil pressing are over, and they bring to him a cask of wine..., he does not receive it from him, but he leaves it for the next vintage[9].   R. Shesheth's disciples asked him, Suppose that it is over, and yet he receives it, what about the law that he shall leave it for the next vintage?   He said to them, Ye have this teaching[10] already. Take the case of a learned and observant man and a common person who are their father's joint heirs. The common person may say to him[11], Take thou the wheat that is in such a place[12], and I will take the wheat that is in

and stands all night upon the table. Just before the filling of the cups of the guests the fourth time there is an interval of dead silence, and the door of the room is opened for some minutes to admit the prophet."

[1] See p. 133.
[2] Lit., But I throw upon it.
[3] Lit. eye, but a final ' seems to have accidentally dropped out of the mss. The argument is; the presentation to the priest that he might test it shewed that the man was not necessarily to be believed.
[4] When they are believed.
[5] When they have to be shewn to the priest.
[6] He is said to have been born on the day that Rabbi died. He was a pupil of Rab at Sora. See Wolf, ii. 867; *Juch.* p. 106.
[7] Says the Talmud editor.
[8] i.e., by Nachman.   [9] See p. 133.
[10] viz., the teaching which immediately follows, and which unfolds the duty of the priest, as a learned and observant man, under such circumstances.
[11] His brother.
[12] Less likely to be liable to uncleanness, though perhaps of less value also.

25 b, i. 4. such a place; take thou the wine that is in such a place, and I will take the wine that is in such a place. But he may not say to him, Take thou the liquid and I will take the dry; take thou the wheat, and I will take the barley. And there is a further teaching with regard to it. That same learned and observant man burns the liquid and leaves the dry. Why? Let him leave it for the next vintage. It may be one of the things which have no vintage¹. Let him leave it for one of the great Feasts². It may be one of the things which will not keep till the Feast. But if he say, I have separated and put into the midst of it the fourth part of something consecrated for hallowed things, he is believed.

P'sachim 92 b, i. 1. We have a canonical Mishnah elsewhere³, viz., The house of Shammai and the house of Hillel agree, that we are to investigate a field in which a person is buried⁴, for those who are keeping the Passover, but we do not investigate for those who desire to eat heave-offering. What is the meaning of investigate? R. Jehudah said that Samuel said, A man blows upon the unclean place⁵ as he walks along. And R. Chia bar Abba in the name of Ola said, An unclean place of this sort that is trodden⁶ is clean. For those keeping Passover they⁷ did not insist upon their decisions, as it was a case of cutting off, but for those who desired to eat heave-offering they did insist on their decisions, as it was a case of death⁸. It was a question for them, In the case of a man who has investi-

---

¹ i.e., which are not wine; e.g., leguminous crops.

² Passover, Pentecost, Tabernacles, when even the common person (see p. 133, note 6) is held to be clean. For the Hebrew רגל, here translated "one of the great Feasts," see pp. 1, note 4, and 7, note 1.

³ Lit., there.

⁴ Inasmuch as to pass through such a field makes a man unclean.

⁵ Lit., house (place) of separation.

⁶ Lit., thrashed, e.g., the *threshold* of a door, which is accustomed to be trodden.

⁷ The Rabbis.

⁸ In the case of heave-offering, to eat when ceremonially unclean involved death (Lev. vii. 14, 20). Yet on the other hand in the matter of heave-offering it was not essential to go and eat, while in the case of Passover, inasmuch as to abstain from eating involved for those not exempted cutting off (Ex. xii. 19), it was essential that a person should go and eat. Hence in the former case, unlike the latter, the provision of means, by which the person might pass through a place unclean by reason of a dead body, was not needful, for he need not go at all. Therefore in the case of heave-offering they insisted on the law that to pass through a place thus unclean involved defilement.

gated for his Passover, what about his eating his heave-offering[1]. 25 b, i. 23.
Ola said, He who has investigated for his Passover is free to eat his heave-offering, but Rabbah bar Ola[2] said, He who has investigated for his Passover is forbidden to eat his heave-offering. That old man[3] said to him, Do not thou contradict Ola's assertion, for there is a canonical Mishnah which bears him out[4], viz., But if he say[5], I have separated and put into the midst of it a fourth part of something consecrated for hallowed things, he is believed. Consequently, seeing that he is believed about hallowed things, he is believed also about heave-offering[6]; and so here too, seeing that he is believed about passover, he is believed also about heave-offering. Chag. 24 b, ii. 15.

In the case of vessels of wine and vessels of oil etc.[7] There is a Baraitha, viz., They are not believed either about the cans or about the heave-offering. Cans belonging to what? If I say, cans belonging to hallowed things; but in that case, seeing that he is believed about the hallowed things, he is believed also about cans which belong to those hallowed things. But are they cans belonging to heave-offerings that are meant? But then it is a clear case. Look now. About heave-offering he is not believed. Shall he be believed about cans that belong to it? But it is a case of cans which are empty of hallowed things, and it is during the remaining days of the year[8]. But in the case of those full of heave-offering and at the time of the vintage they are believed.

---

[1] i.e., may he take advantage of the same blowing to obtain heave-offering?

[2] Ola's son. See Wolf, ii. 880, who however spells רבא, and so too in *Juch.* p. 183 *b.*

[3] Traditionally said to be Elijah.

[4] Lit., like unto him.

[5] See p. 133. The quotation here omits "to him."

[6] As being thus mixed with it. For the presence of the hallowed things in it proves that care has been taken. The hallowed things are offered *to God*, and therefore, where they are concerned, the man may be trusted to have used proper precautions. The heave-offering is given to the *priest*, a fact which may make all the difference as regards the man's care.

[7] See p. 133.

[8] And therefore he must not be believed. The heave-offering however, which is brought to the priest in cans which for these reasons cannot be regarded as certainly clean, may itself be received on condition that it be emptied into the priest's cans. This may seem inconsistent, but then we must remember that there are inconsistencies also in the Scriptures (see p. 71, note 1), and the Rabbis relax in this case for the priest's sake, that the man, who may be very poor, may not be deprived of the heave-offering.

25 b, ii. 12. We have a canonical Mishnah, viz., vessels of wine and vessels of oil which are mixed[1], why should they not be mixed as regards heave-offering? Those of the house of R. Chia say, Mixed as regards hallowed things. But how can there be a mixture as regards hallowed things[2]. Those of the house of R. El'ai[3] say, Yes, in the case of one who is in the act of purifying his untouched[4] produce, to take out of it the libations[5].

For seventy days before the vintage[6]. Abai said, Learn from this that it is decided[7] that the farmer shall go up[8] to cleanse the casks seventy days before the time of the presses.

Mishnah.

III. (5) From Modiim[9] and inwards[10] men are believed with regard to earthenware vessels; from Modiim and outwards they are not believed. How is that made out[11]? The potter who is selling the pots goes inwards from Modiim. That is the potter, and those are the pots, and those are the buyers[12]. He is believed. If he goes out, he is not believed.

---

[1] i.e., which have not yet paid their tithe (to the Levite) nor heave-offering (to the priest), but still have these (not the hallowed things, which the man is not bound to pay) "mixed" up in them.

[2] For that which is consecrated for hallowed things becomes so in the act of separation, and is not, like tithe, a thing which a man is bound to pay.

[3] Father of the R. Jehudah ben El'ai, who, when arrayed in his robes, is said by the Gemara to have looked like an angel of the Lord.

[4] i.e., which has not yet paid dues of any kind.

[5] Because in such a case it is as good as consecrated.

[6] See p. 133.

[7] Lit., the judgment (decision).

[8] Lit., it is incumbent upon him, the farmer, to go up etc.

[9] See Neubauer's *Géog. du Talmud*, p. 99. Modiim (= Modin, the dwelling-place of the Maccabees, 1 Macc. ii. 1) was fifteen miles N. of Jerusalem; now known as *El-Mediyeh*. It was the burial place of Mattathias, father of Judas Maccabæus, and his sons (ibid. xiii. 25—30). His son Simon is said to have adorned the tomb with pillars and carvings of ships, placed so as to be visible from the sea.

[10] i.e., between it and Jerusalem.

[11] מִ, as, אַן, where? עַד, side, part. Of these three the word in the original is compounded.

[12] i.e., all are well known.

Gemara.

There is a Baraitha, viz., Modiim is sometimes within, sometimes without. How is that made out? The potter goes out, and the merchant goes in. In that case it is considered within. Both go in or both go out. It is considered without. Abai said, We also have a teaching, viz., as above. The potter who sells the pots, and goes inwards from Modiim, is believed. The reason is that he has gone inwards from Modiim. Lo, by inference Modiim itself is not believed. Nay, but let me tell you the end of the same teaching. If he goes out, he is not believed. Lo, by inference Modiim itself *is* believed. But do we not learn it[1] thence? The one case[2] is when the potter goes out and the learned and observant man goes in; the other is when they both go out or both come in. Learn it hence.

There is a Baraitha. Men are believed as regards small earthen vessels for hallowed things. Resh Laḳish said, And provided that they are such as are taken in one hand[3]; but R. Jochanan said, Even though they are such as are not taken in one hand. Resh Laḳish said, They do not teach this except as regards empty vessels, but full ones not; but R. Jochanan said, Even though they be full, and even though its veil[4] be within it; and Rabba says and R. Jochanan admits it, even in the case of drinkables which are actually unclean. And be not surprised at this; for lo, in the case of bowls full of drinkables the bowls may be unclean with an uncleanness of seven days[5], while the drinkables are clean[6].

Mishnah.

III. (6) The tax-collectors who have gone into the midst of a house, and so too the thieves who have restored the vessels, are believed, when they say, We have not touched[7]. And in

---

[1] viz., that this is the explanation.

[2] That in which Modiim is reckoned as inside, or, in other words, that in which the potter is believed.

[3] For the use of two hands increases risk.

[4] אֲפִיקַרְסוּת, as an illustration taken from what such a vessel often carried.

[5] i.e., requiring seven days for their purification.

[6] This apparent inconsistency arises from the enactments of the Law, behind which we cannot go. See p. 137, note 8.

[7] In such a way as to render unclean.

26 a, i. 17. Jerusalem they are believed as regards hallowed things, and at the time of a Feast as regards heave-offering also.

Gemara.

But against this I adduce the following Baraitha, viz., In the case of the tax-collectors who have gone into the midst of the house, the house is wholly unclean.   There is no difficulty.   The one is when there is a stranger with them, the other, when there is not a stranger with them.   For there is a canonical Mishnah, If there is a stranger with them, they are believed, when they say, We did not enter, but they are not believed, when they say, We entered but we did not touch.   But, it is asked, What does this mean, "if there is a stranger with them"?   Behold, R. Jochanan and R. El'azar reply. The one says, When a stranger stands beside them; and the other says, When the government official stands beside them.   What is the difference between them?   There is this difference between them. A stranger is not of importance[1].

Taharoth, vii. 6.

And so too the thieves, who have restored the vessels. But against this I adduce the following Baraitha, viz., In the case of the thieves who have gone into the midst of the house, only the place where the thieves' feet trode is unclean.   R. Phinehas[2] said in the name of Rab, They are to be believed only in case they have repented.   You can even press it out from the language of the Mishnah, for the teaching is, *Who have restored the vessels*.   Learn it thence.

And in Jerusalem they are believed as regards hallowed things. There is a Baraitha, viz., They are believed as regards large earthen vessels for sacrifice.   And why all this discussion?   Because they do not make ovens[3] in Jerusalem.

And at the time of a Feast as regards heave-offering also. Whence these words?   R. Joshua ben Levi[4] said, Because the Scripture

---

[1] While the government official is of importance.

[2] For the several Rabbis of this name see Juch. 177 *b*.

[3] To bake earthenware. The object was to avoid smoke, which might deface the beauty of the buildings. Thus they had to be made fifteen miles away. Otherwise (the Talmud means) the question would not have arisen.

[4] Head of the Academy at Lod (Lydda), and teacher of Jochanan (for whom see p. 11, note 7). He lived soon after Rabbi and is accordingly placed by some with the Tannaim, by others with the Amoraim. See Wolf, ii. 812, 874; Etheridge, p. 145.

says, "So all the men of Israel were gathered against the city, *knit together* as one man¹." The Scripture makes them all learned and observant men. 26 a, ii. 3.
Jud. xx. 11.

Mishnah.

III. (7 a) He that opens his cask and he that commences his dough at the time of a festival, R. Jehudah says, he shall finish it, but wise men say, He shall not finish it.

Gemara.

R. Ami and R. Isaac Naphcha sat at the portico of R. Isaac Naphcha. One began² and said, What is the meaning of the words, He shall keep it for another festival? He said to him, Every one's³ hand has been handling it, and dost *thou* say, He shall keep it for another festival? He said to him, Nay, but hitherto as well has not every one's hand been handling it? He said to him, That is quite true⁴; yet hitherto the uncleanness of a common person in a festival the Merciful One cleanseth. But now⁵ it is a case of uncleanness. Shall we say so? For we have one Baraitha which teaches, He shall leave it for another festival, and another Baraitha, He shall not leave it for another festival. Is not this a non-canonical Mishnah? Nay, it is older⁶. Lo, the Baraitha, "He shall leave it," is identical with the teaching of R.

---

¹ The Heb. root means, to join. The substantive, rendered in the above passage, "knit together," came in the later Heb. to denote a man learned in Rabbinic rules and observant of them. The argument deduced from the above-quoted passage is that in any assembly (whether, as there, brought together for a bad, or, as at a Festival, for a good purpose) Israel thus united consists of learned and observant men, who may therefore be trusted to use all precautions. Cf. the fanciful inference from Numb. xiv. 27 (עֵדָה) that ten (the number of the spies, when Caleb and Joshua are subtracted from them) is the *minimum* which constitutes a congregation. See *Pirķe Aboth*, iii. 9.

² Lit., opened (his mouth).
³ Including the hands of the common people.
⁴ Lit., Thus now (הכי השתא, more literally, at this hour) it is all right.
⁵ After the Festival.
⁶ For it is substantially identical with the words of the canonical Mishnah above, since it can, though not at first sight, be derived from the words of that Mishnah.

26 a, ii. 15. Jehudah, and the Baraitha, "he shall not leave it," with that of our Rabbis[1]. But[2] bring your reasoning powers to bear. Lo, R. Jehudah said, Let him finish; but this, which is equivalent to the Baraitha, "let him not leave," is identical with the teaching of R. Jehudah; and the other, which is equivalent to the Baraitha, "let him leave," is identical with the teaching of our Rabbis.

And why shall he not leave it? Because it is not necessary to leave it.

MISHNAH.

III. (7 b) As soon as the festival is over, they make them pass on to the cleansing of the court. But if the festival is over on the sixth day, they do not make them pass on, on account of the honour of the Sabbath. R. Jehudah says, Also not on the fifth day, for the priests are not at leisure.

GEMARA.

There is a Baraitha which says that the priests are not at leisure because of the removing of the fat.

MISHNAH.

III. (8) How is that made out, that they make them pass on to the cleansing of the court? They dip the vessels which 26 b were in the sanctuary, and say to them[3], Be ye clean that ye touch not the table. All the vessels that were in the sanctuary had second and third sets, so that, if the first became unclean, they might bring the second instead of them. All the vessels which were in the sanctuary were subject to dipping, except the altar of gold and the altar of bronze, because that they were like the floor. These are the words of R. Eliezer. But wise men say, Because they were overlaid.

[1] i.e., the other wise men, quoted above.
[2] This is spoken by the Talmud editor. He means that the precepts, Leave, and, Do not leave, are to be assigned indeed to the above-mentioned authorities, but conversely (to the statement just made), and in accordance with the Mishnah given above.
[3] The priests.

Gemara.

There is a Baraitha, Be ye clean, lest ye touch the table or the lamp. And yet we have a Baraitha to this effect, viz., What is the reason that we are not taught this with reference to the lamp? It is because the table is called in Holy Writ perpetual, the lamp is not called in Holy Writ perpetual[1]. And another says, Since Holy Writ says, "and the lamp over against the table," it is as though it were called in Holy Writ perpetual. But another says, It was only to fix its place that it comes. But you may get it out for me in this way. For it is a vessel of wood which is made to rest; and every vessel of wood which is made to rest, is not liable to uncleanness. What is the reason then that it is liable to uncleanness? Because it is like a sack in this respect, and therefore can contract uncleanness. As a sack is moveable, whether empty or full, so also everything which is moveable whether empty or full is liable to cleansing. This[2] also is moveable, whether empty or full[3]. As is the teaching of Resh Lakish; for Resh Lakish said, What is the meaning of the passage, "upon the clean table?" Undoubtedly it implies that it might be unclean. And why? It is a vessel of wood made to rest, and as such it does not receive uncleanness; but it informs us that they raise it up, and exhibit the shewbread on it to those who come up to the festival, and one says to them, Look at the love of God in giving you food. Its end[4] was like its placing[5]. For R. Joshua ben Levi said, A great miracle was wrought in the shewbread.

26 b, i. 8.

Ex. xxvi. 35.

Lev. xxiv. 6.

---

[1] Lit., (As for) the table there is written in (its case) "perpetual;" (as for) the lamp, there is not written in (its case) " perpetual."

[2] The table.

[3] The argument may be stated thus. Holy Writ shews us what is capable of impurity by saying, "Upon whatsoever any of them, when they are dead, doth fall, it shall be unclean; whether it be any vessel of wood, or raiment, or skin, or sack, etc." (Lev. xi. 32.) From this verse it is inferred that nothing is liable to contract uncleanness that does not correspond in its mobility to a sack. Now the mobility of a sack is of this nature, that it can be moved, either empty or full. Such also is the nature of a table's mobility. Therefore, we conclude, a table is liable to contract uncleanness.

[4] Removal.

[5] Arrangement in order.

26 b, ii. 3.
1 Sam.
xxi. 6.

Kelim,
xxii. 1.

As its placing was miraculous, so was its end; for it is said, "to put hot bread in the day that it was taken away¹." But you may get it out for me in this way. It is because it is overlaid. For lo, there is a canonical Mishnah, The table or the tripod table², which have had a piece broken off, or have been covered with marble³, and there has been left on them a place to rest cups, may become unclean. R. Jehudah says, A place to rest cakes. And if thou sayest, It is a different matter with shittim wood, which is esteemed highly, and is not valueless, this is all right according to what Resh Lakish says. For he said, Their teaching only refers to tables made of woods⁴ that come from the province of the sea⁵. But in the case of a vessel of Mismim⁶ it is not valueless. This is very good. But according to R. Jochanan who says, Even in the case of a vessel of Mismim also it is valueless, what is there to say? And if thou sayest, The one is the case of an overlaid article which stands, and the other, of an overlaid article which does not stand. Lo, Resh Lakish asks from R. Jochanan, Does the Mishnah treat of an overlaid article which stands, or of an overlaid article which does not stand? of one which has its extremities covered, or of one which has not its extremities covered? And he said to him, There is no difference in this respect between an overlaid article which stands and an overlaid article which does not stand. There is no difference in this respect between one which has its extremities covered, and one which has not its extremities covered. But it is the table itself which makes

27 a the difference. For the merciful One calls it wood, as it is written,

Ezek. xli. 22.

"The altar was of wood, three cubits high, and the length thereof two cubits; and the corners thereof, and the length thereof, and the walls thereof, were of wood: and he said unto me, This is the table

---

¹ The word חם, from its position in the Heb. sentence, may be made to belong to either of the two verbs. The Rabbis take it as belonging to both.

² Greek δελφική.

³ A material which on account of the closeness of the texture cannot be made unclean.

⁴ אַכְסְלֹגָּיִם (also written אכסלגס and אכסלגיא) is probably connected with ξύλον, wood, and may have meant a special kind of wood. Some take it as the name of a city or other place from which tables of this material were procured.

⁵ i.e., from over the Mediterranean.

⁶ The locality thus named has not been identified.

that is before the LORD." He began with "altar," and he ended with "table." R. Jochanan and Resh Laḳish say both of them, At the time that the Holy House was set up, an altar made atonement for a man; now a man's table makes atonement for him. 27 a, l. 5.

All the vessels that were in the sanctuary had second and third sets etc.[1] The altar of bronze, how had this a counterpart? Because it is written, "An altar of earth thou shalt make unto me." The altar of gold, how had this a counterpart? Because it is written, "the lamp and the *altars*." The altars are placed in comparison one with the other. But wise men say, Because they are overlaid. So much the worse for your argument[2]. Since they are overlaid, they may become unclean. I will tell you the true explanation, viz., the wise men pronounced them capable of becoming unclean[3], because they were overlaid; or, if you like, our Rabbis said to R. Eliezer, What is thine opinion? Is it because they are covered over? No, their covering is of no avail in respect of them[4]. Ex. xx. 24. Numb. iii. 31.

R. Abohu said that R. Eliezer said, As to the disciples of the wise, the flame of Gehenna has no power over them. For this is shewn by an *a fortiori* argument drawn from the salamander. And what is the salamander? It is a creature of fire. He that anoints himself with its blood, flame has no power over him. How much more the disciples of the wise, whose whole body is fire, as it is written, "Is not my word like as fire[5], saith the LORD?" Resh Laḳish said, The flame of Gehenna has no power over the transgressors of Israel. How much less over the altar of gold! As in the case of the altar of gold, upon which is only about the thickness of a denarius of gold, for ever so many years the flame has had no power over it, how much less can it have power over the transgressors of Israel, who are full of the commandments as a pome- Jer. xxiii. 29.

---

[1] See p. 142.
[2] On the contrary; lit. אַד (= עַל דְּ) and רַבָּא. *On the other* side is a *stronger* claim. For the wise men seem to have meant that the overlaying makes them to be free from the liability to contract uncleanness, whereas metal has the opposite effect.
[3] Lit., made them unclean.
[4] i.e., in my comparison between the wood of which they are formed, and the gold with which they may be overlaid, the wood prevails.
[5] Lit., thus, like a fire.

27 a, ll. 10. granate is full of seeds, as it is written, "Thy temples are like a
Cant. iv. 3. piece of a pomegranate." Read not, "thy temples¹" but, the vain
fellows² that are in thee.

May our return be to thee, "Weightier rules hold in hallowed things³ etc."

¹ רַקָּתֵךְ.
² רֵקָנִין.   Cf. "Raca" (Mt. v. 22).
³ See p. 55, note 2.

GLOSSARY.

BARAITHA (בְּרַיְתָּא, pl. בְּרַיָתוֹת) denotes a law or principle extraneous (בְּרָא, בַּר, = outside) to the Mishnah, in other words, one which was not included in the collection made by R. Jehudah ha-Nasi (see MISHNAH). In Mishnic times it was the custom for the Tanna (תַּנָּא) or head of the Academy to lecture in a low voice in Hebrew, while another learned man, named the *Amōra* (אֲמוֹרָא; אָמַר, *he said, discoursed*), "received the law from his lips," and delivered it in the vernacular and in a loud voice to the assembled students. The Amora was on this account named also *M'thurg'man* (תּוּרְגְּמָן, מְתוּרְגְּמָן), interpreter (תִּרְגֵּם, Chaldee, *he interpreted*; cf. מְתָרְגָּם, Pu'al part. in Ezra iv. 7, and *Targum*, = *interpretation, commentary*). Sometimes however, in the absence of a Tanna, the *Amora*, especially if eminent for learning, took the lead, and himself set forth new principles or fresh applications of old ones. These Baraithas are constantly cited in the Gemara, introduced by some such form as T'no Rabbanan (תְּנוּ רַבָּנָן), "Our Rabbis have taught," and they are considered practically as authoritative, unless they plainly contradict some Mishnic teaching. "Besides the Baraithas constituting Tosiphtaoth (see TOSIPHTA), Mechilta[1], Siphra and Siphre[2], there are hundreds of other Baraithas found scattered about in both Talmuds. These are however mere fragments of the vast Mishnayoth (entire Mishnic works) composed by Bar Kappara, R. Hiyya [Chia] and hundreds of other teachers, which in course of time must have perished." Art. *Mishnah* (Schiller-Szinessy) in *Encycl. Brit.* 9th ed.

CHAGIGAH (חֲגִיגָה) is a substantive, derived from the Biblical root חגג (used, e.g., of the Passover in Exod. xii. 14), but not itself occurring in the Old Testament. According to its derivation, its primary sense is, *rejoicing*, festival-*joy*. It seems however to have acquired early a special sense in connexion with the Passover Feast[3], viz., a voluntary peace-offering made

[1] A treatise on Exodus xii—xxiii with other fragments ascribed, at least in part, to Ishmael ben Elisha ha-Kohen, who died A.D. 121.

[2] See p. 5.

[3] The Chagigah however was connected with the other great Feasts (Weeks, and Tabernacles) as well.

by individuals. It had to be without blemish, might be either male or female, and could be taken from the herd as well as from the flock. This is shewn by the passage "thou shalt sacrifice the passover unto the Lord thy God, of the flock and the herd, etc.," which most probably[1] refers to the Chagigah, while subsequent verses (5—7) of that passage have to do with the Paschal lamb, with the eating of which it was associated. The manner of offering the Chagigah followed the ritual provided for other private peace-offerings, in all of which the sacrificial meal was the point of main importance. The regulations for these offerings are given in Lev. iii. 1—5, vii. 29—34 (see also 1 Sam. ii. 16). The animal was slain at the sanctuary door, the offerer resting his hand upon the head of the victim. The sacrificer was allowed the flesh (to be eaten within the Temple courts, or in the city, Deut. xxvii. 7), and apparently the skin. The fat and "the inwards" were burnt by the priest as an offering to the LORD, Who granted him as his portion the breast, after he had presented it as a wave-offering. The right-shoulder[2] was presented direct from the sacrificer to the priest. The offerer and his friends might eat their share of the victim on the day on which it was offered or on the day following. Any part that remained till the third day was to be burned[3]. Other passages which are thought to have reference to the Chagigah-offering are Numb. x. 10, Deut. xiv. 26, 2 Chr. xxx. 22, xxxv. 7, 13, which last verse has been adduced to shew that the Chagigah (as included among "other holy offerings") might be boiled as well as roast. Two Chagigah-offerings are spoken of in this treatise, viz., the Chagigah of the 14th and that of the 15th day of the month Nisan. The former was offered towards the end of that day which with the preceding evening constituted, according to the Jewish mode of reckoning[4], the 14th day, and, after sunset had introduced the 15th, it was eaten with the Passover meal. This Chagigah, as being a voluntary offering, might be brought from animals which had been already dedicated under some other head, e.g., as tithe. That of the 15th day on the other hand was considered obligatory, and therefore must consist of what had not yet been consecrated (חוּלִּין). This Chagigah was not necessarily confined to the 15th, although that was the principal day for it. It might also be brought on any subsequent day of the festival. For further remarks on these two Chagigah-offerings, see notes on pp. 35, 36.

If the 14th of Nisan fell on the weekly Sabbath, its Chagigah, unlike the Paschal lamb, could not be slain.

See farther in Edersheim, *The Temple, its Ministry, etc.*, pp. 186, 217.

GEMARA (גְּמָרָא) is the name of the later in date of the two parts of which, speaking generally, each of the Talmudic treatises is composed. (See

---

[1] Onkelos however denies this interpretation, making "flock" to refer to the Paschal lamb, and "herd" alone to denote the source of the Chagigah offering.

[2] Or, right thigh.

[3] See Lev. vii. 16—18, 30—32.

[4] See Gen. i. 5, etc.

Deut. xvi. 2.

MISHNAH.) It contains the decisions and other sayings of the Amoraim (A.D. 220—500. See BARAITHA and Introd. p. vii). The root (נמר), from which it is derived, denotes *completion*, and the word accordingly has been usually taken to indicate the collection of comments upon the Mishnah, which were needful by way of further exposition, in order to set forth, and *complete*, its sense.

But it is very possible that the word may rather be connected with the sense *to learn by rote*, which its root also bears. If so the Gemara will be that which, as being authoritative, is *learned*, as contrasted with that which consists of matters for speculation, i.e., the sayings of the Sabborâim (סבר = to speculate, reason), who[1] followed the Gemaric teachers (Amoraim).

HAGGADAH (הַגָּדָה) from the root נגד, *to extend, to flow*, and hence, *to speak*, is according to Levy (s. v.), quite distinct from אֲגָדָה (never אַגָּדָה), which is from the root גד with א prefixed (cf. for this derivation his article on אֲגָדָה). Haggadah denotes, as opposed to HALACHAH (which see), those parts of the Rabbinic writings, which are not concerned with the development, discussion, and solution of legal matters as such, but confine themselves on the contrary to "the realms of fancy, of imagination, feeling, humour[2]." Thus the Haggadah (*Legend, Saga*) "was only a 'saying,' a thing without authority, a play of fancy, an allegory, a parable, a tale, that pointed a moral and illustrated a question, that smoothed the billows of fierce debate, roused the slumbering attention, and was generally...a comfort and a blessing[3]." While not absolutely restricting itself to subjects suggested by the historical and prophetical Books, it dealt but little with the Torah. (See HALACHAH.) The unseen world, angels, demons, the future glories of Israel, these were subjects on which it allowed the imagination absolutely unfettered licence. It thus presents to us a curious and interesting picture of the speculations, in the weaving of which the Jewish mind of those days found delight and oftentimes doubtless a real relief from the sufferings belonging to their actual surroundings[4].

HALACHAH (הֲלָכָה, הָלַךְ, he went, walked) denotes first the laws according to which a man's conduct, his *walk* in life, is to be ruled, and hence the Rabbinic rules, or decisions, with the discussions through which they are reached, "the process of evolving legal enactments and the enactments themselves"[5] as contrasted with Haggadah (which see). Just as to the mind of the Jew there was a well-defined distinction between the subject-matter and the comparative importance of the Torah ("Books of Moses") on the one hand

---

[1] See Introd. p. viii.
[2] Deutsch, *Literary Remains*, p. 16.
[3] Ibid. p. 17.
[4] See Morrison, *The Jews under Roman Rule* (The Story of the Nations Series), pp. 268 sqq., for illustrations of the nature of Haggadah.
[5] Deutsch, p. 17.

and the remainder of the Old Testament on the other, so the oral tradition differed in its character according as its main concern was with one or the other of these. If it dealt with the Torah, it was called Halachah. In that case "the oral Law had to answer all questions on which the written law was silent. It had to adapt some parts of the written Law to altered social conditions; it had sometimes to modify the rigour of written precepts, and to bring them by a process of interpretation into harmony with the feelings of the age; it had to adjust the written Law to the practical necessities of the times; it had to define the scope of the written Word, and to shew in what circumstances it should be applied; and it had also to solve all difficulties and obscurities in the written text[1]."

MISHNAH (מִשְׁנָה) is the name of the earlier in date of the two parts of which, speaking generally, each of the treatises of the Talmud is made up. It was brought into shape by R. Jehudah ha-Nasi (see p. 2) by selection from the materials existing in his day. The word itself is not found in the Bible, but the cognate form, Mishneh (מִשְׁנֶה), occurs in the following senses, (a) double (Exod. xvi. 5), (b) a copy (Deut. xvii. 18), (c) a secondary (? suburban) portion of Jerusalem (2 Kings xxii. 14), (d) the second rank (2 Kings xxv. 18), (e) one who holds the second rank (2 Chr. xxviii. 7). The primary sense of the root (שׁנה) is *repetition*. Hence comes the meaning of instruction by repetition, which seems to be the underlying notion of the word (compare שׁנּ in Deut. vi. 7), rather than that it is itself a repetition of the written Law. It consists of the sayings of the Tannaim or Chăkamim (A.D. 70—220) and relates as a rule not to dogma but to rites and legislation. Accordingly it contains but little Haggadah. The Gemara, when quoting a fragment of Mishnah belonging to some other Talmudic treatise, introduces it by the word תְּנַן, "we have learnt," as opposed to תַּנְיָא, (there is) "a teaching," or תָּנוּ רַבָּנָן, "our Rabbis have taught," these latter phrases being reserved for Baraithas (= extra-canonical Mishnahs. See BARAITHA).

A cognate word מַתְנִיתָא occurs three times in the Gemara of this treatise (12 a, ii. 34; 13 b, ii. 1, 21) to denote an extra-canonical Mishnah. Many such, not having been included in the collection made by R. Jehudah ha-Nasi, were brought together by Chia[2] and Oshaia[3], but held only a secondary place in Jewish esteem.

RABBAN. The exact limits of this title are difficult to determine.

The facts, as far as they can be ascertained, seem to be as follows. The title was given to the princes (נשׂיאים) of the house of Hillel, down to, but exclusive of, R. Jehudah ha-Nasi, whose son Gamaliel however also bore it (*Pirḳe Aboth*, ii. 8). The princes from Hillel to Jehudah were probably five in number, though others (see Wolf, iv. 389) would make them seven, by inserting another Gamaliel and Simeon between (3) and

---

[1] Morrison, p. 266. [2] See p. 25. [3] See p. 31.

(4) of the following list, viz. (1) Simeon ben Hillel[1], (2) his son, Gamaliel ha-Zaken, (3) Simeon ben Gamaliel, (4) his son Gamaliel the second, or Gamaliel of Jabneh, (5) Simeon, son of Gamaliel the second. These five, together with the son of Jehudah ha-Nasi above referred to, and Jochanan ben Zakkai, constitute the seven Rabbanan.

That the last-named should have acquired the title, though outside the family of Hillel, was probably due, as Levy says (s.v. רַבָּן), to the fact that at the time of the destruction of the Temple, when the succession of princes was interrupted, he, as having been the friend and colleague of (1) and (2), who died violent deaths, as well as from his being from a political point of view the leading man in the nation, was naturally recognised as the most fitting person to preserve the ecclesiastical and literary continuity.

There is a Rabbinic tradition (quoted by Levy, *ibid.*) to the effect that a higher title than Rab is Rabbi; a higher title than Rabbi is Rabban; while greater even than Rabban is the name without any prefix.

The title Rabban was a later word for any prominent teacher. See Introd. p. vii. note 4, and also passages quoted by Levy (s.v.) See also further for the whole subject, R. David Ganz, *Chronologia sacra-profana* (צמח דוד), in Vorst's Latin transl., Leyden, 1644, pp. 87 sqq.; and Schürer's *History of the Jewish People etc.*, Div. II. vol. i., pp. 315, 316 with notes (T. and T. Clark, Edinb. 1885).

R'IYYAH (רְאִיָּה) is a substantive not found in Biblical Hebrew, but, like Chagigah, derived from a verbal root which is familiar in the Old Testament (רָאָה, *to see*; in the passive, *to appear*). In Exod. xxiii. 17 we read, "Three times in the year all thy males shall *appear* before the Lord God." The occurrence of the above-mentioned root in this command suggested the substantive, meaning an *appearing*, a presenting of oneself, a seeing, and being seen in return by God (see p. 16). At the Passover, as well as at the two other great Feasts (Weeks and Tabernacles), there was further obligatory in connexion with this "appearing," a burnt offering, called עוֹלַת רְאִיָּה, "the burnt offering of appearing," or, more briefly, הָרְאִיָּה, "the appearing." This sacrifice, as the word עוֹלָה implies, was wholly consumed on the altar, and thus R'iyyah attains to the secondary sense of holocaust, which it so often bears in this treatise.

TOSIPHTA (תּוֹסִפְתָּא, pl. תּוֹסִפְתָּאוֹת) denotes an *appendix* (יסף, *to add*) to the Mishnah. It is therefore somewhat of the nature of a Baraitha (see that word), but its application is confined to those of the Baraithas which are arranged as supplements to the several Mishnahs to which they belong. These additions to the Mishnah are to be distinguished from the Tosaphoth (תּוֹסָפוֹת), or comments on the Gemara by later Rabbis. See Etheridge, p. 178.

[1] So Ganz, but others (see Dr Ginsburg's article "Gamaliel I." in *Dict. Chr. Biog.*) would make the title begin with (2), thus limiting the total number of Rabbanan to six.

I. INDEX OF BIBLICAL QUOTATIONS.

For the notation here adopted see Introd. pp. xv, xvi.

Genesis i. 1 ... 12 a i 20, 12 a ii 24, 36
i. 2...12 a i 21, 22, 23, 12 b i 2, 15 a i 11
i. 3 ...... 12 a i 23
i. 4 ...... 12 a ii 8
i. 5 ...... 12 a i 24
i. 6 ...... 15 a i 15
i. 7 ...... 15 a i 15
i. 17 ...... 12 a ii 2, 12 b i 32
i. 19 ...... 12 a ii 3
ii. 4 ...... 12 a ii 26
viii. 21 ...... 16 a ii 17
xvii. 1 ...... 12 a ii 21
xxxiii. 12 ...... 5 b i 20
xxxv. 11 ...... 12 a ii 21
xxxvii. 24 ...... 3 a ii 24
xlv. 3 ...... 4 b ii 8

Exodus v. 1 ...... 10 b i 7, 25
v. 25 ...... 6 b i 13
x. 25 ...... 10 b i 9
xii. 14 ...... 9 a i 31, 10 b i 5
xii. 17 ...... 11 b ii 16
xv. 1 ...... 13 b i 28
xx. 1 ...... 3 b i 23
xx. 7 ...... 14 a ii 31
xx. 24 ...... 27 a i 11
xxi. 23 ...... 11 a i 27
xxiii. 14 ... 2 a i 10, 3 a ii 8, 4 a ii 28
xxiii. 15 (beg.) ...... 18 a i 15
xxiii. 15 (end) ...... 7 a ii 7, 15
xxiii. 16 ...... 18 a i 3

Exodus xxiii. 17 ... 2 a ii 16, 4 a i 10, 4 a ii 11, 17, 7 a ii 18, 19, 7 b i 6
xxiii. 18 ...... 10 b i 12
xxiv. 5...6 a ii 19, 20, 6 b ii 12
xxvi. 35 ...... 26 b i 12
xxix. 42 ...... 6 a ii 22
xxxi. 14 ...... 11 b ii 15
xxxv. 5 ...... 10 a i 17

Levit. i. 2, 4 ...... 16 b ii 18
i. 5 ...... 11 a i 34
i. 13 ...... 11 a i 36
vi. 2 (E. V. 9) ...... 10 b i 18
vii. 19 ...... 24 a i 22
xi. 26, 43 ...... 11 a ii 13
xi. 32, 33 ...... 11 a ii 13
xv. 5 (6, 7, 8, 10, 11, 13, 16, 21, 22, 27) ...... 11 a ii 5
xv. 6 ...... 23 b i 11, 14
xviii. 6 ...... 11 b ii 3
xviii. 30 ...... 11 b ii 13, 15
xx. 2 ...... 11 b ii 8
xxii. 4 ...... 4 b i 10
xxii. 24 ...... 14 b ii 15
xxiii. 4 ...... 18 a ii 14
xxiii. 8 ...... 18 a ii 11
xxiii. 16 ...... 17 b ii 6
xxiii. 21, 22 ...... 17 b ii 10
xxiii. 41 (beg.)...9 a i 31, 10 b i 5
xxiii. 41 (end) ...... 9 a ii 6
xxiv. 6 ...... 26 b i 22

INDEX OF BIBLICAL QUOTATIONS.

Levit.	xxiv. 15 .... 11 b ii 7
	xxvii. 2 .... 10 a i 13
Numb.	iii. 31 .... 27 a i 13
	vi. 2 .... 10 a i 14
	vii. 14 (20, 26, 32, 38, 44, 50, 56, 62, 68, 74, 80)...23 b i 19
	vii. 15, 17, etc. .... 6 a ii 2
	xiv. 34 .... 5 b ii 32
	xviii. 5...............11 b ii 16
	xxvii. 20 .... 16 a ii 8
	xxviii. 6 .... 6 b i 9
	xxx. 3 .... 10 a i 21
Deut.	iv. 32 ... 11 b ii 27, 29, 30, 31, 12 a i 1, 2, 6, 12
	vi. 4 .... 3 a ii 37
	x. 14............... 12 b i 28
	xii. 5, 6 .... 4 b i 5, 12
	xvi. 4 .... 10 b i 22
	xvi. 7............... 17 b i 1
	xvi. 8 (beg.) .... 18 a ii 18
	xvi. 8 (end) .... 9 a i 28
	xvi. 9 .... 17 b ii 8
	xvi. 10 .... 8 a i 12, 8 a ii 1
	xvi. 14 .... 8 a ii 16, 8 b i 8
	xvi. 16 ...... 2 a ii 16, 4 a i 11, 4 a ii 11, 7 a ii 18, 19, 7 b i 6, 17 a i 17
	xvi. 17 .... 8 b i 16
	xxvi. 15 .... 12 b ii 15
	xxvi. 17, 18 .... 3 a ii 34
	xxvii. 7 .... 4 b ii 4
	xxviii. 12............... 12 b ii 18
	xxxi. 11.........3 a i 9, 3 a ii 1
	xxxi. 12 (beg.)...3 a i 8, 3 a ii 31
	xxxi. 12 (mid.) ....3 a i 10
	xxxi. 17 .... 5 a ii 30, 34
	xxxi. 18 .... 5 b i 9
	xxxi. 21...............5 a ii 21
	xxxii. 8...............12 b i 24
	xxxiii. 2...............16 a i 2
	xxxiii. 26...............12 b ii 38
	xxxiii. 27...............12 b i 22
Judges	vi. 24 .... 12 b ii 31
	xx. 11 .... 26 a ii 3

1 Sam.	i. 22 .... 6 a i 7
	xxi. 7 (E. V. 6).........26 b ii 3
	xxv. 29...............12 b ii 32
	xxviii. 13 .... 4 b ii 15
	xxviii. 15 .... 4 b ii 12
1 Kings	viii. 13 .... 12 b i 36
	viii. 39, 43, 49 ...... 12 b ii 25
	xix. 11, 12...............16 a i 7
Isaiah	i. 11...............4 b ii 6
	i. 12 .... 4 b i 1, 4 b ii 1
	iii. 1—4 .... 14 a i 31
	iii. 3 .... 13 a ii 1
	iii. 5 .... 14 a i 30
	iii. 6...............14 a ii 26
	iii. 7...............14 a ii 29
	iii. 10...............12 a ii 8
	vi. 2 .... 13 b ii 7
	vi. 3...............13 b ii 15
	xiv. 14 ....13 a i 13
	xiv. 15 .... 13 a i 27
	xxii. 12 .... 5 b i 34
	xxvi. 6 .... 3 a ii 12
	xxxiii. 7 .... 5 b ii 2
	xxxiii. 18...............15 b ii 15
	xxxiv. 11 ....12 a ii 1
	xl. 22 .... 12 b i 31
	xliii. 12 .... 16 a ii 26
	xlv. 18...................... 2 b i 5
	xlviii. 2 .... 16 a i 5
	xlviii. 10 .... 9 b ii 14
	xlviii. 13...............12 a ii 30
	xlviii. 22...............15 a ii 16
	li. 16 .... 5 b i 12
	lvii. 16...............12 b ii 33
	lviii. 2 .... 5 b ii 29
	lix. 17 ....12 b ii 29
	lxi. 7...............15 a i 33
	lxiii. 15...............12 b ii 37
	lxvi. 1 ... 12 a ii 29, 14 a i 28, 16 a i 32
Jerem.	ii. 5 .... 9 b ii 33
	ii. 22 .... 15 a ii 18
	iii. 4...............16 a ii 20
	iii. 14 .... 15 a i 23
	iv. 30 .... 15 b i 1

INDEX OF BIBLICAL QUOTATIONS.

Jerem.	v. 1 .... 14 a ii 36
	xiii. 17 a .... 5 b i 27
	xiii. 17 b .... 5 b ii 4, 9, 10
	xvii. 18 .... 15 a ii 2
	xxiii. 19 .... 13 b ii 33
	xxiii. 29 .... 27 a ii 3
	xlix. 7 .... 5 b i 19
Ezek.	i. 4 .... 13 b i 10
	i. 6 .... 13 b ii 8
	i. 7 .... 13 b ii 18
	i. 10 .... 13 b i 32
	i. 14 .... 13 b i 5
	i. 15 .... 13 b i 19
	i. 22 .... 13 a i 4
	i. 27 .... 13 a ii 26 (bis)
	i. 28 .... 16 a i 29
	ii. 1 (or 3) .... 13 a ii 23
	iii. 12 .... 13 b i 23
	x. 14 ...... 13 b i 34, 13 b ii 3
	xli. 22 .... 27 a i 1
Amos	iv. 13 .... 5 b i 22, 12 b i 18
	v. 15 .... 4 b ii 23
	v. 25 .... 6 b i 13, 10 b i 26
	ix. 6 .... 12 a ii 27
Micah	vii. 5 .... 16 a ii 14
Nahum	i. 4 .... 12 a ii 23
Hab.	ii. 11 .... 16 a ii 21
Zeph.	ii. 3 .... 4 b ii 21
Zech.	viii. 10 .... 10 a i 3
Mal.	ii. 7 .... 15 b i 26
	iii. 5 .... 5 a i 30, 34, 36
	iii. 18 .... 9 b ii 2
Psal.	v. 5 (E. V. 4) .... 12 b ii 23
	xviii. 12 (E. V. 11) ... 12 a i 26, 12 b ii 39
	xxiv. 5 .... 12 b ii 31
	xxv. 6 .... 12 a ii 17
	xxv. 14 .... 3 b ii 1
	xxxiii. 6 .... 14 a i 16

Psal.	xxxvi. 9 .... 12 b ii 30
	xxxviii. 14 (E.V.13) ... 2 b ii 10
	xlii. 9 (E. V. 8) ...... 12 b i 39
	xlv. 10 .... 15 b i 30
	xlvii. 9 .... 3 a ii 19
	xlix. 10, 11 (E. V. 9, 10) ... 5 b ii 24
	l. 16 .... 15 b i 7
	lxv. 7 .... 12 a ii 15
	lxvi. 13 .... 7 a ii 26
	lxviii. 5 (E. V. 4) ... 12 b ii 37
	lxviii. 10 (E. V. 9) ... 12 b ii 34
	lxxviii. 23, 24 .... 12 b i 34
	lxxxix. 15 (E. V. 14) ... 12 a ii 17, 12 b ii 29
	xc. 10 .... 13 a i 16
	xci. 11 .... 16 a ii 24
	xcv. 11 .... 10 a i 16
	xcvi. 6 .... 5 b i 32
	ci. 7 .... 14 b ii 6
	civ. 6 .... 12 b i 18
	cxvi. 15 .... 14 b ii 8
	cxix. 106 ... 10 a i 19, 10 a ii 15
	cxxxvi. 6 .... 12 b i 16
	cxxxix. 5 .... 12 a i 9, 16
	cxlvii. 20 .... 13 a ii 4
	cxlviii. 7, 8 .... 12 b ii 20
	cxlviii. 7, 9, 14 ...... 14 b i 19
	cxlviii. 8 .... 12 b i 20
Prov.	iii. 19 .... 12 a ii 14
	iii. 20 .... 12 a i 15
	ix. 1 .... 12 b i 26
	ix. 5 .... 14 a i 37
	x. 25 .... 12 b i 27
	xiii. 9 .... 12 a ii 9
	xiii. 23 ...... 4 b ii 25, 5 a i 5
	xvi. 10 .... 14 a ii 5
	xxii. 17 .... 15 b i 28
	xxiii. 5 .... 13 b ii 16
	xxv. 16 .... 14 b ii 11
	xxv. 17 .... 7 a ii 24
	xxvii. 26 .... 13 a ii 20
	xxvii. 8 .... 9 b ii 32
Job	ii. 3 .... 5 a i 13
	ix. 6 .... 12 b i 14
	xii. 4 .... 5 b ii 27

Job	xv. 15	5 a i 15	Lam.	iii. 23	14 a i 13
	xviii. 19	15 b i 22		iii. 29	4 b ii 20
	xxii. 16	13 b ii 35, 14 a i 8			
	xxv. 3	13 b ii 26	Eccles.	i. 4	5 a i 6
	xxvi. 11	12 a ii 16		i. 15	9 a i 9, 9 b i 14
	xxviii. 17	15 a ii 3		v. 6	15 a i 18
	xxx. 4	12 b ii 13		vii. 14	15 a i 28
	xxxviii. 15	12 a ii 7		xii. 11	3 b i 2
				xii. 14	5 a ii 2
Cant.	i. 4	15 b ii 28			
	iv. 3	27 a ii 11	Esth.	x. 1	8 a ii 14
	iv. 11	13 a ii 17			
	v. 10	16 a i 4	Dan.	ii. 22	12 b ii 40
	v. 11	14 a i 18		vii. 9	14 a i 17, 21, 22
	vi. 11	15 b i 33		vii. 10	13 b ii 25, 31
	vii. 1	3 a ii 13			
			1 Chr.	xvii. 21	3 b i 1
Ruth	ii. 14	22 b ii 9			
Lam.	ii. 1	5 b ii 14	Ecclus.	iii. 21, 22	13 a i 8

II. INDEX OF PERSONS AND PLACES[1].

For the notation here adopted see Introd. pp. xv, xvi.

Abba, 8 b ii 5, 10 a ii 21, 16 a i 28
Abba Saul. See Saul.
Abai, 4 a i 23, 6 a i 1 (10), 22, 6 a ii 24, 7 b i 1, 10 b i 4, 16 b ii 2, 17 b ii 5, 22 b i 25, 22 b ii 1, 23 b i 10, 24 a ii 2, 25 a ii 9, 25 b ii 16, 26 a i 1
Abohu, 13 a ii 20, 13 b i 37
Abtalion, 16 a ii 31
Acha bar Ada, 19 b i 12
Acha bar Jacob (see also Papa bar Jacob), 13 a i 2, 13 b ii 34, 15 a i 16
Acha bar Rabba, 6 b ii 16, 16 b i 25
Acher. See Elisha ben Abuyah
Ada bar Ahăbah, 25 a ii 7
Ahithophel, 15 b ii 20
Akiba, 4 b i 10, 6 a ii 28, 12 a ii 35, 14 a i 23, 14 b i 34, 14 b ii 4, 15 a i 29, 15 a ii 6, 18 a ii 14, 23 b i 22, 23 b ii 5
Alcasnadri, 5 a i 25
Alexis, 18 a ii 27
Ami, 4 b ii 19, 21, 13 a i 31, 15 b ii 19, 16 b ii 34, 24 b i 9, 26 a ii 7
Asi (אסי), 4 b ii 23, 13 a ii 8, 15 a i 17, 22 b ii 10
Ashi (אשי), 3 a i 24, 7 b ii 20, 8 a ii 10, 8 b i 2, 10 b ii 17, 11 b ii 17, 16 b i 25, 17 a i 1
Azzai. See Ben Azzai

Bar-Channa. See Rabbah bar bar-Channa
Bar He He, 9 b i 15, 9 b ii 1, 13

Bar Kaphra, 23 b ii 6
Bardala bar Tabyumi, 5 a ii 32
Baybi bar Abai, 4 b ii 26, 5 a i 3
Ben Azzai, 14 b ii 3
Ben Zoma, 14 b ii 3, 17, 15 a i 9

Caesar, 5 b i 12, 14 a ii 13
Chănaneel, 13 b ii 13
Chănaniah, 10 a i 18
Chănaniah ben Akbia, 23 a i 6
Chănaniah ben Chăkinai, 14 b i 35
Chănaniah ben Hezekiah, 13 a ii 37
Chanin, 23 b i 19, 24 a i 11
Chănina, 15 b i 30
Chănina bar Papa, 5 a i 35, 21 b i 5
Chănina ben Antigonus, 24 b i 24
Chănina ben Dosa, 14 a ii 12
Chasda, 5 a ii 19, 6 b ii 11, 8 b i 20
Chia (Rabba bar Abba), 5 b ii 15, 13 a i 28, 16 a i 7, 24 a i 12, 25 b i 17
Chia bar Rab, 14 a i 9

Daniel bar Kattina, 8 b i 6
Dimi, 14 a i 28, 15 b i 31
Doeg, 15 b ii 20

Ela, 5 b i 21, 21 a ii 1, 21 b i 4, 22 a i 8, 31, 23 a i 28
El'a, 16 a i 33
El'ai, 25 b ii 14
El'azar ben Arach, 14 b i 5, 35
El'azar ben Azariah, 3 a ii 30, 3 b i 28, 14 a i 26

---

[1] See also General Index.

El'azar ben Chisma, 3 a ii 27
El'azar ben Jacob, 17 b ii 9
El'azar (ben Shammua'), 4 b ii 7, 11, 5 b ii 5, 6 a ii 25, 12 a i 4, 12 b i 26, 13 a ii 6, 13 b i 20, 14 a ii 18, 17 a i 15, 17 b ii 13, 20 a i 6, 26 a i 23
El'azar ben Zadok, 20 a i 18, 20 a ii 20
Eliezer (ben Hyrkanus), 9 b ii 13, 10 a i 13, 16 a i 25, 19 a i 33, 23 a ii 2, 25 a i 11, 26 b i 7, 27 a i 17, 19
Elijah, 9 b ii 12, 25 a ii 2
Elisha ben Abuyah (=Acher), 14 b ii 3, 15 a i 18, 15 a ii 2, 10, 15 b i 12, 20, 25, 15 b ii 4, 22
Ezekiel, 13 b i 26

Gamzu. See Nachum Gamzu
Gidel, 10 a ii 13

He He. See Bar He He
Hezekiah, 8 a i 6, 8 b i 28, 9 a ii 19
Hillel (or house of H.), 2 a i 8, 2 a ii 25, 6 a i 6, 32, 9 b i 15, 9 b ii 1, 16 a ii 31, 17 a i 5, 17 b i 4, 22 a ii 18, 25 b i 14
Hunna, 3 b ii 17, 4 a i 3, 4 a ii 16, 4 b i 18, 4 b ii 3

Idi, 5 b ii 25
Isaac, 10 a i 17, 13 a ii 26, 16 a i 31
Isaac bar Abdimi, 11 b i 2
Isaac Naphcha, 20 b i 7, 26 a ii 7
Isaiah, 13 b i 26
Ishmael, 6 a ii 25, 9 a i 19, 12 a ii 35, 16 b ii 20, 20 a ii 3, 12

Jacob, 12 a ii 11
Jacob bar Idi, 5 b ii 25
Jacob of K'phar Chatyah, 5 b ii 21
Jannai, 5 a ii 9
Jehudah, 2 a ii 14, 4 b i 15, 7 a ii 16, 10 a i 20, 10 a ii 26, 11 a ii 17, 12 a i 10, 17, 12 a ii 18, 12 b i 28, 12 b ii 22, 13 a ii 31, 13 b i 7, 14, 14 b i 33, 15 b ii 12, 16 a ii 2, 12, 19 a ii 7, 22, 22 b ii 8, 27, 23 a i 20, 24 b i 21, 25 b i 16, 26 a ii 6, 14, 19, 26 b ii 8. See also under Rabbi.

Jehudah ben Lakish, 9 b ii 31
Jehudah ben Tabbai, 16 a ii 29, 16 b i 7
Jehudah ben Tema, 14 a i 35
Jeremiah, 9 a ii 22, 20 a i 25
Jeshaiah, 18 a i 17
Jochanan (ben Eliezer), 3 b ii 18, 5 a i 12, 15, 29, 5 a ii 1, 20, 5 b ii 28 (bis), 7 a i 3, 7 a ii 19, 8 a i 8, 8 b i 28, 8 b ii 4, 9 a i 19, 9 a ii 11, 10 a i 7, 13 a ii 5, 15 b i 16, 25, 16 a i 7, 16 b ii 8, 18 a i 7, 19 a ii 21, 20 a ii 27, 22 b ii 10, 24 a i 13, 24 b i 1, 26 a i 11, 27 a i 6
Jochanan ben Berukah, 3 a ii 27
Jochanan ben Dahābai, 2 a ii 13, 4 b i 14
Jochanan ben Gudgodah, 3 a i 16, 18 b i 10, 20 a i 10
Jochanan ben Zakkai, 3 b ii 4, 5 a i 33, 13 a i 11, 14 b i 3, 34, 16 a i 25, 26 b ii 13
Jonah, 24 b i 8
Jonathan, 14 a i 15, 18 a i 17
Jonathan ben Amram, 20 a i 17, 20 a ii 23
Jonathan ben El'azar, 20 a i 15, 20 a ii 25
Jordan, 23 a i 8
Jose (ben Chelpetha*), 7 a ii 16, 11 a ii 17, 12 b i 9, 14 b i 33, 16 b ii 20, 22 a ii 10, 16, 24 a i 15, 24 a ii 4, 24 b i 21
Jose ben Chănina, 12 a ii 33, 13 b i 9
Jose ben Dosai, 13 b i 29
Jose bar Jehudah, 25 a i 10
Jose ben Joezer. See under Joseph ben Joezer
Jose, son of a Damascene woman, 3 b i 29
Jose the Galilaean, 6 a ii 28, 14 a i 23, 18 a ii 13
Jose the priest, 14 b i 25
Joseph (bar Chia), 4 b ii 25, 5 b i 11, 7 a ii 31, 9 b i 13, 9 b ii 18, 13 a ii 10, 16 a i 29, 25 a ii 9

* Or Chalaphta. See Wolf's *Biblioth. Hebr.* ii. 846.

Joseph ben Joezer, 16 a ii 27, 18 b i 9, 20 a i 8
Joseph ben Jochanan, 16 a ii 27
Joshua (ben Chănania[h]), 3 a ii 28, 5 b i 12, 18, 10 a i 15, 14 b i 25, 34, 15 a i 8, 22 b i 2, 17, 23 a ii 4, 24 b i 14
Joshua ben Levi, 26 a ii 2, 26 b ii 1
Joshua ben P'rachyah, 16 a ii 28

Ḳaphra, 23 b ii 5
Ḳ'phar Chatyah, 5 b ii 22
Ḳetina, 14 a ii 24
Kohăna, 3 a ii 22, 5 b i 25

Levi, 7 a ii 25, 12 b ii 11
Lod. See General Index.

Mar Zot'ra, 3 a i 23, 6 b ii 15, 15 a i 17
Mari, 19 b ii 2
Mary of Magdala, 4 b ii 28
Mattai. See Nittai.
Meir, 15 a i 27, 15 a ii 3, 11, 15 b i 14, 24, 28, 32, 15 b ii 2, 25, 16 b i 7, 18 b ii 2, 19 a ii 29, 19 b i 9
Menahem, 16 a ii 31, 16 b ii 1
Mesharshia, 15 a i 33
Mismim. See General Index.
Modiim. See General Index.
Mothnah, 23 a i 33, 23 a ii 10

Nachman, 18 b ii 16, 22, 19 a i 23, 19 a ii 13, 22 a i 2, 22 b ii 12, 24 a i 6, 25 a ii 6
Nachman bar Isaac, 10 a ii 17, 14 a i 3
Nachmani, 16 a ii 3, 12
Nachum Gamzu, 12 a ii 36
Nathan bar Minyumi, 3 a ii 23
Nebuchadnezzar, 13 b i 15
Nimrod, 13 a i 14
Nimus, 15 b ii 25
Nittai (for Mattai), 16 a ii 29

Ola, 8 a i 5, 8 b ii 1, 19 a ii 21, 25 a ii 1, 25 b i 18, 23
Oshaia, 7 a i 5, 9 a ii 12, 17 a i 15, 17 b ii 13, 20 a i 21

Papa, 4 a i 2, 5 b i 32, 9 a ii 24, 10 b i 4, 11 a i 20, 13 b ii 2, 14 a i 35, 16 b ii 35, 22 a ii 15
Papa (false reading for Acha) bar Jacob, 14 a ii 19
P'dath, 19 a ii 6
Pekün, 3 a ii 28
Phinehas, 26 a i 28
Pumbeditha, 13 a ii 12

Rab, 5 a ii 5, 25, 33, 5 b i 24, 29, 5 b ii 26, 8 b i 7, 10 a i 4, 10 a ii 13, 11 a i 8, 12 a i 10, 18, 12 a ii 12, 18, 12 b ii 22, 13 a ii 25, 13 b i 14, 13 b ii 13, 33
Raba (Rabo), 21 b ii 2, 22 a i 8, 14, 30
Rabba, 2 b ii 16, 3 a ii 14, 4 a ii 30, 5 a ii 16, 28, 5 b i 1, 10, 10 a i 22, 10 a ii 17, 10 b ii 8, 11 b i 2, 13 b i 25, 15 b i 32, 16 b ii 3, 17 b ii 3, 19 a i 23 (רבה), 22 b i 25, 26 a i 13
Rabbah bar Abuah, 19 a ii 13, 20 a ii 1, 22 a i 3, 22 b ii 19, 24 a i 7
Rabbah bar bar-Channah, 15 b i 25, 16 a i 1
Rabbah bar Ola, 25 b i 25
Rabbah bar Samuel, 17 b i 18
Rabbah bar Shela, 5 b i 21, 15 b i 35, 23 a i 32, 23 a ii 9
Rabbi, 3 a i 15, 5 b ii 13, 15, 11 a i 27, 13 b ii 28, 15 b i 20, 24 b i 21, 25 a i 7. See also Jehudah
Rabbin, 8 b ii 15
Rabena, 2 a ii 5, 2 b ii 16, 4 a ii 22, 20 a i 31
Ramai bar Chama, 10 b ii 3, 16 b ii 14
Resh Lakish, 5 a i 34, 7 a i 10, 7 a ii 19, 8 b ii 1, 12 a ii 21, 32, 12 b i 29, 13 b i 27, 36, 15 b i 28, 16 a i 5, 16 a ii 3, 13, 18 a i 2, 23 b ii 5, 24 a ii 10, 24 b i 8, 25 a i 4, 26 a i 10, 26 b i 21, 26 b ii 10, 27 a i 6, 27 a ii 5
Ribbi Jehudah, 24 a ii 4

Samuel, 5 a ii 7, 26, 9 b ii 18, 10 a i 6, 20, 10 a ii 8, 10 b ii 25, 14 a i 9, 14 b ii 18, 15 b ii 11, 22 b ii 8, 27, 23 a i 33, 23 a ii 10, 25 b i 16
Samuel bar Inya, 5 b i 28

Samuel bar Isaac, 5 b i 29
Samuel bar Nachmani, 5 b i 31, 14 a i 14
Saul (Abba), 22 a i 33
Shabur (Sapor), 5 b i 4
Shammai (or house of S.), 2 a i 8, 2 a ii 25, 6 a i 7, 16, 26, 7 b i 9, 18, 7 b ii 10, 17, 16 a ii 32, 16 b ii 2, 17 a i 3, 17 b i 3, 22 a ii 18, 25 b i 13
Shemaiah, 16 a ii 30
Shemen (=Simon) bar Abba, 8 b ii 19, 16 b ii 7
Shesheth, 8 b i 21, 25 a ii 17
Shezbi, 24 a i 27
Shila, 5 a ii 14
Shimi bar Ashi, 18 b ii 10
Shisha ben R. Idi, 9 b i 12
Simeon, 6 a i 15, 10 a ii 24

Simeon ben Betheyra, 23 b ii 2
Simeon ben Jochai, 9 a i 15, 9 b ii 28
Simeon ben Manasseah, 9 a i 11, 9 b ii 21
Simeon ben Shetach, 16 a ii 30, 16 b i 8
Simeon the Holy, 13 b ii 36
Simeon bar Abba. See Shemen bar Abba

Tanchum, 3 a i 29, 3 a ii 7, 24
Tarphon, 10 a ii 2, 18 a ii 28

Zadok, 20 a i 7
Zareka, 16 a ii 23
Zera, 5 b ii 36, 9 a ii 13, 13 a i 29, 23 a i 29
Zoma. See Ben Zoma
Zot'ra bar Tobiah, 12 a ii 12, 13 b ii 33

III. INDEX OF HEBREW WORDS.

70, גְנוּזִים

הַגָּדָה, see *Haggadah*
הַדְרָן וְגוֹ', 55, 115, 146
הכי דמי, 11, 27
הכי השתא, 141
הֲלָכָה, see *Halachah*
הניח, 13
חרדלית, see חרדלית
הָרוּגֵי מַלְכוּת, see "Slain etc."

ואלא, 40
והתני, 123
וחב"א, 94
ויש אמרים, 91
ולטעמיך, 113
ומאי נפקא מינה, 53
גְּמָה, 25

זעירא, 26

חָבֵר, see "Learned and observant man"
חֲגִינָה, see Chagigah
חרדלית, 109, 111

טירמויי"א, 9

116, אַב הַטּוּמְאָה
117, אָבֵל
אֲגָדָה, see *Haggadah*
אדרבא, 145
40, אַהֲדָדֵי
אהלות, 77. See also Tents etc.
117, אוֹגֵן
86, אוֹר הָעוֹלָם
איבעי, 12
איכו, 25
איתמר, 131
אִכְסַלְגִּיס, 144
אֲמוֹרָא, vii. and see Gloss. BARAITHA
139, אֲפִיקַרְסוּת

124, בית הצבטה (הצביעה)
בנא, vii
בָּרַיְתָּא, see Glossary
בשלמא, 13

גָּאוֹן, viii
גּוֹי, xiv, 134
31, גְּמִילוּת חֲסָדִים
גְּמָרָא, see *Gemara*

INDEX OF HEBREW WORDS.

בֵּיפִים, 109
כָּל־הַמּוֹסִיף גּוֹרֵעַ, 101
כָּלֵךְ, 77

מַגְרֵפָה, 113
מוֹעֵד, 34
מַחְלְתָּא, 55
מְטִי, 19
מַטְרוֹנִיתָא, 79
מִינָא (מִין), xiv, 22
מִכְּדִי, 12
מַמְזֵר, 46
מְנַהֲנִי מִילֵי, 41
מַסְכְּתָּא, xii
מַצּוֹת, 105
מִקְרָא הַקֹּדֶשׁ, 34
מַר, 12
מִשְׁנָה, see *Mishnah*
מְתוּרְגְּמָן, see *M'thurg'man*
מַתְנִיתָא, 61 and Gloss. MISHNAH

נִנְעִים, 77
נְדָבָה, 34
נֶגֶר, 34

סָבַר, viii
סֵדֶר עוֹלָם, 32
סְדָרִים, xii
סַלְקָא דַּעְתָּךְ אָמִינָא, 13
סַנְדָּל, 91
סִפְרָא, see *Siphra*
סִפְרֵי, see *Siphre*
עִגּוּת מַצּוֹת, see מַצּוֹת
עֲצֶרֶת, 27, 41, 42
פּוֹ"ד קִט"ב, 100
פֶּחוֹת, 78
פָּטוּר, 27

פַּיִס, 100
פִּיּוּסִי, 97
פַּלְטֵרִין, 92
פֶּסַח קָטָן, 43
פְּשִׁיטָה, 33

צְבַט, 124
צֶבַע, 124
צְדָקָה, 31
צָרַף, 97

קַטִּינָא, 26
קָרְבָּן, 101
קרטבלא, 129

רַבִּי, 31
רֶגֶל (רְגָלִים), 1, 7, 15, 101, 136
רֶמֶס, 15
רְאִיָּה, see Appearing etc.

יִשְׂדִּי, 60
שׁוֹנִין, 134
שָׁמַיִם, 61
שְׁנֵי הַטּוּמְאָה, 116
שַׂר הָעוֹלָם, 85

תּוֹסֶפְתָּא, 63 and Gloss.
תּוּרְגְּמָן, see *M'thurg'man*
תּוֹרָה שֶׁבִּכְתָב, vi
תּוֹרָה שֶׁבְּעַל פֶּה, vi
תֵּיקוּ, 12
תְּמִימֹת, 103
תַּנָּא, vii and see Gloss. BARAITHA and MISHNAH
תָּנוּ רַבָּנָן, 11 and see Gloss. MISHNAH
תַּנְיָא, 134 and see Gloss. MISHNAH
תַּרְבּוּת, 97
ת"שׁ, 77, 102

S. CH.   11

IV. GENERAL INDEX

(Including those names of persons and places which occur in the Introduction and notes).

⁎ *Transliterations of Hebrew words, Latin words, modern names of places, and titles of books, are in italics.*

Abba, application of the title, 75
Abel, 117
Abraham, a prince, 7
Accents, reference to, 30
Affirmative commandments. See Commandments, etc.
Agadah. See *Haggadah*
ἀγαπᾷ, 36
Ahab, 90
Ahithophel, 90
Aloes, 77
Ammon and Moab to pay tithe, 10
Amora. See Gloss. BARAITHA.
Amos quoted as tradition, 51
Angels, silent in the day, 64; manner of creation of, 76; eager for knowledge, 81; have eyes all round, 85; have only one foot, ib.; compared with demons and with men, 92; guardian angels, 94; Angel of death, 17, 81
Appearing before the Lord, 1, 13, 16, 31, 32. See also Gloss. R'IYYAH
Aquila's Greek Version, reference to, 62
Araboth, 63
Arbela, 95
Aryoch, 20
ἀθυμεῖν, 25
Ashi, x
Augustine, St, referred to, 16

Balaam, 90
Baldacchino, 109

Balloon, 90, 134
Banaim, vii
Baraitha. See Gloss.
Bath-Ḳol, 67, 82
Beasts compared with men, 92
Bekiin. See Pekiin
Ben Stada, 10
Beth-din, 123
"Bitters," 77
Blacksmith, 11, 115
Blessedness, degrees of, 82
Blind in one eye, 2, 3, 16
Blind Rabbis, stories of, 17, 25, 38
B'ne Berak (*Ibn Ibrak*), 15
"Bridegroom and bride," festivities of, 82
βυρσεύς, 14

Calf, allusion to the golden, 73
Censorship, xiii, 69, 134
Chăkhamim, vii and Gloss. MISHNAH. See also "Wise men".
Chagigah, compared with holocaust, 27 sqq; notes on, 35, 36, and Glossary
Chalk (to mark animals), 37
Chaos (תֹהוּ), a green line, 58
Chaplain. See Private chaplain
"Chariot, The" 55, 81
Chashmal, 70 sqq.
Cherub, derivation of, 73, 74
Cherubim, discrepancy as to number of wings of the, 74
Child, definition of, 1, 26

Child that is lame, case of, 27
Christ supposed to be possessed of magical powers, 95
Commandments, affirmative and negative, 50
"Common person," 114 sqq., 133, 135
"Continual burnt offering," 28 sqq.
Cordwainer, etc. 14, 34
"Curtain, behind the," 87, 92

David, as a title of Messiah, 77
Deafness, definition of, 3 sqq.
Degrees of blessedness, seven, 82
δελφική, 144
Demons compared with angels and with men, 92
Derivations, examples of fantastic, 22, 60, 61, 71, 74
Desolation (בהו), nature of, 59
Diospolis. See Lod
Doeg, 90
Domestic chaplain. See Private chaplain
"Draw and go down," 111
"Draw and go up," 111
Dualism, 83, 84, 85
Dumah, 18
Dumb men, story of two, 5
Dumbness, definition of, 4
Duties transferable from one day to another. See Substitutions etc.

Earthen vessel, its outside cannot become unclean, 121
Ecclesiasticus, note on versions of, 66
Edersheim, reference to, 67
Elijah, reference to supposed occasional appearances of, 12, 45, 89, 135, 137
El-Mediyeh, 138
Enoch, 85
ἐπίχυσις, 9
Epicurus, 22
Errors of reading. See Variants
Esau = Rome, 23
Euphemisms, 10, 23, 88, 90, 96
Evil eye, fear of, 33

Ezekiel, apparent discrepancies between the Law and, 71 (cf. pp. 137, 139); compared with Isaiah, 73

Familia, 75
Faust in connexion with Acher, 83
Figs, story of man gathering unripe, 18
Firmaments, the seven, 63
"Foot, a straight." See Cherubim
"Forks, needles and," 111
Fourth part, the smallest suitable for a libation, 133, 136, 137
Funnel, by which corn enters a mill, 9

Gandrippus, 12
Gehazi, 90
Gehenna, 26, 55, 75, 86, 88, 92, 145
Gemara, 6, 80, and Glossary
Gematria (substitution of letters), instance of, 44
Generations held back from being created, 75
Geonim, viii
Giza, viii
Goethe. See Faust etc.
"Going down of the sun," 117, 126
Golah, 69
Grammar, lapses of, in Mishnah, 96, 122
Grammatical forms, notes on, 2, 5, 9, 12, 21, 22, 33, 40, 55, 77, 97, 114, 118, 122, 138, 145
Greek words, certain or probable transliterations of, 9, 12, 14, 20, 22, 45, 59, 72, 82, 85, 91, 109, 144 (bis)

Haggadah, 77, 78, and Glossary
Halachah (Halachoth), 5, 47, 49, 52, 53, 97, and Glossary
Half a slave, and half free, case of one who is, 2, 3
"Hallowed things." See Ḳodesh
Hattin, 25
Heave-offering, 115
Heaven, distance from earth to, 58, 67
Heavens, supposed diurnal revolution of, 62
Hiatus in the teaching, 4, 35

GENERAL INDEX.

Holocaust compared with Chagigah, 27 sqq.
Hormouz, 20, 21
Hyrcanus, John, viii

'Ina. See Giza
Intercalary month, 10
Interpretation, the four methods of, 83
Interpreter. See *M'thurg'man*
Irbid, 95
Isaiah compared with Ezekiel. See Ezekiel
Israel = videns Deum, 16

Jabneh (Jabneel, Jamnia), 7, 10, 23, 45
Jacob's ladder, 67
Jehudah the Holy, ix
Jeroboam I., 90
Jochanan ben Eliezer, x

Ḳabbala, 47, 81, 82, 83
Keble, quotation from, 19
Ḳodesh, 115
Ḳorban, 100
κυνάνθρωπος, 12

"Lacking the time," 44
Lacuna in the teaching. See Hiatus, etc.
Lame in one foot, case of one who is, 6
Latin words, transliterations of, 63, 75, 79, 85, 92
Law, inconsistencies in the, 137, 139
Lay the hands on (an animal brought for sacrifice), 35, 98
"Learned and observant man" (חָבֵר), 127, 133, 135, 136, 141
Lentil, 54
Lilith, 11
Limit, things that have no prescribed, 31
Lod (Lydda, Diospolis), 7, 9, 45, 48, 105, 140
Longfellow quoted, 47, 72, 76
Lunel, 9

Maccabees, viii, 138
Magical powers ascribed to Christ, 95
Makhon, 63

Manasseh, 90
Ma'on, 63
Margoliouth, Prof., referred to, 67
Marriage a duty, 3
Massoretic text, variations from (See also Readings, etc.), 53, 64, 65, 66, 68, 93, 94
Maxim, Rabbinic, 36
Meah, 2, 27, 38
Mejdjel, 95
Men compared with angels, with beasts, and with demons, 92
Messiah, David as a title of, 77
Metatron, the, 85, 91
M'thurg'man, 79, 125 and Gloss. BARAITHA.
Middle holiday (מוֹעֵד), note on, 34
Mishnah, 80, and Glossary
Mishnahs, conflicting, 3, 107; inaccurate quotations of, 15, 46, 97, 105, 111, 117, 137
Mismim, 144
Mnemonic, 4, 71
Moab. See Ammon, etc.
Modiim, 138
Moist things specially liable to uncleanness, 117, 123, 131
Mosaib, 6
Mule-drivers, 45, 114

Nahras. See Neresh
Nazirite, 43, 48
Nebuchadnezzar, 67, 72
"needles and forks," 111; "needles and pipes," 119
Negative, positive commandments compared with, 50
Nehardea, 11, 20, 21, 69
Neresh, 6, 12
Nero, a Roman general, 86
New Testament words or thoughts, expressions or passages illustrating, 9, 14, 25, 46, 60, 62, 64, 68, 69 (bis), 70 (bis), 72, 81 (bis), 82, 89, 91, 102, 129, 146
Nimrod, 67

ξύλον, 144

Olive, 126
"One hundred and one things," 107
Onen, 117
Osha, 7, 104
Ovens not made in Jerusalem, 140
Ox changed to a cherub, 73

Pairs (Prince-presidents and Vice-presidents), 95
Palatia, 92
Paradise, Rabbinic use of the word, 83
παρασάγγης, 45
παρρησίᾳ, 20
Passage called after a prominent word, 70
Passover, a second, 43
Paul, St, 120
Pekiin, 7
πήλωμα, 59
"Pentecost is after the Sabbath," 100, 105, 106
"Pipes, needles and," 119
Pirḳe Aboth quoted or referred to, 48, 59, 62, 80, 107
Play on words, 22, 76, 77, 91 (bis)
πλήσμη (πλημμυρίς), 59
Pomegranate, illustrations from, 79, 146
Positive commandments compared with negative, 50
Postponement of offerings. See Substitutions etc.
Poverty connected with Israel, 45
Priest, how restricted as to marriage, 84
Prince-presidents, 96, 97
Private chaplain, 103, 124, 129
Proselytes in Caesar's household, 79
Protest against the Christian Sunday, 106
Proverbial sayings, 21, 45, 49, 69, 101
Pumbeditha, 5, 13, 17, 21, 69
Purgatorial flame, 88

Quotations (Biblical) differing from Massoretic text, 53, 64, 65, 66, 68, 93, 94

Rab, application of the title, 26
Rabban, application of the title, 10 and Gloss.
Rabbanan, vii
Rabbi, application of the title, 26, 118
Rabena, viii, x
Rainbow not to be gazed into, 93
Rakia', 63
Rashi referred to, 9, 62, 63, 76, 90
Readings, conjectural emendations by the Rabbis in Biblical, 44, 78, 146. See also Massoretic text, variations from
Rejoicing, an integral part of the Feast, 4
Religious bath, rules for size of, 54, 119
Ribbi, application of the title, 31
R'iyyah. See Appearing etc.
Roman rule, See Veiled etc.
"Rooter up of mountains," 13

Sabbath day's journey, 87
Sabbath work, 49, 98
Sabboraim, viii
Sack, 143
Sacrifices not to be offered during the night. See Sunset, etc.
Sadducees' view as to sunset rule, 127
Salamander, 145
Sandalphon, 72
Satan, reference to, 88
Sayings of the Jewish Fathers. See Pirke Aboth
Scorpion. See Wasp and the Scorpion
"Scraper," 113
Scripture and tradition, comparative estimate of, 47; all rules must be finally traced back to, 110
Seahs, 108, 110, 111, 120
Sepharvaim, vi
Septuagint, illustration from, 11
Seven degrees of blessedness, 82
Shares, to everyone belong two, 86
Sh'chaḳim, 63
Sheba, Queen of, 83
Shechinah, 77, 81, 93
Showbread, 143

Shili, 17
Sifra (Sivra), 6
Simeon ben Lakish, vi
Simon the Just, vi
Simona, viii
Siphra, 5, 55
Siphre, 5, 55
"Slain on account of the kingdom," 16, 22, 27, 63, 78
Smoke going up from a grave, meaning of, 88
Sopherim, vii, 120, 129
Sora, viii, ix, 6, 11, 20, 21, 26, 30, 69
Substitutions of one day for another, 2, 41 sqq., 100, 103
Sunset, offerings not to be made after, 40, 43, 44, 117, 126, 128, 130. See also "Lacking the time".
Superfluous expressions impossible in Holy Writ, 6, 14, 42, 50, 101, 105, 117
Supplementary offerings, 38 sqq.
"Supporting peg," 14
Synagogue, men of the Great, vii
Synonyms, 13

"Take up and give," 78, 80
Tallith, 81
Talmud in sense of *Gemara*, 47, in the general sense, 78
Tanna. See Gloss. BARAITHA.
Tarphon, quotation from, 48
Tautology. See Superfluous expressions, etc.
Ten, the minimum constituting a congregation, 141
Tents in connexion with ceremonial uncleanness, 53, 77, 90

Testaments of the xii Patr. referred to, 63
Tiberias, 11, 26, 32
Titus, veiled reference to, 67
Tosiphta, 63 and Glossary
Tower, 90, 134
Trade, learned Jews practised a, 91
Tradition, Scripture outside the Torah called, 51
Tremueia, 9
Trespass, how different from a sin, 52
τρικλίνια, 82
Two days (in case of Festivals) kept, 39

Unclean thing, minimum size for, 54, 126

Variants and erroneous readings, notes on, 5, 14, 18, 26, 40, 56, 74, 94, 95, 103, 109, 112, 122, 134, 135
Veiled references to Roman rule, 23, 67
Vice-presidents, 96, 97
Vilon (=*velum*), 63
Vows, 47 sqq.

Wasp and the Scorpion, 21
Waters, interval between the upper and the lower, 84
"Weighing and giving," 57
Wet. See Moist things, etc.
"Wise men," 59, 61, 94, 105
Witnesses, method of dealing with perjured, 96
Wright's *Comp. Gram.* referred to, 21

Z'bul, 63
Zouza, 20, 45

SOME PUBLICATIONS OF
THE CAMBRIDGE UNIVERSITY PRESS.

The Palestinian Mishna. By W. H. LOWE, M.A., Lecturer in Hebrew at Christ's College, Cambridge. Royal 8vo. 21s.

Sayings of the Jewish Fathers, comprising Pirqe Aboth and Pereq R. Meir in Hebrew and English, with Critical and Illustrative Notes. By CHARLES TAYLOR, D.D., Master of St John's College, Cambridge. Demy 8vo. 10s.

The Old Testament in Greek according to the Septuagint. Edited by H. B. SWETE, D.D., Regius Professor of Divinity and Honorary Fellow of Gonville and Caius College.
Volume I. Genesis—IV. Kings. Crown 8vo. 7s. 6d.
Volume II. I. Chronicles—Tobit. By the same Editor.
[*Nearly ready.*

The Book of Psalms in Greek according to the Septuagint, being a portion of Vol. II. of the above. Crown 8vo. 2s. 6d.

The Greek Liturgies. Chiefly from Original Authorities. By C. A. SWAINSON, D.D., late Master of Christ's College, Cambridge. Crown 4to. Paper covers. 15s.

London: C. J. CLAY AND SONS,
CAMBRIDGE UNIVERSITY PRESS WAREHOUSE,
AVE MARIA LANE.

www.ingramcontent.com/pod-product-compliance
Lightning Source LLC
Chambersburg PA
CBHW020248170426
43202CB00008B/270